The Stalinist Era

Placing Stalinism in its international context, David L. Hoffmann presents a new interpretation of Soviet state intervention and violence. Many "Stalinist" practices – the state-run economy, surveillance, propaganda campaigns, and the use of concentration camps – did not originate with Stalin or even in Russia, but were instead tools of governance that became widespread throughout Europe during World War I. The Soviet system was formed at this moment of total war, and wartime practices of mobilization and state violence became building blocks of the new political order. Communist Party leaders in turn used these practices ruthlessly to pursue their ideological agenda of economic and social transformation. Synthesizing new research on Stalinist collectivization, industrialization, cultural affairs, gender roles, nationality policies, World War II, and the Cold War, Hoffmann provides a succinct account of this pivotal period in world history.

David L. Hoffmann is Distinguished Professor of History at the Ohio State University. He has authored three books on Stalinism, *Peasant Metropolis: Social Identities in Moscow, 1929–1941* (1994), *Stalinist Values: The Cultural Norms of Soviet Modernity, 1917–1941* (2003), and *Cultivating the Masses: Modern State Practices and Soviet Socialism, 1914–1939* (2011), and edited two further books, *Russian Modernity: Politics, Knowledge, Practices* (2000) and *Stalinism: The Essential Readings* (2002). He has held fellowships from Harvard University, Cornell University, Stanford University, the Woodrow Wilson Center, the National Endowment for the Humanities, the International Research and Exchanges Board, the Mellon Foundation, and the Social Science Research Council.

NEW APPROACHES TO EUROPEAN HISTORY

Series editors

T. C. W. Blanning, *Sidney Sussex College, Cambridge*
Brendan Simms, *Peterhouse, Cambridge*

New Approaches to European History is an important textbook series, which provides concise but authoritative surveys of major themes and problems in European history since the Renaissance. Written at a level and length accessible to advanced school students and undergraduates, each book in the series addresses topics or themes that students of European history encounter daily: the series embraces both some of the more 'traditional' subjects of study and those cultural and social issues to which increasing numbers of school and college courses are devoted. A particular effort is made to consider the wider international implications of the subject under scrutiny.

To aid the student reader, scholarly apparatus and annotation is light, but each work has full supplementary bibliographies and notes for further reading: where appropriate, chronologies, maps, diagrams, and other illustrative material are also provided.

For a complete list of titles published in the series, please see:
www.cambridge.org/newapproaches

The Stalinist Era

David L. Hoffmann

The Ohio State University

CAMBRIDGE
UNIVERSITY PRESS

CAMBRIDGE
UNIVERSITY PRESS

University Printing House, Cambridge CB2 8BS, United Kingdom

One Liberty Plaza, 20th Floor, New York, NY 10006, USA

477 Williamstown Road, Port Melbourne, VIC 3207, Australia

314–321, 3rd Floor, Plot 3, Splendor Forum, Jasola District Centre, New Delhi – 110025, India

79 Anson Road, #06–04/06, Singapore 079906

Cambridge University Press is part of the University of Cambridge.

It furthers the University's mission by disseminating knowledge in the pursuit of education, learning, and research at the highest international levels of excellence.

www.cambridge.org
Information on this title: www.cambridge.org/9781107007086
DOI: 10.1017/9781139017503

First published 2018

Printed in the United Kingdom by TJ International Ltd. Padstow, Cornwall

A catalogue record for this publication is available from the British Library.

Library of Congress Cataloging-in-Publication Data
Names: Hoffmann, David L. (David Lloyd), 1961– author.
Title: The Stalinist era / David L. Hoffmann.
Description: Cambridge, United Kingdom ; New York, NY : Cambridge University Press, 2018. | Series: New approaches to European history | Includes bibliographical references and index.
Identifiers: LCCN 2018025220| ISBN 9781107007086 (hardback : alk. paper) | ISBN 9780521188371 (paperback : alk. paper)
Subjects: LCSH: Soviet Union – History – 1925–1953. | Soviet Union – Politics and government – 1917–1936. | Soviet Union – Politics and government – 1936–1953.
Classification: LCC DK267 .H615 2018 | DDC 947.084/2–dc23
LC record available at https://lccn.loc.gov/2018025220

ISBN 978-1-107-00708-6 Hardback
ISBN 978-0-521-18837-1 Paperback

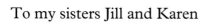

To my sisters Jill and Karen

Contents

Illustrations

Maps

Acknowledgments

I wrote this book under very difficult personal circumstances. Shortly after I agreed to write it, my wife Patricia Weitsman was diagnosed with myelodysplastic syndrome, a pre-leukemia condition. She had to undergo a stem cell transplant, which was initially successful thanks to Dr. William Blum and the staff at the James Cancer Hospital. This transplant would not have been possible without Yaakov Brisman, Patricia's only perfect match in a database of 17,000 potential stem cell donors. I am forever grateful to Yaakov and his wife Miriam for their life-saving generosity. Patricia recovered from the transplant and our family had three precious years together before she relapsed and died in 2014.

Because my work on this book was delayed for a number of years, I deeply appreciate the understanding of Michael Watson, Executive Publisher of History and Area Studies at Cambridge University Press. He remained enthusiastic about the project long after the completion deadline had passed, and thanks to his patience, I was able to complete it. I would also like to thank Liz Friend-Smith, the editor at Cambridge in charge of the New Approaches to European History series, for all of her help preparing this book for publication. I am also grateful to others who were involved with production of the book, including Allan Alphonse, Ian McIver, Abigail Walkington, copyeditor Matthew La Fontaine, and cartographer David Cox. I also acknowledge the anonymous referees for the project; in record time, they strongly endorsed the book and provided insightful suggestions to improve it.

My colleagues at The Ohio State University were extremely supportive during this difficult period in my life. Christopher Otter taught an entire course for me in order to give me time to care for my family. Colleagues in the Russian, East European, and Eurasian history field – Nicholas Breyfogle, Theodora Dragostinova, Scott Levi, and Jennifer Siegel – likewise took over a number of my academic responsibilities. Other Ohio State colleagues also helped, lending both moral and practical support, and I would like to thank Angela Brintlinger, Alice Conklin, Steven Conn, Jane Hathaway, Ted Hopf, Robin Judd,

Margaret Newell, Geoffrey Parker, Nathan Rosenstein, Tina Sessa, Birgitte Soland, and Judy Wu.

Many friends provided assistance as well. In particular, I would like to thank Adam Baker and Linda Zionkowski, Ly Burnier, Jean and David Comer, Lois Doxey, Lori Dunlap, Jillian Gustin, Vince Jungkunz, Danielle Leshaw, Ginger Moodie, Kristen and Nathan Peters, David Rader and Terre Vandervoort, Renee and John Reilly, Mary Travis, Michael and Wendy Travis, and Susan Varisco. I owe special thanks to Jody and Paul Baxter, Vivian Moore, and Madge and Peter Vail for their help over many years.

Most of all, I would like to thank my relatives for their love and support. During Patricia's illness, a number of them traveled to Ohio and helped out in countless ways. In particular, I acknowledge my parents, George and Irene Hoffmann; my sisters, Jill and Karen Hoffmann; my brothers-in-law, Gordon Strain and Jeffrey Schang; my father-in-law and his wife, Allen Weitsman and Wei Cui; my mother-in-law, Judith Evans; Patricia's aunt, Carol Franco; and especially my sisters-in-law, Stacy Young, Susan Huter, and Deborah Ogawa. In the aftermath of Patricia's death, my mother helped me deal with my grief and my children's grief. For decades she had volunteered with hospice organizations doing grief support work, and both her words of understanding and the books she sent were invaluable. Sadly, just a year after Patricia's death, my mother became ill with ALS, and she died the following year. During this time my sisters Jill and Karen gave me vital emotional support, as they have throughout my life. It is to them that I dedicate this book.

Finally, I would like to acknowledge my children, Sarah and Jonah. When I began this book they were still in elementary school, and now they are teenagers, with their own ideas, interests, and opinions. I love to spend time with them, including going to watch their performances and sports events. We have taken family trips together on four continents, and they are the best traveling companions I could imagine. Even more than that, they never cease to amaze me with their intelligence, their talents, and their resilience. I am very proud of both of them, and I know their mother would be too.

Abbreviations

GARF   Gosudarstvennyi Arkhiv Rossiiskoi Federatsii (State
        Archive of the Russian Federation)
RGAE   Rossiiskii Gosudarstvennyi Arkhiv Ekonomiki (Russian
        State Archive of Economics)
RGASPI Rossiiskii Gosudarstvennyi Arkhiv Sotsial'noi i Politicheskoi
        Istorii (Russian State Archive of Social and Political History)
TsMAM   Tsentral'nyi Munitsipal'nyi Arkhiv Moskvy (Central
        Municipal Archive of Moscow)

Introduction

In 2010, Communist Party members in Zaporizhia, a city in southeastern Ukraine, erected a statue of Joseph Stalin. Nearly a thousand people attended the monument's unveiling, including many World War II veterans bedecked with medals. After the playing of the Soviet national anthem, one speaker called out "Long live Stalin!" and the audience responded "Hurrah, hurrah, hurrah!" Not all of the city's residents welcomed the Stalin monument with such enthusiasm. Several months later, unidentified protesters used a hacksaw to cut off the statue's head. A few days after that, the decapitated statue was blown up completely by a homemade bomb. Where the Stalin statue once stood, only an empty pedestal remains.

Few historical figures inspire more adoration and loathing than Joseph Stalin, dictator of the Soviet Union from 1928 until his death in 1953. Under his rule, the Soviet Union was transformed from an underdeveloped, agrarian country into a military superpower that defeated Nazi Germany and rivaled the United States for world domination. But this transformation was accomplished through massive state violence and bloodshed. Stalinist methods included deportations, incarcerations, and executions. Literally millions of Soviet citizens suffered arrest, starvation, or death as a result of Stalinist policies. While Stalinism modernized the Soviet Union and changed the course of world history, it did so at tremendous human cost.

For students of Soviet history, no problem looms larger than that of Stalinism. How was it that the October Revolution of 1917, which seemed to promise human liberation and equality, resulted not in a communist utopia but in a Stalinist dictatorship instead? Why did this attempt to create a perfect society lead to Gulag prison camps, bloody purges, and unprecedented levels of state repression? To answer these questions, it is imperative to study the origins of Stalinist methods and to examine the combination of forces that led to the establishment of such a repressive political system. It is also important to discuss the

1

consequences of Stalinism – the impact it had upon the lives of Soviet people and the suffering that it inflicted.

Before proceeding to explain what caused Stalinism, let us pause for a moment to define it. Stalinism was a set of tenets, policies, and practices wielded by the Soviet government during the years in which Stalin was in power (1928–53) – policies characterized by extreme coercion employed for the purpose of economic and social transformation. Among the particular features of Stalinism were the abolition of private property and free trade; the collectivization of agriculture; a planned, state-run economy and rapid industrialization; the wholesale liquidation of so-called exploiting classes through dispossessions and incarcerations; widespread repression of alleged enemies, including those within the Communist Party itself; a cult of personality deifying Stalin; and Stalin's virtually unlimited dictatorship over the country.

What caused Stalinism? The simplest explanation is Joseph Stalin himself – his personal vindictiveness, his skillful political infighting, his accumulation of power and excessive use of coercion. Stalin was a ruthless dictator, someone who personally signed the death warrants of thousands of people and who ordered secret police operations that resulted in countless arrests and executions. There is no question of Stalin's guilt or responsibility for the state violence of his era. And there is no doubt that as a dictator he wielded unchallenged authority within the Soviet Union. As a historical explanation, however, blaming only Stalin for the crimes of Stalinism is incomplete. The Soviet state was a massive bureaucratic apparatus overseen by the Communist Party, with more than a million members. Stalin's fellow Communist Party leaders shared not only his belief in Marxism-Leninism but much of his worldview, with its focus on class struggle and internal enemies. While Stalin personally played a pivotal role in the system that bears his name, an understanding of Stalinism must go beyond the thoughts and actions of a single person.[1]

Another possible explanation is that Stalinism derived from Russia's autocratic traditions, as both the prerevolutionary tsarist government and the Stalinist dictatorship were characterized by authoritarian rule, extensive use of police powers, disregard for individual rights, and state control of information.[2] It is true that the tsarist autocracy was an absolute monarchy that denied its subjects basic rights and liberties. Centuries of autocratic rule did nothing to establish democratic traditions and hence provided no basis for the development of representative institutions. This legacy contributed to the authoritarianism of the Soviet state. At the same time, any sort of facile equation of tsarism and Soviet socialism is highly misleading. Not only were these systems based on diametrically opposed ideologies, but the degree to which they intervened in society was drastically different. While the tsarist police sent a few thousand political prisoners into administrative exile (where they lived among the popula- tion in Siberia), the Soviet secret police under Stalin imprisoned several million "class enemies" and "enemies of the people" in Gulag prison camps. The tsarist government had no ambition to reshape the population or refashion individuals, as did the Soviet government, and accordingly its social interventions were limited. So along with Stalin's personality, Russian political traditions contributed to Stalinism, but they do not fully explain it.

To understand Stalinism, it is important to consider the geopolitical context in which it arose. By 1900, the Russian empire had fallen far behind the more developed countries of western Europe. An overwhelmingly peasant country, Russia largely lacked the factories, burgeoning cities, and railway networks that characterized the United Kingdom, France, and Germany. Much of Russia's population remained impoverished and illiterate. Its military did not have adequate artillery, munitions, or warships. In order to compete both economically and militarily, Russia needed to industrialize quickly.[3] But how could this be accomplished? In western Europe, industrialization had taken place over a century and it was based on free market capitalism. A gradual approach, however, would not allow Russia to catch up, and moreover, many Russian observers were repulsed by the exploitation and class antagonism that accompanied capitalist industrialization.

The fact that Russia was a late-developing country meant that its intelligentsia could draw upon a preexisting critique of industrial capitalism.[4] Leftists in western Europe had condemned capitalist inequality and proposed various alternatives labeled "socialism," which generally sought political and economic equality for workers. One branch of socialist thought was Marxism, based on the writings of German philosopher Karl Marx. Marx envisioned violent proletarian revolution as the means to overthrow the capitalist system and establish socialism. Many Russian intellectuals were drawn to Marxism, given its scientific critique of capitalism and its conviction that socialism was inevitable. The more radical wing of Russian Marxists, called the Bolsheviks and later renamed the Communists, ultimately came to power in the Russian Revolution of 1917.

Here, then, we have another possible explanation for Stalinism: Marxist ideology.[5] Lenin, Stalin, and other Soviet leaders were Marxists – they employed Marxist categories and viewed the world in terms of class struggle.[6] They saw history progressing along a Marxist timeline to socialism and ultimately to communism. And they believed that, as the vanguard of the proletariat, the Communist Party could push the Soviet Union along this timeline through a process of economic and social transformation. Soviet leaders' sense of historical progression also guided their cultural and nationality policies.[7] In these ways, Marxism infused the thinking of Communist leaders and played a crucial role in the Soviet system.

Marxist ideas alone, however, do not explain the genesis of Stalinism. Marxism provided no blueprint for how to construct a socialist state. In fact, Marx's writings gave only a vague description of what life would be like under socialism. It is true that Marx endorsed violent proletarian revolution as the means to overthrow the old order, but nowhere did he discuss the scale or types of violence that would be used. Moreover, none of the Stalinist state's institutions or methods came from Marxist ideology. Features of Stalinism such as the planned economy, deportations, and Gulag prison camps were state practices that had their origins elsewhere. We must therefore look further to account for the extreme social intervention characteristic of the Stalinist system.

To provide a new perspective on Stalinism, this book will place it in an international, comparative context. While often viewed as anomalous, Soviet history actually had striking parallels, as well as important differences, with the histories of other countries. In the twentieth century, a sharp rise in state intervention occurred not only in the Soviet Union but in countries across Europe and around the world. In an age of industrial labor and mass warfare, governments increasingly sought to manage and mobilize their populations. In this sense, Stalinism represented a particularly violent incarnation of state practices that developed over several centuries and reached their culmination during and after World War I.

Efforts to shape populations first began in early modern Europe, when cameralist thinkers argued for a greater state role in fostering a productive society. Eventually, the narrow fiscal interests of cameralists were superseded by broader ideals of improving the population's welfare for its own sake. In the nineteenth century, social science disciplines and modern medicine offered new means to identify and solve social problems. A wide range of professionals – social workers, urban planners, public health inspectors – intervened in people's lives to safeguard the population's health and wellbeing. Some reformers were altruistic and sought to ease the suffering of the urban poor, while others were more concerned with economic productivity and public order. In themselves social reform efforts were generally benevolent and did much to reduce disease and poverty. But by the twentieth century, some governments launched more coercive and sweeping attempts at social transformation.[8]

World War I marked a dramatic increase in coercive state intervention. Many "Stalinist" practices – the state-run economy, widespread surveillance, propaganda campaigns, large-scale deportations, and the use of concentration camps – did not originate with Stalin or even in Russia, but were instead tools of governance that became widespread throughout Europe during World War I. The Stalinist planned economy was modeled on the German World War I economy where the government established extensive control over the production and distribution of goods. The Soviet welfare system, which included full employment, universal health care, and old age and disability pensions, reflected a pan-European trend toward mutual obligations between the state and its citizens. The Soviet use of surveillance followed practices established by the governments of all major combatants in the war.[9] The establishment of Soviet concentration camps – what became the Gulag – was based on a method of European colonial warfare that was utilized (in the form of internment camps) during World War I by the United Kingdom, France, Germany, Austria-Hungary, and the United States.[10]

The Soviet system was formed at a moment of total war – the juncture of World War I and the Russian Civil War – and wartime institutions and practices became the building blocks of the new political order. Although the Soviet government, once in power, ended involvement in World War I, it almost immediately began mobilization for the Civil War, and it continued many wartime practices. State bureaucracies and agencies, including the Soviet secret police, were established to enact these measures, and they soon became institutionalized as permanent means of rule. The revolutionary origin of the Soviet state also meant that its leaders could act with no traditional or legal limits on their authority. So while state interventionism increased throughout Europe at this time, it assumed a particularly virulent form in the case of Stalinism.

To understand Stalinism as one particular version of modern state practices is not to exonerate Stalin and his fellow leaders for the death and suffering they caused. Wartime practices such as deportations and incarcerations were tools of social control that leaders could choose to use or not. The actualization of Stalinist state violence resulted from the Soviet Union's type of government and the decisions of its leaders. The Soviet government was a dictatorship with no constitutional constraints on its power. Stalin and his fellow leaders chose to use instruments of state violence to pursue their agenda of rapid industrialization and social transformation.

No single factor caused Stalinism. As with all complex historical phenomena, a range of factors contributed to the coercive set of policies enacted under Stalin. While Stalin's vindictiveness, Russian authoritarian political traditions, and Marxist ideology all played a role, we must also take into account the wider international context in which Stalinism developed. The Stalinist era was one of acute international tensions and military aggression. The Soviet Union, like other underdeveloped countries, needed to industrialize quickly for the sake of national defense. The mass warfare of this era also led political leaders throughout Europe to enact new state practices of mobilization and social intervention. Such practices included both positive interventions (welfare programs and public health measures) and negative interventions (surveillance, deportations, and incarcerations). This book will explore these causes of Stalinism, and it will also describe its social consequences. Among those consequences were the death and suffering of millions of people.

Overview of Chapters

To examine the roots of Stalinism, Chapter 1 begins with a description of the tsarist empire on the eve of World War I. At that time, Russia was an underdeveloped country with a government that thwarted reform efforts. It was only with the enormous demands of World War I that the tsarist autocracy undertook state welfare and public health initiatives. Foreshadowing future Stalinist policies, the wartime tsarist government also implemented coercive measures of economic and social control. The chapter then discusses the Russian Revolution and its two stages – first, the collapse of the tsarist autocracy and its replacement by the Provisional Government; and second, the October Revolution when the Bolsheviks took power. The chapter goes on to discuss the Russian Civil War as well as the 1920s, the period of the New Economic Policy.

Chapter 2 describes the first period of Stalinist rule, 1928–33, what Communist Party leaders called "the era of building socialism." In these years, the Soviet government eliminated capitalism and launched a crash industrialization drive intended to catch up with the more industrialized countries of western Europe. These economic policies triggered massive social upheaval. Millions of peasants moved to cities to find work constructing new factories, and large numbers of urban women took jobs in heavy industry. Many workers received educational opportunities as the Stalinist leadership, distrustful of "bourgeois specialists," sought to create a new technical elite from the ranks of the proletariat. Rapid industrialization was made possible by state control of the economy and the channeling of all resources into the building of steel mills and machine plants. An end to private farming meant the forced collectivization of agriculture, an extremely coercive Stalinist policy that saw the dispossession and deportation of several million peasants labeled kulaks. Overall this period was a time of severe economic deprivation – the Soviet government introduced rationing, living standards fell sharply, and famine in the countryside resulted in nearly 6 million deaths.

Chapter 3 covers the period after Stalin declared that the foundations of socialism had been built, 1934–38. With the end of capitalism and the establishment of a state-run economy, Soviet leaders believed that they had attained a new stage in world history – the era of socialism. As Marxists, they felt that a new economic base should dictate a new political and cultural superstructure. Accordingly, they issued a new constitution, the Stalin Constitution of 1936, and reoriented official Soviet culture away from iconoclastic avant-garde art toward socialist realism. Having eliminated those people deemed class enemies – kulaks and petty capitalists – Soviet leaders thought the time of open class struggle had passed. But secret police officials warned that there remained hidden enemies who would seek to sabotage the Soviet state. In the late 1930s, with the growing threat of war from Nazi Germany and fascist Japan, Stalin launched a massive wave of state violence to incarcerate or execute potential traitors, in particular former oppositionists within the Communist Party, petty criminals and former kulaks, and members of diaspora national minorities.

Chapter 4 covers World War II, beginning with the Nazi-Soviet Pact. After the signing of this treaty, Germany invaded Poland from the west, while the Soviet Union invaded eastern Poland, the Baltic countries, and Finland. The chapter goes on to discuss the Nazi invasion of the Soviet Union in June 1941 – an invasion the country barely survived. The German army drove deep into Soviet territory and within a few months had reached the outskirts of Leningrad and Moscow. To mobilize for the war effort, Soviet leaders relied upon the same state practices they had used during the Civil War and the 1930s – state control of economic resources, surveillance and propaganda to ensure the loyalty of the population, and secret police arrests to neutralize any potential dissent. While the Soviet Union ultimately defeated Nazi Germany, 27 million Soviet citizens lost their lives during the war. For the Soviet people, the story of World War II is not only one of victory, but also of repression, sacrifice, and death.

Chapter 5 analyzes the postwar Stalin years, 1946–53. As a result of the wartime victory, the Soviet Union attained the status of a superpower within the international system, rivaling the United States for world domination. This international prominence profoundly affected both Soviet foreign and domestic policy. The Soviet Union imposed Communist governments upon eastern European countries, an act that fueled Cold War tensions with the United States and its allies. In domestic policy, the mammoth task of rebuilding the country, where millions were homeless and hungry, was accomplished through continued state economic controls and coercion. Despite people's hopes for political liberalization after the war, the Stalinist regime remained just as repressive. The wartime victory seemed to vindicate the Stalinist system, and the Cold War dictated continued vigilance.

The conclusion considers the legacy of Stalinism, a legacy that cast a long shadow over the remainder of the Soviet period and even beyond. Nikita Khrushchev, Stalin's successor, embarked on a contentious campaign of de-Stalinization, denouncing Stalin's cult of personality and his use of violence against Party members. But with Khrushchev's ouster in 1964, discussion of Stalinist repressions ceased, to be revived only in the late 1980s under Mikhail Gorbachev. At that time, fuller disclosure of Stalinist repressions discredited the Soviet government and, along with a host of economic and ethnic discontents, contributed to the rapid demise of the Soviet system. The end of the Soviet Union, however, did not end the debate over Stalinism, which is bitterly contested in Russia even to this day.

Stalinism is of central importance to our understanding of twentieth-century world history. During the Stalinist era, the Soviet Union became a military and industrial superpower, capable of winning World War II and rivaling the United States during the Cold War. But Stalinism is not simply a tale of industrial modernization and military triumph. While the Stalinist system represented an alternative model of development and a grave ideological challenge to liberal democracy and capitalism, it also exacted an appalling human toll. Our obligation to study the Stalinist era stems not only from its importance, but also from our responsibility to come to terms with one of the darkest pages in all human history.

1   Prelude to Stalinism

In his 1835 book *Democracy in America*, French political thinker Alexis de Tocqueville predicted that Russia and the United States would eventually become the most powerful countries on earth. He wrote, "There are at the present time two great nations in the world ... the Russians and the Americans ... Each of them seems marked out by the will of heaven to sway the destinies of half the globe."[1] By the middle of the twentieth century, his prediction had come true. The United States and Russia, by then called the Soviet Union, had emerged as the world's two super-powers, and they were locked in a Cold War struggle for world domination. But fifty years earlier, at the dawn of the twentieth century, few observers could foresee this. True, Russia was an enormous land empire and was considered one of the Great Powers of Europe. But the country's economic and military strength seemed to be diminishing compared to the United Kingdom, France, Germany, and the United States. Whereas these countries were undergoing rapid industrialization, Russia remained an agrarian country, in only the early stages of industrialization. Militarily the country was also falling behind. In 1905, Russia endured a humiliating loss in the Russo-Japanese War. A decade later, the Russian army suffered crushing defeats at the hands of the German army in World War I. How was Russia going to defend itself in this era of industrial production and mass warfare? How was it going to mobilize its vast human and natural resources to fashion a modern military capable of preserving its national sovereignty?

Stalinism was not inevitable. We need to explain how and why it developed. But part of this explanation involves understanding the international context in which Russia operated in the early twentieth century. World War I ushered in a new era of international rivalry and mass warfare, and Russia's lack of industrial development left it militarily vulnerable. Rising international tensions were accompanied by growing interventions by political leaders to ensure the economic capacity and war readiness of their populations. Here too the Russian monarchy had lagged behind western European governments. But once World War I broke out, the tsarist state vastly expanded its social reach. After the Bolsheviks seized power during the Russian Revolution, they further expanded state control and coercion as they fought a bloody civil war. The Soviet bureaucracy and secret police were formed during the Civil War, and they went on to become fundamental components of the Stalinist state. The origins of Stalinism are complex, and to understand these origins we must consider the prelude to the Stalinist era.

Russia on the Eve of War and Revolution

At the beginning of the twentieth century, Russia was a vast yet under-developed empire. The largest country on earth, it stretched 9,000 miles – nearly halfway around the world – from west to east. It extended across the Eurasian land mass, from the Baltic Sea all the way to the Pacific Ocean (see Map 1.1). The northern reaches of Siberia were a seemingly endless expanse of frozen tundra, while the Central Asian part of the Russian Empire was desert and arid steppe. Only 14 percent of the empire's 125 million inhabitants were urban dwellers, meaning that most of the population lived in villages scattered across this enormous region. Transportation and communication remained very poor, so that many of these villages, even in European Russia, were connected to the larger world only by dirt roads, some of which turned to mud and became impassable during spring rains. A decree issued by the tsar, the country's hereditary monarch, might take weeks or months to reach his subjects.

The empire was inhabited by a wide range of ethnic and religious groups. Russians made up just more than 40 percent of the population. Together with other Slavic peoples – Belorussians, Ukrainians, and Poles – they constituted around 70 percent. Although the tsarist state had coopted some ethnic elites, many nationalities felt oppressed by Russian rule. Among Poles, Finns, Estonians, Latvians, and Lithuanians there was a strong desire for independence, something these nationalities achieved following the Russian Revolution. Other nationalities also had aspirations for independence, including those in the Caucasus such as Georgians and Armenians, both of whom possessed distinct political and cultural heritages. A majority of people in the Russian empire were Christian, including ethnic Russians who overwhel-mingly were members of the Eastern Orthodox Church, but there were also large Jewish and Muslim populations. Jews felt oppressed by the tsarist regime, as its laws restricted both where they could live and what occupations they could take up. The many Muslim peoples of the empire, including Tatars on the Volga River, ethnic groups in the Caucasus, and

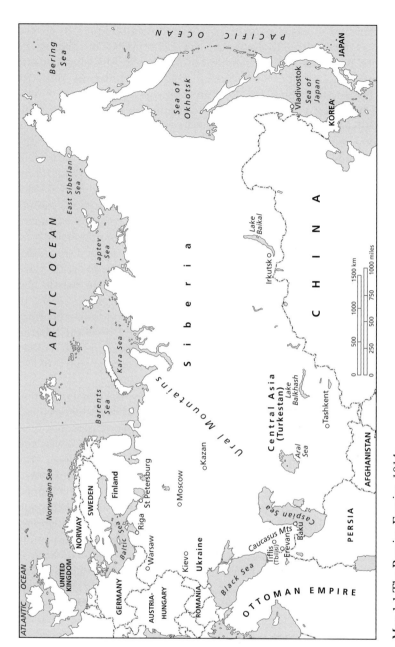

Map 1.1 The Russian Empire, 1914.

the Turkic and Persian peoples of Central Asia, frequently viewed Russians as imperialists. In theory the tsar was supposed to stand above nationality, but in the late nineteenth century the tsarist regime became increasingly nationalistic. Government attempts to Russify minority groups, by teaching them the Russian language or trying to convert them to Orthodox Christianity, only confirmed in the minds of non-Russian subjects the oppressive imperialism of the tsarist state.[2]

By 1900, western portions of the empire were developing economically. The Polish provinces and the Baltic states, as well as St. Petersburg itself, had substantial numbers of factories and slightly higher standards of living. But most of the empire remained poor and underdeveloped. In provincial European Russia and Ukraine the majority of peasants engaged in subsistence agriculture. Nationalities in the Caucasus region, apart from those in a few urban centers, lived in remote mountain villages. Some residents of Central Asia were nomads who engaged in animal herding, while others relied on agriculture, though in arid, non-prosperous conditions. Given land shortages in European Russia and Ukraine, increasing numbers of peasants migrated to western Siberia to farm there, though the short growing season made conditions far from favorable for agriculture. In the far north of European Russia and Siberia, the Chukchi and other "small peoples of the north" lived in even harsher climatic conditions and subsisted primarily on hunting and reindeer herding.[3]

In addition to deep ethnic and religious divisions, the Russian empire suffered from severe social stratification. At the top of its hierarchical, caste society was the nobility, which made up less than 2 percent of the population yet controlled much of the country's political power and wealth. In European Russia, the provincial nobility were the landlords for the largest social group, the peasantry, which constituted more than 80 percent of the population. Most Russian peasants farmed the land communally – the peasant commune was an institution through which peasant elders apportioned both land and tax obligations among members of their village. But much of the land in the Russian countryside was owned by the nobility, and peasants had to lease this land or work as sharecroppers in order to feed their families. Peasants generally believed that all the land should belong to those who worked it, and accordingly they felt enormous antipathy toward noble landowners. While some peasants by the late nineteenth century had become involved in trade, handicraft labor, and temporary work in cities, others continued to engage in subsistence agriculture, eating the crops they grew and endangered by periodic crop failures and famines.[4]

Russia lacked the sizeable middle class that had developed by this time in many western European countries. Merchants and industrialists represented only a tiny fraction of the population, and Russia had little in the way of entrepreneurial traditions – in fact, most Russians detested profit seeking and the accumulation of wealth.[5] With a scarcity of private capital and entrepreneurship, much of what little industrial development occurred was the result of state investment. In the 1880s and 1890s, the tsarist government embarked upon a program of railroad construction and state-sponsored industrialization. While still small relative to Russia's size, factory output increased. Coal, iron, and steel industries arose alongside preexisting textile mills, and the number of industrial workers grew substantially.

Although nascent industrial growth boosted the country's economy, it did little to ease social tensions. In fact, the early stages of industrialization and urbanization only made differences in wealth and status more glaring. Whereas for centuries peasants had lived in poverty, their misery had been dispersed across an enormous rural expanse. Industrial workers crammed into urban slums and tenements were far more visible, and the contrast between the workers' poverty and the wealth of urban nobles and merchants highlighted the country's social polarization. Dangerous factory conditions, long hours, and low wages further added to workers' discontent.[6] Workers' proximity to one another also offered greater possibilities of collective organizing and political action. The tsarist government increasingly saw the growing working class not only as a social problem but as a political threat as well.

Russia's political system provided no outlet for social grievances and no democratic basis to resolve tensions. Until 1905 it was an absolute monarchy, which meant that the people had no voice in their government and all power rested with the tsar. It was also a hereditary monarchy – the eldest son of the tsar inherited the throne, whether or not he was competent to lead the empire. Russia's last tsar, Nicholas II, who reigned from 1894 to 1917, was a weak ruler (see Figure 1.1). He was devoted to his family and was known for his good horsemanship and ballroom dancing. But he completely lacked the will and ability to reign. Upon inheriting the throne, he confided to his brother-in-law, "I am not prepared to be a Tsar. I never wanted to become one. I know nothing of the business of ruling. I have no idea of even how to talk to the ministers."[7] Government ministers soon discovered that Nicholas II constantly changed his mind, agreeing with whomever he had spoken to last. Dim-witted and indecisive, Nicholas II provided no leadership for an empire that desperately needed it. He proved resolute only in his resistance to political reforms, despite the fact that monarchical institutions were becoming obsolete.

Figure 1.1 Tsar Nicholas II, ca. 1900.

The tsar ruled the empire through a huge bureaucracy, which had grown to nearly 400,000 officials by the early twentieth century. Most tsarist bureaucrats worked in St. Petersburg, the capital city located in the far northwest corner of the country. They generally had little knowledge of the local conditions of the empire's various peoples, many of whom lived thousands of miles away. As ethnic Russians, central bureaucrats tended to be disdainful of ethnic minorities and their customs, contributing to the imperialist nature of the tsarist government. Moreover, tsarist administrators were notoriously incompetent and corrupt, as people learned to expect inefficiency and bribe-taking when trying to deal with government officials.

The intelligentsia, the relatively small number of highly educated people in Russia, despised the tsarist autocracy and longed for political and social reform. In the early nineteenth century most members of the intelligentsia had come from the nobility, but by 1900 there were growing numbers of educated professionals – doctors, lawyers, teachers, engineers, agronomists – who were not of noble birth. Some were the sons and daughters of the clergy, while others had come from less privileged groups but had managed to get a university education. These people often felt alienated from both the government elite and the lower classes. Yet members of the intelligentsia were also characterized by a sense of obligation to help peasants and workers. They were aware of the wretched living conditions, widespread malnutrition, and high rates of infectious diseases among the lower classes.

In 1887, life expectancy in the Russian empire was only 32 years, and Russia's infant mortality rate was the highest in Europe – one-quarter of all infants died in their first year of life. Nearly three-quarters of all peasants were illiterate, though with the spread of new schools, literacy rates were increasing at the end of the tsarist era.[8] Peasant villages were characterized by poverty – dank, smoky huts with dirt floors, farm animals living alongside humans, swarms of flies in the summer, cold and darkness in the winter. Drunkenness was widespread among the peasantry, as was superstition and domestic violence. Educated Russians hoped to uplift the masses and to improve their lives and living conditions.[9]

The intelligentsia's efforts at social amelioration mirrored reform movements in western Europe, where public health specialists, social workers, and educators sought to teach hygiene, sobriety, and literacy to the burgeoning ranks of urban, industrial workers. But the Russian intelligentsia hoped to avoid many of the pitfalls of Western modernization. The fact that Russia industrialized later than the countries of western Europe meant that its intelligentsia was aware of the problems associated with industrialization and urbanization, including overcrowding, exploitation, crime, and social strife. Industrialization had seemingly destroyed the organic unity of traditional societies. Educated Russians could draw upon socialist thought, which proposed an alternative to industrial capitalism and class antagonism. The intelligentsia, then, was eager to modernize, but sought Russia's own path to modernity, one that might avoid the social disruption and alienation of industrial capitalism. They wanted to modernize the country not only to bolster national defense, but to improve people's lives and overcome the population's high rates of illiteracy and infectious disease.[10]

Members of the Russian intelligentsia had much in common with reformers in other late-developing countries, such as the Ottoman Empire, Persia, Japan, and Mexico. In those countries too, educated professionals were aware of their populations' "backwardness" and were eager to modernize. They too looked at "the West" with a mixture of admiration and apprehension. While they hoped their societies would emulate Western material progress and education, they wished to avoid the capitalist exploitation they witnessed in western Europe. The Russian intelligentsia and their counterparts in other developing countries placed their faith in the transformative powers of science and culture as the means by which they might uplift the people. And given that all these countries lacked well-developed civil societies and civic institutions, many of their educated elites hoped to use the power of the state to help enact this social transformation. In the case of Russian intellectuals, they did not look to the tsarist autocracy, but rather to some future, progressive state that would give them a leading role in developing the country.

The Revolutionary Movement

Some members of the intelligentsia went beyond calls for reform and pushed instead for revolution – the violent overthrow of the tsarist order. The origins of the Russian revolutionary movement may be traced to the rise of utopian thought in western Europe. The notion of radically restructuring society had been inconceivable within a traditional world-view that saw God as the sole arbiter of worldly affairs. But Enlightenment thinkers in eighteenth-century France began to question both the existence of God and the sanctity of tradition. And if there were no God to manage society, then should not humankind construct its own rational social order? If there were no heaven above, should not people seek to create a heaven on earth – a perfect society, with liberty, equality, and prosperity for all?

By the nineteenth century, social thinkers in western Europe had developed utopian ideas, and these ideas began to spread to Russia. Some Russian intellectuals found these ideas alluring, but they confronted an enormous gulf between their aspirations and the reality around them. While they hoped to create a perfect society, everywhere they saw poverty, disease, and illiteracy, all presided over by the tyrannical and corrupt tsarist bureaucracy. For them to bridge this gulf and make the leap to a utopian future, it seemed that small incremental steps were too little. Instead, the more radical among them dreamed of bold, dramatic action – something that in one apocalyptic moment might wipe away all of the injustices of the old world and create something entirely new. In other words, they dreamed of a revolution. And if that revolution were to achieve their utopian goal, where all future generations would live in harmony, then any action including violence seemed justified in order to realize it.

Russian radicals of the 1870s formed a terrorist organization called the People's Will. Its members plotted to assassinate the reigning tsar, Alexander II, in the hopes of sparking a political uprising. In 1881, a member of the People's Will threw a bomb under the tsar's horse-drawn carriage in the streets of St. Petersburg. The explosion injured several guards, but the tsar stepped out of the splintered carriage unhurt. As he thanked God for sparing his life, another terrorist ran up shouting, "It is too early to thank God," and threw a second bomb. This one exploded at the tsar's feet and killed him.[11] The assassination of Alexander II, however, did not trigger a revolution. Instead, the next two tsars, Alexander III and Nicholas II, sought to reinforce the monarchy with conservative policies and repression. The tsarist police arrested hundreds of suspected revolutionaries and hanged those involved in terrorist activities. A range of revolutionary groups nonetheless continued to struggle for the overthrow of the autocracy.

Some Russian radicals turned to the ideas of Karl Marx. Like other socialist thinkers, Marx hoped to overcome the social stratification and antagonisms that had accompanied the rise of industrial capitalism in western Europe. He believed that the path to equality and social harmony could be found via proletarian revolution that would usher in an era of socialism. Marx put forward a theory of history according to which humankind was progressing through stages – feudalism to capitalism to socialism, and ultimately to communism, a utopian final stage in which all people would live in prosperity and harmony. Many Russian leftists were drawn to Marxism due to its emphasis on environmental factors as the determinants of human consciousness. They blamed the wretched condition of the masses not on peasants and workers themselves, but on imperial Russia's oppressive economic and social environment. Marx promised the replacement of the old order with freedom and equality under socialism. The particular context in which Marxism took root, then, was one in which members of the Russian intelligentsia fought simultaneously to overcome the tsarist autocracy and to uplift the people. To view Marxism as an ideology artificially imposed on Russia ignores both the reasons it was adopted and the fact that many non-Marxist intellectuals shared this wish for revolutionary change.

Russian Marxists were divided into two factions, the more radical being the Bolsheviks, later renamed the Communists. Vladimir Lenin, the leader of the Bolsheviks, was uncompromising in his push for a socialist revolution in Russia. Unlike the more moderate Marxist party, the Mensheviks, Lenin and the Bolsheviks did not see the need for Russia to pass through a long stage of capitalism. Flaunting traditional Marxist thought, which saw proletarian revolutions starting first in the industrialized countries of western Europe, Lenin argued that the working classes in developing countries could become the vanguard of world revolution. In his article, "Imperialism, the Highest Stage of Capitalism," Lenin stated that because capitalism was most exploitative in colonial settings (including in Russia), workers there would be the first to rise up against it.[12]

Many Bolsheviks were from non-Russian minorities within the empire, including Georgians, Latvians, and Jews. The fact that these groups were disproportionately represented in this revolutionary political party is not surprising, given that they were largely excluded from positions of power and privilege under the tsarist government. Discrimination toward national and religious minorities naturally aroused opposition within these groups. Among the Bolshevik Party members was a young Georgian named Joseph Djugashvili, alias Joseph Stalin. Stalin came from a poor, working-class family. His mother wanted him to become a priest, and he attended an Orthodox seminary. There he received an education and was also exposed to Marxist ideas. After he left the seminary, he joined the Bolshevik Party and became a revolutionary organizer who planned strikes and protest marches. Like many of the Bolsheviks, he suffered arrest and exile to Siberia several times, but persecution by the tsarist police only heightened his commitment to violent revolution.[13]

Had the tsarist autocracy provided for national defense and increasing prosperity, the Bolsheviks and other radical groups in Russia might never have had the opportunity to carry out a revolution. But instead, military failures combined with widespread privation undermined people's faith in the tsar's ability to lead the country. In the Russo-Japanese War of 1904–05, Russia was badly defeated by a country that was not yet considered a leading military power. The Baltic Fleet – the pride of the Russian navy – sailed halfway around the world to engage the Japanese, only to be annihilated in the Battle of Tsushima. Tales of government incompetence coupled with military defeats eroded people's confidence in their government.

The Revolution of 1905 broke out during the Russo-Japanese War. On January 9, 1905 – Bloody Sunday, as it became known – a crowd of demonstrators marched toward the royal palace to petition the tsar. They sought improved working conditions, better wages, and an end to the war with Japan. Some of the demonstrators carried portraits of the tsar to emphasize their loyalty to him and to plead for his assistance. To prevent the marchers from reaching the palace, tsarist soldiers fired on the crowd, killing and wounding hundreds of people. This massacre of peaceful demonstrators provoked widespread outrage, and workers throughout the country organized strikes and demonstrations in response. As rebellions escalated, tsarist officials seemed paralyzed and unable to quell the unrest. Mutinies broke out in the military. Peasants began to seize land and drive nobles from the countryside. In addition to widespread antipathy toward the monarchy, the Revolution of 1905 revealed the deep social antagonisms between Russia's upper and lower classes. Finally in October 1905, Nicholas II issued the October Manifesto, which promised the creation of a national parliament (the Duma).[14]

The October Manifesto divided the revolutionary forces and allowed the autocracy to endure, but it did not lead to a stable constitutional monarchy. Nicholas II and his advisors subsequently limited the Duma's powers and (after dissolving it twice) decreed new electoral regulations that guaranteed conservative noble landowners a majority in the Duma. This change meant that while a Russian parliament existed, it had limited authority and did not democratically represent the population. While the tsarist government carried out harsh repressive measures against revolutionaries, social discontent increased further, particularly among workers after the Lena goldfields massacre in 1912 – another large-scale shooting of peaceful demonstrators by tsarist soldiers.

As if the tsar's authority were not discredited enough, he fell under the influence of a self-proclaimed holy man from Siberia named Grigory Rasputin (see Figure 1.2). Rasputin had gained a reputation as a mystic healer, and in 1907 he was brought to the royal palace to help the tsar's son. Nicholas II's only son and the heir to the throne, Aleksey, suffered from hemophilia, a serious medical condition in which one's blood does not clot properly. Like other hemophiliacs, Aleksey was prone to internal or external bleeding, and doctors at the time could do little to help him. Rasputin seemed to be the only person who could soothe and heal the boy, and in this way he gained influence first over the tsar's wife, Alexandra, and then over Nicholas II himself. Rasputin used this influence to meddle in politics and sway the tsar's decisions.

Prime Minister Peter Stolypin warned the tsar that Rasputin's presence at the palace was discrediting the monarchy. He even showed him police reports on Rasputin's orgies with prostitutes, and agreed to confront Rasputin himself. Stolypin later described their meeting: "Rasputin ran his pale eyes over me. He mumbled mysterious and inarticulate words

Figure 1.2 Grigory Rasputin, 1916.

from the Scriptures and made strange movements with his hands." Stolypin sensed Rasputin was trying to hypnotize him, but he threatened "this vermin" and banished him from the capital.[15] Nicholas II promised not to see Rasputin again, but Tsarina Alexandra defended "Our Friend," and Rasputin was soon back at the palace. At times, Rasputin would go into holy fits, when he would writhe on the floor and speak as if possessed. Nicholas II and Alexandra interpreted Rasputin's words as the voice of God, and they heeded his advice.

Even among the nobility, many began to doubt the tsar's ability to lead the country. The fact that a dissolute adventurer like Rasputin could gain such influence over the tsar revealed a fundamental flaw in Russia's monarchical government. Personalized rule concentrated in the hands of one person – someone chosen based on heredity, not merit – meant that decisions of the utmost national importance could be made capriciously. Opportunists and charlatans manipulated the tsar and his policies in harmful ways. The Russian monarchy was not only undemocratic, it was arbitrary and corrupt, and clearly unequal to the task of governing a vast empire.

To sum up, Russia on the eve of World War I was the world's largest country, comprised of many different national and ethnic groups. It was primarily an agrarian country, with an overwhelmingly peasant population and high rates of illiteracy and infectious disease. Compared with western European countries, it was underdeveloped – lacking in industry, infrastructure, transportation, and communication networks. As a consequence, Russia had fallen behind Germany and other countries in terms of military capability. Politically, Russia also seemed backward – a monarchy with weakly developed institutions of civic engagement. Ethnic tensions, social strife, and a growing revolutionary movement increasingly endangered the existing social and political order. Overall the country was ill-prepared for the cataclysm of World War I, a war that the tsarist regime would not survive.

World War I

Never before in history had there been a war fought on the scale of World War I. Nearly 70 million soldiers fought in the war, with more than 9 million of them killed and more than 20 million wounded. Traditionally, European warfare had been the business of professional armies, and the civilian population was largely insulated from wars. But the conscription of millions of young men into armies during World War I, and the mobilization of civilians to produce weapons for the war, changed the face of both warfare and politics. The advent of mass warfare led to the politicization of the masses. Governments could not continue fighting the war without maintaining the morale and support of their populations. Nowhere did this fact become clearer than in Russia, where World War I led to the overthrow of the tsar and eventually to the founding of the Soviet regime. In addition, the mobilizational demands of war led to expanded government control over the economy and the population. World War I, then, not only led to the Russian Revolution, it also established a range of interventionist practices that would become prominent features of Stalinism.

The iconic images of World War I come from the western front, where soldiers were mired in trenches and the battle lines changed very little in four years of war. Infantry charges were repeatedly repulsed as soldiers were slaughtered by machine guns and artillery. On the eastern front, soldiers also suffered slaughter by artillery bombardment and machine gun fire, but the character of warfare was different. The battle lines there were much more fluid, and vast swathes of territory changed hands in the course of the war. Unfortunately for the Russian army, most of its movement was in retreat. At the outset of the war, the Russian army invaded German territory, only to suffer a catastrophic defeat in the Battle of Tannenberg. While the Russian army did have some success against the Austro-Hungarian army to the south, it was no match for the German army. Because Germany was much more industrialized than Russia, its artillery and munitions were far superior. In addition, Russia's railway network was less developed, so the Russian military had trouble moving troops and supplies. Russia soon began to run short of rifles and ammunition, and by 1915, one-quarter of Russian soldiers were sent into battle without guns.

The tsarist autocracy was clearly not up to the task of mobilizing the vast human and material resources needed for World War I. Indeed, this unprecedented mobilization proved a challenge for all countries, and it deeply affected governments and societies throughout Europe. All major combatants in the war extended the reach of state authority. Governments initiated economic controls, surveillance mechanisms, internment camps, welfare programs, and public health measures. The expansion of state control was dictated by the demands of mass warfare, as political leaders sought to safeguard their countries' "human capital" and "military manpower." New government programs also arose in response to security concerns and social problems caused by the war.

Russia had lagged behind many other European countries in terms of government welfare programs. But wartime mobilizations, widespread epidemic diseases, and massive social displacements required the Russian government to augment state intervention. Government policies included a range of public health and welfare measures. When, for example, locally based physicians proved unable to cope with the millions of war wounded and the spread of epidemic diseases, the tsar finally agreed to the creation of a state ministry of health in 1916 – similar to countries throughout Europe that created ministries of health in the wake of World War I.[16] To provide for the welfare of disabled soldiers, war widows, and refugees, the Russian government replaced private charities with parastatal organizations (nominally independent bodies connected to the state). These organizations offered medical aid, food, and shelter for the hundreds of thousands of citizens in need during the war.[17]

Countries involved in World War I all increased government control of their economies. Germany went the furthest, with government planning of industrial production and, in late 1916, universal labor conscription. The United Kingdom's Defence of the Realm Act gave the government power to manage key sectors of the economy. Russia likewise moved toward centralized economic controls through the creation of the War Industries-Committees – organizations of industrialists who worked closely with the government to manage Russia's economy for the war effort.[18] Governments also intervened to manage food supplies, through both rationing and the requisitioning of grain. In Germany, Austria-Hungary, and the Ottoman Empire (and later in Russia under the Provisional Government), political leaders replaced free-market economies with government grain monopolies, state food supply bureaucracies, and the use of military units to requisition grain.

Governments throughout Europe also vastly expanded surveillance of their populations during World War I. Previously, police in many countries, including Russia, had monitored the activities of small numbers of people – suspected revolutionaries and opponents of the regime. During World War I, governments of combatant countries began to monitor the "political moods" of their entire populations through perlustration of letters, the use of informants, and intelligence reports. The French government in 1915, for example, introduced military postal censorship and perlustration of mail, whereby censors would secretly open soldiers' letters. Initially these measures were simply to prevent soldiers from revealing sensitive military information, but soon censors began to compile and analyze information on sentiments within the French army. Other countries including Russia similarly began perlustration of letters, use of informants, and reporting on the political moods of the population. Surveillance became much more than an effort to keep tabs on subversive individuals. Instead, it embodied an effort to map and mold people's thinking.[19]

Hand in hand with surveillance came massive government propaganda efforts. During World War I, political and military leaders throughout Europe came to see the national will as crucial to victory. To maintain their civilians' morale and their soldiers' will to fight, governments formed state bureaucracies or parastatal organizations to produce propaganda posters, leaflets, and films. The British War Cabinet formed the National War Aims Committee, the Austro-Hungarian High Command created the Enemy Propaganda Defense Agency, and the Italian government established the Commissariat for Civilian Assistance and Propaganda. In Russia, the Skobelev Committee, a parastatal organization with close ties to the tsarist government, produced films and posters to promote patriotism and subservience to the tsar.[20]

Governments also used new forms of state violence against civilian populations, in particular deportations and concentration camps. The incarceration of civilians in concentration camps first occurred during colonial warfare around 1900 – in Cuba during the Spanish–American War and in South Africa during the Boer War. All major combatant countries then used concentration camps during World War I. German military commanders created a network of civilian labor camps in Belgium and northern France, while Russia, Germany, the United Kingdom, France, Canada, and the United States all established internment camps for "enemy aliens" (citizens of opposing countries) residing on their soil.[21] Governments of multinational empires – Russia, Austro-Hungary, and the Ottoman Empire – also deported and interned segments of their own populations, namely ethnic and religious minorities that they did not trust. The tsarist government deported nearly 1 million of its subjects – ethnic Germans, Jews, and Muslims – from regions near the front.[22]

Like other combatant countries, then, Russia instituted a range of total war practices – economic controls, grain requisitioning, government health and welfare programs, surveillance, deportations, and concentration camps. All of these practices would become institutionalized features of the Soviet system and key elements of Stalinism. The fact that they arose outside Russia and prior to 1917 indicates that the origins of Stalinism went beyond Marxist ideology and Stalin himself. Instead, Stalinism represented a system of government mobilization and repression based on wartime practices. As we will see, what distinguished Stalinism was the fact that Stalin and his fellow leaders continued these total war practices during peacetime and used them to pursue their ideological agenda.

World War I in Russia also led to the increasing politicization of the masses. While industrial workers had already been politically active, the peasantry now became politically aware as well. This was particularly true of the roughly 15 million peasants drafted into the army during the course of the war. But even back in the villages there was heightened political awareness, as peasants eagerly gathered to hear newspapers read in order to learn about the course of the war.[23] As the war dragged on and Russian losses mounted, morale in the army began to fall. By the end of 1916, the Russian army had lost 5.7 million men, 3.6 million killed or seriously wounded and the rest prisoners of war. The politicization of soldiers meant that they discussed the failures of the tsarist government and increasingly questioned the authority of their officers. Some soldiers began to desert from the army while others defied their officers and mutinied. Soldiers garrisoned in Russia's cities were exposed to propaganda by socialist agitators who denounced the war effort and called for revolution. Whereas in 1905 the army had ultimately played a decisive role in crushing rebellions, in 1917 soldiers could no longer be counted on to shoot protesters. On the contrary, many soldiers became a revolutionary force, deserting from the army and taking their guns with them back to their villages.[24]

Among the civilian population, unrest also began to grow. The continuing war effort caused severe shortages of fuel and food, so that urban residents were cold and hungry. Workers repeatedly engaged in strikes, literally thousands of which had occurred by 1917. Increasingly they put forward not only economic but political demands. Peasants, who for decades had been wanting more land, began to seize the property of noble landowners. Some non-Russian nationalities began to rebel against tsarist authority. A large-scale revolt took place in Central Asia when the tsarist government tried to conscript Muslims into the Russian army in 1916.[25] When the tsarist autocracy finally collapsed in February 1917, Russia entered a period of revolution and civil war – the moment in which the Soviet state would be born.

The Russian Revolution

The overthrow of the monarchy came not at the hands of revolutionary groups, but rather as the result of spontaneous protests. By the beginning of 1917, demonstrations had become regular occurrences in the Russian capital, Petrograd (previously named St. Petersburg). On International Women's Day in February 1917, a group of women workers called for a strike and began marching through the streets demanding bread and an end to the war. Their protest in the context of worker militancy ignited a political revolution. Marching past factories, the women strikers were joined by more and more workers. By the end of the day, more than 100,000 workers (a third of the city's workforce) were on strike. During the next few days, the strikes grew into large demonstrations against the war effort and the tsarist regime. Nicholas II ordered authorities to disperse the demonstrators, but after some initial bloodshed, soldiers refused to fire on crowds and instead joined the revolution. The military high command then rejected the tsar's order to move new troops to the capital. Having lost all authority, Nicholas II abdicated the throne, and the Russian monarchy came to an end.[26]

When the tsarist autocracy collapsed, Russia was left with a power vacuum. If the Duma had been a truly democratic parliament with the confidence of the people, then it might have formed a government with popular legitimacy. Members of the Duma did form the Provisional Government, with the idea that it would rule until national elections could be held and a constitution written. But the Provisional Government never gained popular legitimacy or full administrative control over the country. The lower classes did not trust the Provisional Government, and workers and soldiers elected delegates to their own representative bodies, the soviets. Historians have termed the uneasy coexistence of the Provisional Government and the soviets "dual power," because political power was divided. These political divisions reflected the deep social divisions in Russia, particularly between the upper classes on one hand, and the mass of peasants, soldiers, and workers on the other.[27]

The Provisional Government continued the wartime trend of expanding state responsibility for the population's welfare. It established ministries of health, state welfare, and food supply, and placed many professionals in the positions of leadership they had so long desired. Politically, however, the Provisional Government failed to win a broad base of support. The country's lower classes had their own revolutionary agendas that included an end to the war, immediate land redistribution, and workers' control of factories, none of which the Provisional Government delivered. As soldiers deserted, peasants seized land, and workers pledged loyalty to the soviets, Provisional Government officials became disillusioned with the masses for refusing to conform to liberal ideals of patriotism and civic consciousness. Increasingly the Provisional Government resorted to coercive means of governance, for example the use of military force to requisition grain.

The most pressing issue facing the Provisional Government was World War I. After three years of warfare and literally millions of casualties, both soldiers and civilians wanted the war to end. But Provisional Government leaders instead continued the war effort. The leader of the liberals, Pavel Miliukov, assured Russia's allies that his country would fight on to a decisive victory.[28] Alexander Kerensky, a moderate member of the Socialist Revolutionary Party and the leader of the Provisional Government, in June launched a new military offensive that proved to be another disaster for the Russian army. More soldiers deserted and returned to their villages, where they spread the revolution.[29] The Provisional Government also failed to meet the peasantry's demand for land redistribution. Government leaders postponed action on this issue, and in the summer of 1917, peasants took matters into their own hands by seizing the nobility's land.

Moderate socialists, including Mensheviks and Right Socialist Revolutionaries, participated in the Provisional Government, and as hostility toward the government grew, their popularity declined. But the Bolsheviks, after Lenin's return from exile in April, took a militant stance against the Provisional Government. They instead called for "All Power to the Soviets!" The Bolsheviks also coined another slogan, "Peace, Land, and Bread." This slogan promised the lower classes what they wanted: peace – an immediate end to the war; land – the redistribution of the nobility's land to the peasants; and bread – an end to food shortages in the cities. As disenchantment with the Provisional Government grew, the Bolsheviks' popularity among workers and soldiers soared.[30]

The Bolsheviks were also responsive to the demands of non-Russian nationalities within the empire. The collapse of the tsarist regime had given non-Russian nationalities the opportunity to articulate their aspirations for self-rule. While most Russian politicians insisted on maintaining a strong, centralized Russian state, Lenin supported non-Russians' demands for greater autonomy. At Lenin's urging, Stalin had written a treatise on Marxism and nationalism in which he argued that national minorities should, within a larger state structure, have regional autonomy, including the right to use their own languages and administer their own schools. He did not advocate national independence, arguing that nationalism was only a temporary phase under capitalism that would fade under socialism. But unlike many political leaders in 1917, Lenin and Stalin recognized that Russian chauvinism and attempts to suppress national minorities would only inflame nationalist separatism.

In an atmosphere of crisis and political polarization, the Provisional Government's authority rapidly eroded. In September, a right-wing general named Lavr Kornilov attempted to carry out a military coup. To defend the revolution, railway workers refused to transport Kornilov's troops to Petrograd, and Bolshevik agitators quickly convinced the troops not to follow their officers' orders. Following their prominent role in defeating Kornilov's coup attempt, the Bolsheviks gained even greater support among workers and soldiers. They achieved a majority in the Petrograd Soviet and Lev Trotsky, a prominent Bolshevik leader, was elected chairman. "All Power to the Soviets" now effectively meant power to the Bolsheviks themselves. By October, a majority of soldiers in the Petrograd garrison supported the Bolsheviks. Though the Provisional Government continued to rule in name, real political and military power in the capital had shifted to the Bolsheviks.

In late October, Lenin decided the time had come to overthrow the Provisional Government. The Second Congress of Soviets – a meeting of representatives from soviets around the country – was set to convene on October 25. Lenin sought to seize power on the eve of this assembly.

On the night of October 24, Bolshevik paramilitary units known as Red Guards began to take control of key points in Petrograd – railway stations, telegraph offices, and government buildings.[31] By the following evening, the Bolsheviks controlled the Russian capital with the exception of the Winter Palace, the seat of the Provisional Government. That night, Bolshevik Red Guards "stormed" the Winter Palace and overthrew the Provisional Government. In reality, the Palace was virtually undefended and Red Guards and other rebels entered the building uncontested. At this critical moment there were almost no troops willing to defend the Provisional Government. The long-awaited socialist revolution had finally taken place, but it occurred in a power vacuum, in a country wracked by war and growing anarchy.[32]

The next day, Lenin took the stage at the Second Congress of Soviets and proclaimed, "We shall now proceed to construct the Socialist order!"[33] But what would a socialist order look like? Never before in world history had there been a socialist state, and Marxism provided no blueprint for how to create one. Marx had written little about what would happen after a successful proletarian revolution – most of his focus had been on the unsustainability of capitalism and the inevitability of revolution. Lenin and other Bolsheviks likewise had focused on bringing about the revolution, not what they would do next. Once they had seized power, the Bolsheviks had to govern the country – a country that, in part due to their own actions, was rapidly heading toward civil war.[34] The measures they took and the state institutions they created were shaped not only by their ideology, but by the desperate circumstances they faced and by state practices already established during World War I.

When the Bolsheviks announced their takeover to the Second Congress of Soviets, moderate socialists – Mensheviks and Right Socialist Revolutionaries – walked out to protest what they saw as a Bolshevik coup. Lenin had long fought factional battles with fellow socialists, and he showed no inclination to work with them now. The fact that he did not wait for the Second Congress of Soviets to convene before seizing power confirms that he in fact preferred one-Party rule. Not all the Bolshevik leaders were so partisan; Grigory Zinoviev and Lev Kamenev had openly opposed the unilateral Bolshevik takeover. But Stalin staunchly supported Lenin, having fought his own factional battles with Mensheviks since first becoming a Marxist revolutionary (see Figure 1.3). Lenin formed a governing executive committee, the Council of People's Commissars, made up almost entirely of Bolsheviks, though he allowed a few Left Socialist Revolutionaries to join them. Two months later, when long-planned elections to the Constituent Assembly (an assembly that was to write a constitution for Russia) were held and the Bolsheviks

Figure 1.3 Joseph Stalin and Vladimir Lenin, 1919.

finished second to the Socialist Revolutionaries, Lenin quickly disbanded the Assembly and retained power for the Bolsheviks. It is not clear that the Constituent Assembly could have established a functional democratic order in the deeply divided Russian empire. But the Bolsheviks' actions certainly heightened political polarization and eliminated any chances for liberal democracy.

Once in power, the Bolsheviks had to make good on their promises of peace, land, and bread. They undertook redistribution of land in their first decree, which gave all land to the peasantry. In effect, this decree only legalized the peasants' seizure of land that had already occurred, but it did demonstrate that the Bolsheviks were willing to take quick action on behalf of the lower classes. Ending the war proved much more difficult. The Germans, who had advanced deep into Russian territory, demanded such humiliating terms of surrender that Trotsky initially walked out of peace negotiations. Ultimately the Bolsheviks accepted huge territorial losses and signed the Treaty of Brest-Litovsk to end the war. Their lone coalition partners, the Left Socialist Revolutionaries, broke with them on this issue and resigned from the government. From that point on, the Soviet state was a one-party dictatorship.[35]

The Civil War

Though the Bolsheviks extricated Russia from World War I, the country was soon embroiled in a bloody civil war in which more than a million people died in battle and several million more succumbed to starvation and disease. The Civil War proved to be a formative event for the nascent Soviet system; it shaped state institutions as well as the political culture and mentality of Bolshevik leaders. To gain administrative rule over the country and to fight the Civil War, they drew upon wartime practices, including centralized economic controls, widespread surveillance, and the use of state violence. The Soviet system was founded not only in the absence of traditional institutional constraints (parliaments, courts, and property rights) but also against the backdrop of a wartime mobilization and a vicious partisan conflict. Significantly, the Bolsheviks' opponents relied on similar practices – grain requisitioning, surveillance, concentration camps, and summary executions – to establish control and eliminate opposition.

Both the Bolsheviks (Reds) and the anti-Bolsheviks (Whites) saw the Civil War as a life-or-death struggle. In his speeches, Lenin bluntly stated that the alternatives facing the Bolsheviks were victory or death. One Russian observer recalled that the Civil War "had no rules of any kind. It was every man for himself; every battle became a matter of individual life and death. No one took prisoners. The wounded were finished off on the spot . . . Kindness, pity, compassion, and justice had been abandoned, to be replaced by cruelty, hatred, and anger."[36] The Civil War was a military conflict, but for many people it was also a fight to survive. As the country descended into anarchy, armed bands roamed the countryside, pillaging villages as they went. Economic collapse in the cities left urban dwellers without food, heat, clean water, or soap. Cities became partly depopulated as thousands fled to villages. Accompanying the flight of starving, lice-covered refugees were widespread epidemics. In his Civil War-era novel, *Doctor Zhivago*, Boris Pasternak describes miles of abandoned trains buried in the snow that served as "strongholds for armed bands of highway robbers, a refuge for criminal and political fugitives in hiding, the involuntary vagabonds of that time, but most of all as common graves and collective burial sites for those who died of cold and the typhus that raged all along the railway line."[37] To win the Civil War, the Bolsheviks had to overcome not only the White armies, but anarchists, foreign intervention, typhus epidemics, and economic collapse.

The most immediate challenge to the Bolsheviks came from the White armies, led by former tsarist officers who did not accept the new Soviet government. These officers, supported by other groups who opposed the

Bolshevik takeover, attempted to win control of the country by force. A White army with about 25,000 soldiers was in the northwest and attacked Petrograd, which only months before had been threatened by the German army. In 1918, the Bolsheviks moved the capital to Moscow, which was more centrally located and less vulnerable. Larger White armies formed in Siberia and in the south. Admiral Alexander Kolchak, leader of the White army in Siberia, declared himself the Supreme Ruler of all Russia, while General Anton Deniken, the leader of the Whites in the south, had 150,000 men under his command. In October 1919, Deniken's army advanced to within 200 miles of Moscow, and until the Red Army counter-attacked, it was not clear that the Soviet regime would survive.[38]

The Bolsheviks also had to contend with foreign intervention, including British, French, American, Czech, and Japanese troops on Russian soil. The initial purpose of intervention by the Allies was to revive the eastern front against Germany, but even after the German surrender on the western front in November 1918, Allied troops stayed on to aid the Whites against the Bolsheviks. While foreign intervention made little difference militarily, it definitely contributed to the Bolsheviks' siege mentality. The lasting legacy of Allied intervention was Bolshevik leaders' memory that, in these early days of the Soviet state, capitalist countries had intervened militarily on the side of their enemies.

The name "Bolsheviks" was strongly associated with the working class, and in order to broaden their support among the peasants, Party leaders renamed themselves "Communists." To fight the Civil War, the Communists formed the Red Army, which they envisioned as a volunteer army with elected officers. The number of volunteers was quite small, however, and the Communists soon instituted conscription. Trotsky, the Commissar of War and head of the Red Army, also abandoned the practice of electing officers and instead strengthened military hierarchy and discipline. Facing a lack of military expertise, he recruited some former tsarist officers (those who had not gone to fight for the Whites). Lenin recognized that the new Soviet state needed technical, bureaucratic, and military specialists. He and Trotsky were willing to appoint former tsarist officers as commanders, provided they were overseen by political commissars. Stalin and other Communists, however, remained deeply suspicious of these representatives of the old regime and repeatedly clashed with them.[39]

The Communists also established a widespread surveillance system during the Civil War. If monitoring "political moods" of the population had been important during World War I, then it was even more vital during the Civil War. Both the Communists and the Whites relied on surveillance to discern people's allegiances and quell opposition. Soviet surveillance techniques replicated those used by governments during World War I and included the perlustration of letters, the recruitment of informants, and the compilation of reports on popular opinion.[40] Soviet postal-telegraph control bureaus employed many of the same bureaucrats who had read letters and written reports for the tsarist regime and the Provisional Government. Soviet leaders did not seek to know popular opinion in order to accommodate it – they labelled people who opposed their policies "counterrevolutionary." But knowledge of soldiers' and civilians' sentiments did guide their propaganda campaigns intended to build support for the Soviet regime.

Surveillance was increasingly carried out by the newly founded Soviet secret police. The Communists had no plan to create a secret police force, but with the widespread political opposition, anarchy, and looting that occurred following the October Revolution, they formed the Cheka (later renamed the OGPU, the NKVD, and eventually the KGB). Intended as a temporary organization with a few dozen employees, the secret police became a permanent fixture of the Soviet system with about 60,000 members by 1921. During the Civil War, the secret police operated tribunals that handed down extrajudicial sentences – including incarceration and execution – to opponents and suspected enemies. In 1918, the Soviet government decreed that "it is essential to protect the Soviet republic against its class enemies by isolating these in concentration camps."[41] The secret police set up a network of concentration camps that held 16,000 people by 1919, and more than 70,000 by 1921. The Whites also carried out summary executions and mass incarcerations against those they saw as enemies. The use of concentration camps to incarcerate civilians deemed a political threat became a fixture of Soviet rule – one that continued long after the Civil War had ended.

At the close of the Civil War, the Communists faced a wave of peasant revolts against grain requisitioning, including a large-scale uprising in Tambov province. General Mikhail Tukhachevsky, the Red Army commander charged with crushing the uprising, relied on deportations and concentration camps to defeat peasant rebels. He ordered the deportation of families and in some cases entire villages suspected of aiding the insurgents. In suppressing the revolt, Soviet authorities carried out summary executions of 15,000 people and imprisoned or deported an additional 100,000. Later, Tukhachevsky wrote that anti-insurgency operations should focus on the entire population rather than on individuals, and that segments of the population deemed unreliable should be physically removed from society – either placed in concentration camps or deported from the region entirely. Thus, for Tukhachevsky, the former tsarist officer and Civil War commander, the keys to establishing Soviet control over a region were techniques of excisionary violence – deportations and concentration camps – that would physically remove hostile segments of the population.[42] An entire cadre of Communist Party members, military officers, government administrators, and secret police agents carried out deportations, incarcerations, and summary executions during this period of total warfare. These practices would continue to inform their behavior, including their readiness to employ state violence in future periods of crisis, particularly during Stalinist collectivization.

To mobilize resources for the Civil War and to govern a vast country in anarchy, the Communists built a huge state apparatus. They employed some former tsarist or Provisional Government bureaucrats, but they also hired non-Communist professional people. The Commissariat of Health, for example, became a large government bureaucracy. Lacking their own ideas and expertise in this area, Communist leaders allowed liberal physicians to play a leading role establishing the Commissariat and its policies. With deadly epidemics sweeping the country, these physician-bureaucrats instituted aggressive public health measures and centralized state control of health care.[43] Similarly, the Soviet government's Commissariat of Social Security, which replaced the Provisional Government's Ministry of State Care, employed non-Communist professionals. These bureaucrats centralized relief efforts for the millions of war wounded, war widows, and refugees.

Government control expanded in the economic realm as well, as the Communists adopted policies that became known as War Communism. They set up the Supreme Economic Council – a body that had authority over the country's entire economy. All economic interests, including those of workers, were thus subordinated to the state bureaucracy. As we have seen, centralized control over the economy was common to many countries during World War I, and it is not surprising that the Communists sought to marshal economic resources during the Civil War. The Supreme Economic Council became institutionalized as a permanent fixture of the Soviet state – one that would continue to oversee the Soviet economy for the entirety of its existence. Economic centralization ended workers' control of factories. In 1917, workers had taken charge of many factories, and the Soviet government sanctioned workers' factory committees in one of its early decrees. But in 1918, the Communists established government management of factories and subordinated workers' wages and hours to government-run trade unions.[44]

The Communists also continued the government grain monopoly, first set up by the tsarist government during World War I. When food shortages continued to worsen, they deployed armed detachments to collect grain, as the Provisional Government had done before them.[45] So, despite the fact that the Communists let the peasants have the land, they did not allow them to profit from it by marketing their grain. Even with grain requisitioning, food shortages in cities continued, and the Soviet government had to ration food, a practice begun in 1916. Commissariats of food supply in towns and cities set bread rations at half a pound per day or lower based on dwindling food stocks.[46] Government control of the economy in all these forms – central planning, state-run industry, grain requisitioning, and rationing – would all become central features of Stalinism as well.

Even before the October Revolution, the Bolsheviks/Communists had expected armed conflict with "class enemies," and indeed their seizure of power helped precipitate the Civil War. But the experience of the Civil War reinforced in them a siege mentality whereby they saw enemies everywhere. After Lenin was seriously wounded in an assassination attempt by the Socialist Revolutionaries (SRs) in 1918, he and other Communists became almost fanatical in their use of terror against opponents. Zinoviev declared, "Comrades, beat the Right SRs mercilessly, without pity; neither courts nor tribunals are necessary . . . Let the blood of Right SRs and White Guards flow. Exterminate the enemies physically."[47] The Communists also came to see the combination of internal and external enemies as a particular danger. In 1920, Poland invaded Ukraine, and Trotsky had to redirect troops fighting the Whites to stop the Polish army. The Red Army successfully drove the Poles back, but the brief war with Poland allowed the White army in the south to regroup. While the Red Army went on to defeat the Whites, the specter of combined internal and external enemies continued to haunt Communist leaders.

The Communists were able to win the Civil War by building an army and a state. From a force of a few thousand Red Guards at the beginning of the war, they fashioned a Red Army of 5 million soldiers.[48] Most of their recruits came from the peasantry, the largest social group in the country, and rates of desertion were very high. But as much as peasants hated Soviet grain requisitioning and conscription, they were more hostile to the White armies which threatened to take away their land and return it to noble landowners.[49] Soviet promises of national autonomy also built support among non-Russian nationalities far more than did the Whites' slogan of "Russia, one and indivisible." To mobilize for war, Communist leaders recruited workers and Red Army soldiers into the Communist Party and appointed many to government positions. Some liberal professionals and former tsarist bureaucrats also served the new Soviet government despite their hostility toward the Communists, in part because of the widespread anarchy within the country. With armed bands roaming the countryside, starvation and epidemics rampant, and the loss of basic urban services, many liberals and even conservatives concluded that the Communists were the only ones who could hold Russia together and re-establish order.[50]

In what ways, then, was the Civil War a formative period for the Soviet system and Stalinism? To win the Civil War, the Communists established a centralized state apparatus, government economic controls, a large secret police force, widespread surveillance, and a network of concentration camps. All of these measures became institutionalized as permanent features of the Soviet system. The Civil War, as part of the lived experience of Soviet leaders and officials, also created a militant tradition within the Communist Party. The Civil War had been a desperate fight to overcome White armies, foreign intervention, and anarchy, but when the Communists won, they could look back on a glorious time when they had laid down their lives to defend the Revolution. This heroic tradition included a cult of will and violence, a sense that if the Communists were ruthless enough they could accomplish anything. As we will see, Stalin and his fellow leaders drew directly on these traditions and institutions to carry out a brutal transformation of the country during the 1930s.

The New Economic Policy

Following their victory in the Civil War, the Communists were faced with the task of rebuilding a country devastated by warfare and economic collapse. Russia had been at war almost continuously from 1914 to 1920. Many sectors of industry had ground to a standstill, and industrial production was only 20 percent of its pre-World War I level. Large cities had lost nearly half their populations due to deaths and flight from starvation. Agricultural production had fallen catastrophically as well, and in 1921–22 a terrible famine swept the Volga region. In the period between 1914 and 1922, roughly 14 million people had died due to war, famine, or disease. So many children had lost their parents that there were some 7 million orphans in the country, many of them homeless and forced to beg or steal to survive (see Figure 1.4).[51]

In addition to economic devastation, the Communists faced a new political crisis at the end of the Civil War. With the White armies defeated, peasants no longer saw the return of landowners as a possibility, and in several regions they rebelled against Communist grain requisitioning. The peasant uprising in Tambov province was but the largest of a number of uprisings that had to be suppressed by military force. In March 1921, sailors at the Kronstadt naval base outside of Petrograd

Figure 1.4 Starving orphans in Samara, 1921.

also revolted against Communist rule. Many of them were from peasant families and opposed Soviet economic controls. The sailors made both political and economic demands, including an end to the Communist dictatorship and a halt to grain requisitioning.[52] Red Army units bloodily suppressed the revolt, but Communist leaders were left deeply shaken. During the Revolution and Civil War, Kronstadt sailors had been among their strongest supporters, so this rebellion compelled them to rethink their economic policies.

Given that there was no model for a socialist economy, Communist Party leaders debated what course to follow. They shared the goals of eliminating capitalism and industrializing the country, but how were they to proceed and at what tempo? Various Party factions put forward programs for creating and administering the new socialist society. The so-called Workers' Opposition argued for workers' participatory democracy with elected representatives in charge of the economy. A faction led by Trotsky advocated a revolutionary transformation based on hierarchy, discipline, and the militarization of labor. Lenin rejected both of these models in favor of a gradualist approach with limited capitalism. At the Tenth Communist Party Congress, meeting during the Kronstadt uprising, he introduced the New Economic Policy (NEP) – a policy that ended grain requisitioning. Peasants now simply had to pay a tax on what they produced, and they could keep surplus grain to sell for a profit. Lenin thus reluctantly allowed the revival of a free-market economy. The Soviet government also abandoned the complete nationalization of industry – while it retained control of large-scale industry and banking, it permitted small-scale capitalist enterprises to operate. Despite strong reservations, Communist Party members accepted the NEP as a necessary retreat given the country's economic devastation and unrest.

At the same time that Lenin pushed through this economic liberalization, he and other Party leaders took no steps toward political relaxation. On the contrary, they maintained vigilance and perpetuated Communist Party dominance over the highly centralized Soviet state apparatus. Lenin even instituted a ban on factions within the Party, and subsequently justified this effort to tighten Party discipline by declaring, "When an army is in retreat, a hundred times more discipline is required than when the army is advancing."[53] Institutions such as the secret police continued to operate, and practices including censorship and surveillance became permanent features of the Soviet state.[54] Whereas the other combatant states of World War I stepped back from total war practices at the conclusion of the war, the Soviet government did not. Communist Party leaders could have disbanded the secret police, lifted censorship, and decentralized political authority. But not only were these institutions and practices firmly entrenched, Party leaders chose to retain them. Given that they were a working-class party ruling a largely peasant country, surrounded by hostile capitalist powers, they continued to feel besieged even after their victory in the Civil War.

While the NEP period was not nearly as violent as the Stalinist era to follow, Party leaders continued to use state violence throughout the 1920s. It was at this time that they institutionalized labor camps within the Soviet system. Already during the Civil War the chief of the secret police, Felix Dzerzhinsky, had introduced forced labor for those incarcerated in concentration camps. In the early 1920s, he and other Soviet officials promoted labor camps not only to isolate class enemies but also to amass laborers for economic projects in remote regions. In 1922, they established a labor camp on the Solovetsky islands in the far north, and this camp became a model for the enormous Gulag prison camp system of the 1930s. Prisoners there were forced to perform hard labor, initially as a tool of reeducation, though beginning in 1926 as a source of revenue for the state.[55]

Soviet officials also continued to use other forms of state violence during the 1920s, particularly on the country's periphery. From 1923 to 1927, the Soviet government undertook large-scale military operations in Central Asia and the Caucasus in order to consolidate control over these regions. Both Red Army units and secret police troops carried out pacification programs that included summary executions, incarcerations, and deportations. In Central Asia, Red Army commander Mikhail Frunze carried out the "complete annihilation" of rebel groups by isolating them from the local population.[56] In the northern Caucasus, some of the same officials who later oversaw the repressions of the 1930s supervised secret police tribunals in the 1920s that handed down thousands of death sentences.[57] Thus, there was significant continuity from the Civil War era to the 1930s both in terms of secret police personnel and repressive practices.

The incorporation of non-Russian nationalities into the Soviet Union was accomplished not only through state violence. As noted earlier, Lenin believed that non-Russians should have the right of national self-determination, arguing that the oppression of national minorities would only inflame nationalist separatism. He wished to retain as much territory as possible under Soviet power but accepted the fact that Poland, Finland, Estonia, Latvia, and Lithuania – all formerly part of the tsarist empire – became independent countries. Lenin believed that if national minorities within the Soviet state were allowed some autonomy that their nationalism would fade over time. Not all Communist leaders agreed with Lenin, as some wished to crush any form of nationalism in favor of proletarian consciousness. Stalin, as Commissar of Nationalities, followed Lenin's general policy of creating non-Russian territorial units within the country, though he remained wary of nationalist separatism and sought greater central control. At the end of 1922, the Communist Party's Central Committee approved Lenin's proposal to form the Union of Soviet Socialist Republics, whereby major nationalities had their own territorial units and became part of a federal system on an equal footing with Russians. In practice, the non-Russian republics did not get political autonomy, but they were allowed to develop, within limits, their own national cultures.[58]

Lenin died in early 1924 after a series of debilitating strokes. Traditionally, Communist leaders were cremated after their deaths, but Party leaders instead decided that Lenin's body should be preserved. They established the Commission for the Immortalization of Lenin's Memory, which was charged with this task. Speaking for the commission, Abel Enukidze stated, "It is of great importance to preserve the physical appearance of this remarkable leader for the next generation and all the future generations."[59] Soviet scientists developed special embalming methods for the long-term maintenance of Lenin's corpse, which was put on display in a mausoleum on Red Square. Poet Vladimir Mayakovsky declared, "Lenin Lived, Lenin Lives, Lenin Will Live!" Lenin's alleged immortality became the basis of a Lenin cult, as portraits and statues of Lenin were displayed and Petrograd was renamed Leningrad.[60] The Lenin cult set a precedent for a subsequent cult of Stalin – a similar deification of the leader, though while Stalin was still alive and ruling the country.

Over time, the New Economic Policy succeeded in reviving the country's economy. By the mid-1920s, agriculture and industry had recovered to their prewar levels. Some scholars have argued that the NEP represented a moderate alternative to Stalinism – a "market road to socialism" that would not have required massive state coercion and economic control.[61] Indeed, Party leader Nikolai Bukharin and his supporters wished to continue the NEP for a long time in order to maintain peace with the peasantry and build economic wealth for the future socialist society. But the NEP system was deeply unpopular among Party members and workers. They resented the capitalists – known as NEPmen – who became rich operating small factories and shops. Some NEPmen flaunted their wealth, wearing fashionable clothing and patronizing expensive restaurants and nightclubs. Party members asked why they had shed blood during the Revolution and Civil War, only to see the capitalists return and exploit workers once again.

The period of the New Economic Policy also presented a myriad of social problems. Workers faced high levels of unemployment, as industry recovered unevenly.[62] Unemployment was particularly bad among women workers, some of whom turned to prostitution to feed themselves and their families. Drug use became rampant, with cocaine abuse among urban youth and rising rates of addiction. Petty crime also spread, a consequence of drug addiction, unemployment, and the uneven distribution of wealth. Rates of juvenile delinquency soared, in part due to the large number of orphaned, homeless children.[63] In the countryside, generational tensions arose between village elders and younger peasants, particularly those who had spent time in the cities or served in the Red Army. Party leaders also imagined that "kulaks" – rich peasants – were exploiting poor peasants and withholding grain. The Revolution was supposed to eliminate the social problems of the tsarist era, but instead these problems persisted, and in many ways worsened. Party members blamed NEP capitalism for social ills, and many of them wished to abandon the New Economic Policy altogether.

Socialism in One Country

Soviet leaders initially believed that their revolutionary regime could only survive if socialist revolution spread to other countries. Prior to 1917, Lenin had stated that "the Russian Revolution can achieve victory by its own efforts, but it cannot possibly hold and consolidate its gains by its own strength. It cannot do this unless there is a socialist revolution in the West."[64] Not only did Marxist theory underscore the importance of international proletarian revolution, but geopolitical realities weighed heavily upon Lenin and his fellow leaders. They were well aware that their country was far weaker militarily than the industrially advanced countries of the world. Moreover, several of these countries – the United Kingdom, France, and the United States – were openly hostile to the Soviet government.

Communist Party leaders hoped that workers' revolutions would spread to other countries. The advance of socialism would serve both their ideological interests and their security needs. Were revolutions to sweep socialists into power abroad, the Soviet Union would no longer be the world's lone socialist state, surrounded by capitalist enemies. To this end, in 1919, Party leaders had created the Communist International (Comintern), an organization that supported foreign communists' efforts to stage their own revolutions. Such hopes had not been unfounded in the immediate aftermath of World War I. After four years of brutal warfare in which millions had been killed, no one was able to give a good reason why the war had been fought. Among European workers there was a sense that the only people who had benefitted from the war were industrialists, who became rich while common men were slaughtered in the trenches. Widespread unrest, including soldiers' mutinies in 1918 and a wave of strikes in 1919, characterized the period at the end of the war. In fact, uprisings in Germany and Hungary (the latter aided by the Comintern) made it appear that socialist revolutions were spreading to other countries. These revolts, however, proved to be short-lived, and Soviet leaders soon had to face the fact that they could not count on help from revolutions abroad.

As hopes for international proletarian revolution dwindled, Stalin began to argue that the Soviet Union could build socialism on its own. Beginning in the mid-1920s, he proclaimed his doctrine of Socialism in One Country, whereby Soviet Communists would not need support from abroad. Trotsky and Zinoviev scorned Stalin's idea as a distortion of Marxism, and they continued to prioritize the spread of revolution to western Europe. But Stalin's stance won the support of rank-and-file Party members, many of whom were not well-versed in Marxist theory and welcomed the view that they could succeed on their own. Stalin and his supporters still believed the revolution would spread eventually, but increasingly they saw the strengthening of their own country as the best way to achieve socialism.

Stalin's doctrine of Socialism in One Country helped him in the succession struggle that unfolded after Lenin's death. Lenin had not designated his successor. In a document known as his "Testament," he had appraised the Party's leading figures but had found fault with each of them. What followed Lenin's death in 1924 was a period of collective leadership while Party leaders grappled for power. Trotsky seemed the most likely heir to Lenin. He was a brilliant speaker and theoretician; he had played a role second only to Lenin during the October Revolution; and he had created the Red Army and won the Civil War. But others did not trust Trotsky and teamed up against him. Wary of the historical example of the French Revolution, they saw Trotsky as a potential military dictator like Napoleon. Zinoviev and Kamenev formed an alliance with Stalin, whom they saw as no threat to themselves.

Stalin lacked oratorical skills and theoretical brilliance. He excelled instead at organizational matters and served as the Communist Party's General Secretary in charge of personnel. This post allowed him to appoint his own loyalists to key positions in the Party. In 1926, two of Stalin's strongest supporters – Viacheslav Molotov and Kliment Voroshilov – became members of the Politburo (the ruling executive body of the Communist Party). That same year, his protégé Sergey Kirov became the head of the Leningrad Party organization. Stalin also benefitted from changes in the composition of the Communist Party. The Party expanded enormously during the Civil War, as many Red Army soldiers gained membership. After Lenin's death more than 400,000 workers were recruited into the Party to guarantee its proletarian character. These new recruits were less educated than Party intellectuals, and for that reason they were drawn to Stalin's blunt style, as well as to his ideas.[65]

Belatedly, Zinoviev and Kamenev recognized Stalin's ascendency, and they formed the United Opposition with Trotsky in 1926. But Stalin outmaneuvered them and cast them as deviationists. While Lenin's 1921 ban on factionalism had not really ended factions within the Party, Stalin used the myth of Party unity to condemn Trotsky, Zinoviev, and Kamenev's opposition movement. He had all three of them expelled from the Communist Party in 1927, and he had Trotsky deported in 1929. By the late 1920s, Stalin was the clear leader of the Soviet Union and ruled in alliance with Bukharin, the leading proponent for continuing the

New Economic Policy. However, neither Stalin's alliance with Bukharin nor his support for the NEP would last for long.

Since its founding, the Soviet state had faced considerable international hostility. The United States, for example, refused to recognize Communist leaders as the legitimate rulers of Russia, and did not establish diplomatic relations with the Soviet Union until 1933. The United Kingdom did sign a trade agreement with the Soviet Union in 1921, but in 1927, conservatives in the British government denounced Soviet spying and broke off diplomatic relations. This action prompted a "war scare," as many in the Soviet Union feared that an invasion by capitalist countries was imminent.[66] The same year, Soviet policy in China suffered a calamitous reversal. After socialist revolutions failed to spread to western Europe, the Comintern had focused much of its attention on China. Soviet leaders instructed Communists in China to ally with the Nationalist (Guomindang) Party there, believing the Communists were too weak to take power on their own. But in 1927, Nationalist leader Chiang Kai-shek turned on the Communists, arresting or killing many of them and bloodily suppressing a workers' rebellion in Shanghai. Soviet advisors left China to return home, while the Chinese Nationalists broke off diplomatic relations with the Soviet Union.[67]

International tensions and setbacks made even more urgent Soviet leaders' need to industrialize the country. Increasingly for them, the building and defending of socialism came to mean rapid industrialization. Through the mid-1920s the Soviet economy had grown gradually under the New Economic Policy, as the country recovered from the devastation of the Civil War. But further industrial growth in the late 1920s required capital investment. With no access to foreign loans, no overseas colonies, and no allies to provide aid, Soviet leaders truly had to build socialism "in one country." Given the Soviet Union's overwhelmingly agrarian economy, the only substantial source of capital was agricultural wealth. Because this capital was thinly distributed amongst the country's 100 million peasants, there was no easy way to reallocate it to industry. Party leaders would either have to postpone industrialization or abandon the NEP market economy. The New Economic Policy was thus fundamentally incompatible with a one-party dictatorship intent on rapidly industrializing the country.[68]

While Party leaders debated the precise pace of development, they all agreed on the need to accelerate industrialization.[69] At the Fifteenth Party Congress in 1927, they resolved to draw up a five-year economic plan, and the result targeted growth rates for heavy industry that could not be achieved within a free-market framework. To accumulate capital for industrialization, the Soviet government raised prices for manufactured goods and set agricultural prices artificially low. Peasants reacted by withholding their grain from the market in the hope that agricultural prices would rise. While Bukharin argued for adjusting prices to maintain market equilibrium, Stalin and a majority of Politburo members were prepared to forge ahead with rapid industrialization, even if it meant destroying the market economy. Stalin broke with Bukharin on this issue, denouncing him as a right deviationist. And as we will see in Chapter 2, Stalin and his supporters soon reverted to total war practices – grain requisitioning, deportations, and government economic control – to implement collectivization and industrialization.

The New Economic Policy helped the country recover from years of war and destruction. For many peasants it was a beneficial time, one in which they could profit from the land they had gained during the Revolution. It was also a period of reduced coercion, though both the institutions and the practices of state violence continued throughout the 1920s. The NEP, however, was also characterized by unresolved tensions. The Revolution had come, but full socialism had not been achieved. A "working-class state" had been established, but many workers were unemployed. The Communist Party had a monopoly on political power, but it did not control the capitalist sector of the economy, where NEPmen and kulaks seemed to flourish. Party members deeply resented the NEP and were eager to proceed with industrialization, both to serve workers' interests and to strengthen the country. Communist leaders remained painfully aware that their country was encircled by hostile capitalist countries. The Soviet Union was an underdeveloped, militarily weak country with an overwhelmingly peasant population. Party leaders needed somehow to provide for national defense in an era of international tensions and mass warfare. The fate of the world's first socialist state seemed to hang in the balance.

2 Building Socialism (1928–1933)

The Stalinist era began in the late 1920s. At this time, Stalin consolidated his power and launched collectivization and rapid industrialization – two central features of Stalinism. Abandoning the New Economic Policy, he and his supporters abolished the free market and private farming. Private businesses were closed and peasants were forced to join collective farms. The Soviet government took charge of the entire economy and launched a crash industrialization drive. Stalin called 1929 "the year of the great break." He meant that this year marked a final break with the capitalist past and its replacement with a socialist economy. Along with this state-run economy, there was to emerge a socialist society, one in which everyone worked for the common good. This new society was supposed to be modern and forward-looking. Party leaders stated that collectivization and industrialization were to end the country's backwardness. Their "socialist offensive" included an assault on religiosity and peasant traditions. Entering this new epoch, the Soviet Union would catapult ahead of industrialized countries and lead the world to socialism.

How did the Soviet government implement this program? Stalin and his fellow leaders drew upon techniques and rhetoric developed during the Civil War. They established in essence a wartime economy, where state officials controlled the allocation of resources and the distribution of goods. They reinstituted grain requisitioning and rationing. On the industrialization "front" they nationalized all industry and mobilized labor and materials for steel and armaments production. They deployed collectivization "brigades" and the secret police to force peasants to join collective farms. Those deemed class aliens – kulaks and NEPmen – were physically removed from society and interned in special settlements or Gulag labor camps. Party leaders also attacked existing cultural and technical elites. As they persecuted "bourgeois specialists," they simultaneously promoted thousands of workers into positions of authority.

Stalinist policies had enormous consequences for the Soviet population. Collectivization forced peasants throughout the country to give up their privately held land and livestock and become members of state-run collective farms. Several million peasants labeled kulaks were not allowed to join collective farms – instead they were dispossessed and many of them were deported from their villages. In addition to those peasants forced to leave, millions voluntarily moved to cities and became industrial workers. The urban population doubled during the 1930s, as former peasants provided the labor to build and staff thousands of new factories. Women were recruited into heavy industrial jobs in large numbers, as gender roles underwent a dramatic change. And many non-Russians were also caught up in the country's economic transformation – some who became industrial workers, and others who perished in the horrendous famine of 1932–33. Stalinist collectivization and industrialization transformed the country through exhortation, coercion, and violence.

Collectivization

When journalist Maurice Hindus returned to visit his native Russian village on the eve of collectivization in 1929, he was amazed by the changes there. For the first time in its history, the village had a schoolhouse, a nursery, and a fire station. Peasant children were learning to read. Young adults talked of moving to the city. Women were interested in urban fashions and showed a new-found independence. Traditional ways seemed to be crumbling. The young generation of peasants no longer heeded their elders. The village church, formerly a bastion of peasant society, had fallen into neglect – even on Sunday mornings it was virtually empty. Agriculture was also changing, as new fertilizers and machinery were introduced. Most significantly, Communist agitators were pressuring peasants to give up individual farming and join the collective farm.[1]

Russian peasant society had long been governed by traditions. For centuries, the peasant commune, which apportioned land, was run by village elders – male heads of households. Their authority rested not only on control over their households, but also on their memory of how things should be done. But by the early twentieth century, the spread of schools and literacy began to erode elders' authority of memory and led peasants to question traditional ways. The Revolution brought political changes to the countryside as noble landowners fled and the Soviet government established rural soviets – local branches of government that rivalled the power of village communes. Soviet schools, nurseries, clinics, and agronomical programs provided sources of knowledge that undercut traditions. In many villages, the Communist Party's presence remained weak, but non-Party specialists staffed new institutions and sought to teach peasants modern ways.

Demographic shifts also undercut village elders' authority. Millions of young peasant men served in the army during World War I and the Civil War, and, having seen the wider world, no longer accepted the authority of village elders. In addition, economic collapse during the Civil War meant that many peasants who had gone to work in cities returned to their native villages. Increasingly, peasants who returned from the army or the city refused to live with their extended families, as was the Russian custom. Instead they started their own separate households. These young male heads of household had the right to attend the assembly of village elders where they contested elders' authority. In some cases, young women also attended the elders' assembly, challenging the gender hierarchy as well as the generational hierarchy of the village. Peasant society in the 1920s was still traditional, but it was in ferment owing to these currents of change.[2]

Communist Party leaders wanted to modernize the countryside, but they lacked a nuanced understanding of peasant society. They viewed the peasantry in rigid Marxist terms and thought that village conflicts were between rich peasants (kulaks) and poor peasants. When they launched the collectivization drive, anyone who resisted was labeled a kulak. In reality, class categories did not fully apply to peasant society, as divisions were primarily generational and between those who had spent time outside the village and those who had not. On visiting his native village, Hindus noted that younger peasants were far more open to the idea of collective farms than were their elders. To a certain extent, generational divisions opened the door to socioeconomic changes in the countryside. But given the Stalinist leadership's crude class understanding of the peasantry, and given its penchant for using force, collectivization resulted in a violent confrontation between the peasantry and the Soviet regime.

The collectivization drive was precipitated by a grain collection crisis in the late 1920s, and by Party leaders' decisions in dealing with it. In 1927–28, state grain procurements fell far below targets. This shortfall jeopardized plans to accelerate industrialization, as it meant insufficient food supplies for urban workers and a lack of grain to export in exchange for foreign industrial technology. During Politburo debates throughout 1928, Bukharin and his allies, Aleksey Rykov and Mikhail Tomsky, proposed slowing industrialization and raising grain prices to induce peasants to sell more grain and maintain the NEP market economy. But a majority of Politburo members, including Stalin's closest allies Molotov, Kirov, Anastas Mikoyan, and Lazar Kaganovich, chose instead to return to the wartime technique of grain requisitioning. Food detachment brigades went to villages and forced peasants to hand over their grain, paying them only a low, fixed price. By 1929, the Politburo ordered officials throughout the country to use the so-called Ural-Siberian method of grain collection whereby quotas were assigned to each peasant household, with particularly high quotas for those labeled kulaks. Peasants who failed to meet their grain quotas could be prosecuted under anti-speculation laws and either fined or arrested.

Grain requisitioning succeeded in increasing state food supplies, but it destroyed the market economy. With no chance to profit from sales, peasants no longer had an incentive to grow more grain. Faced with high quotas and taxes, some wealthy peasants sold off livestock and reduced the land they cultivated in order to escape the "kulak" designation. Not only prosperous peasants but poor and middle peasants resisted grain collections, hiding their grain or seeking to sell it illegally. Given this resistance, Party officials increasingly sought to eliminate private agriculture entirely through collectivization. Under collectivization, the land, equipment, and most livestock were supposed to be owned collectively, though in reality they were controlled by collective farm officials. Peasants worked as employees on collective farms and got paid out of any grain that remained after the government had taken its share.

Collectivization matched both the ideological agenda and practical needs of Party leaders. The elimination of private agriculture was a way to abolish capitalism in the countryside. And the establishment of state-run collective farms gave the government authority over land, livestock, and crops. On collective farms, Soviet officials controlled grain supplies directly and did not need to coerce peasants or search households in order to collect grain. Earlier in the 1920s, a small number of peasants had joined collective farms on a voluntary basis, but the collectivization drive aimed at forcing all peasants to sign over their land and livestock to collective farms. At the November 1929 meeting of the Party's Central Committee, Molotov announced the leadership's decision to launch all-out collectivization on a national scale. Party leaders did not provide a precise timetable for collectivization, leaving much to the discretion of local officials, but clearly their goal was rapid collectivization.[3]

Local Party officials pursued an extremely rapid rate of collectivization. Backed by brigades of urban activists, as well as secret police detachments, they cajoled and threatened peasants into joining collective farms (see Figure 2.1). Peasants who resisted could be labeled kulaks and deported. Within three months, nearly 60 percent of all peasant households nationwide had been collectivized. But this figure did not mean that peasants were committed to collective farming. Under pressure, most had joined with no understanding of how collective farms would function.

Figure 2.1 Collectivization activists speaking to peasants in Ukraine, 1929.

Many peasants slaughtered and ate their livestock rather than turning them over to the collective farm. Other peasants fought back, resisting or even attacking Soviet officials. In 1930, there were nearly 14,000 mass disturbances in reaction to collectivization involving more than 2 million peasants, and this unrest had to be suppressed by secret police forces.[4]

With rising chaos in the countryside, Party leaders began to worry that the collectivization campaign would disrupt spring planting. On March 2, Stalin published his article, "Dizzy with Success: Problems of the Collective Farm Movement." He stated that peasants were supposed to join collective farms voluntarily, and he blamed local Party members for being overzealous, though of course the impetus for all-out collectivization had come from Stalin himself. Peasants responded by quitting the collective farms in droves. By June only one-quarter of peasant households remained collectivized. But peasants who quit did not necessarily get their land back – generally they received a portion of inferior land, while the collective farm retained the most fertile land as well as most livestock and farm equipment. Over the next two years, Soviet officials renewed pressure on peasants to join collective farms. As a concession, they allowed peasants to retain a few livestock (one cow and some chickens), as well as private garden plots to grow produce for themselves. By 1933, two-thirds of peasant households had joined collective farms, and by the end of the decade virtually all peasants had been collectivized.[5]

Ideology and administrative control explain Party leaders' decision to collectivize agriculture, but do not explain how they proceeded with collectivization. Party officials could have collectivized gradually through a series of incentives and penalties to induce peasants to join collective farms. Instead they carried out collectivization as a type of military campaign, with brigades storming the countryside. In keeping with this military mindset, "kulaks" were regarded as an enemy who would sabotage collective farms if not physically removed from the village. As during World War I and the Civil War, deportations and concentration camps provided the means by which to remove and isolate these "class enemies." Party leaders considered this process an integral part of collectivization and they called it dekulakization – the elimination of an entire category of peasants, through dispossession, deportation, and in some cases even execution.

The Elimination of the Kulaks

Even before Party leaders formulated a policy on dekulakization, some regional Party officials began to dispossess and exile kulaks as part of the collectivization drive. Then, in December 1929, Stalin announced "the liquidation of the kulaks as a class." He stated, "Dekulakization represents a component part of the formation and development of collective farms. Therefore it is absurd and frivolous to expatiate now about dekulakization. When a head has been cut off, no one cries over the hairs."[6] Following Stalin's speech, the acting head of the secret police, Genrikh Yagoda, ordered the removal of "kulak elements" from the countryside, warning that kulaks might instigate uprisings against collectivization. The Politburo subsequently designated three categories of kulaks. Those in the first category, considered the most dangerous, were to be arrested by the secret police and sent to Gulag prison camps or executed. Second-category kulaks were to be dispossessed of all but personal items and deported to special settlements. Third-category kulaks were to be dispossessed of their land and livestock and resettled beyond the boundary of the collective farm.

The actual process of dekulakization was extremely violent. In 1930 and 1931, the secret police executed approximately 30,000 people and imprisoned or deported between 1.6 million and 1.8 million more (the first- and second-category kulaks). N. N. Pavlov described his family's deportation as follows:

That morning, father, mother, and we two little brothers got ready to be exiled as kulaks … We were only allowed to bring the clothes on our backs and a small supply of food. They put the four of us … on a cart with two armed policemen for our guards. And just like that we left. Everyone made a fuss, cried for us along the way. The cart set off and a crowd of villagers accompanied us far beyond the [village's] outskirts.[7]

Pavlov and his family, along with other deportees, were then loaded onto a train to be transported to a special settlement. Crammed into an overcrowded boxcar with only a bucket for a latrine, they traveled for days, only occasionally receiving water and some bread.

In addition to those deported, some 3.5 million third-category kulaks were dispossessed by local activists and expelled from their villages, whereupon most made their way to cities. Sometimes dispossessions assumed the form of drunken looting as collectivizers consumed alcohol found in kulaks' homes and ripped shirts off their backs. A. T. Shokhireva was fifteen when her family was dekulakized. "They came and destroyed all the buildings," she recalled. "They took away whatever they could … Our home was ruined."[8] The designation of kulaks was itself quite arbitrary. While authorities in Moscow sought to define, categorize, and enumerate kulaks with great precision, local activists often had no clear idea which peasants were kulaks. Frequently any peasant who resisted collectivization was labeled a kulak, and even Party reports acknowledged that some non-prosperous peasants had been incorrectly labeled kulaks and dispossessed.[9]

Dekulakization triggered a vast expansion of the Soviet labor camp system, now called the Gulag – the acronym for the secret police's Main Administration of Corrective Labor Camps. With thousands of arrests during dekulakization, the Gulag mushroomed into an enormous complex of camps, most located in remote regions of Siberia where labor was needed for mining and logging operations.[10] In theory, forced labor in the Gulag was supposed to transform the mentality of "bourgeois exploiters" and instill in them a proletarian consciousness. Many camp administrators, however, were more concerned with using the convicts' labor to meet production targets. While the practice of isolating segments of the population in concentration camps had its roots in colonial warfare and World War I, the idea of applying this technique to mobilize labor and reeducate people was something new. Soviet leaders thus took an existing wartime practice and applied it to their peacetime program of economic and social transformation.[11]

In addition to the thousands of first-category kulaks sent to Gulag labor camps, more than 1.5 million second-category kulaks were deported to special settlements. These special settlements were similar to the Gulag in that they isolated kulaks and exploited their labor, but they were not formal prison camps with guards and barbed wire. Secret police chief Yagoda pushed the idea of special settlements to send kulaks to do hard labor in Siberia, the Urals, Kazakhstan, and the far north. He argued that kulaks deported to these settlements could support themselves through farming while simultaneously providing a permanent labor force in forestry, mining, and other industries. Government bureaucrats began to draw up detailed blueprints for special settlements. But there was no time to build these settlements before the deportees arrived, as hundreds of thousands of peasants were already being transported to places with little food or shelter. In some cases, dekulakized peasants were taken to industrial sites and crammed into barracks, old churches, or tents. In other cases, they were deported to remote forests of the far north and told to build their own housing.

Incredibly, the secret police deported entire families, including infants and the elderly, to northern forests in the middle of the winter. Varvara Stepanovna Sidorova later recalled how as a girl she and her family were unloaded from a train in the far north with nothing but trees in sight. Along with the other deportees, her parents and elder brother labored knee-deep in snow, cutting timber to meet their work quotas while desperately building a makeshift shelter in their spare time. Within a month, Varvara Stepanovna's father was dead. She and her younger siblings walked miles to the nearest peasant village to beg for food in order to survive.[12] Even some Soviet officials were appalled at the lack of adequate food and shelter for the deportees. Vladimir Tolmachev, the Commissar of Internal Affairs for the Russian Republic, reported that at special settlements along the railroad lines of the far north:

People are billeted in 750 barracks, hastily assembled from logs. The crowding is unbelievable – there are places where each person has one-tenth of a square meter of living space in multi-tiered bunks (the space is smaller than a coffin). There are no floors in the barracks, the roofs are made of poles and loosely sprinkled hay and crumbled mud. As a rule, the temperature does not go above 4 degrees [Celsius]. [Everything] is lice-ridden. Along with the miserly feeding, and for many almost nothing, all this creates colossal [rates of] illness, and death among children."[13]

Thousands of deported kulaks did die of exposure, hunger, and disease. Given the overcrowding, lack of sanitation, extreme cold, and starvation, there were soon epidemics of scarlet fever, measles, diphtheria, and typhus. The deportation of kulaks was one of the most inhumane and lethal of all Stalinist policies.

Collectivization and dekulakization met the objectives of Party leaders; it abolished private farming and gave the government control over grain supplies. But this economic and social transformation was accomplished using extreme violence and coercion. The state violence used to carry out collectivization reflected a fundamental characteristic of Stalinism – the reliance on wartime practices to achieve ideological and administrative goals. Using deportations and concentration camps, now called labor camps, Soviet officials physically removed "class enemies" from society. The class-war mentality behind these operations went beyond Stalin, as shown by the fact that regional Party officials began to exile kulaks from villages even before Stalin declared dekulakization to be the official policy. Party leaders and lower-level officials alike assumed that kulaks could not be reconciled with collective farms. Instead of offering incentives to promote gradual collectivization, they launched an assault on the village and repressed any peasants who resisted.

Collectivization proved immensely destructive – particularly for those executed or deported during dekulakization, but also for peasants who remained behind. Collective farms destroyed traditional rural ways and culture. Deprived of their land and livestock, peasants became sullen and resentful. Young adult peasants were more open to change, but in the early 1930s many of them moved away to work in the cities. This exodus, combined with the deportation of kulaks, meant that far fewer peasants remained to work the land. Those who stayed had less incentive to produce, given that they no longer owned the crops they grew. Agricultural output declined, though state grain requisitions actually increased. By 1932–33, there would be a terrible famine that added further to the horrific death toll of collectivization.

Industrialization

Another centerpiece of Stalinism was rapid industrialization. At the end of the 1920s, the Stalinist leadership launched a drive to industrialize the country within a decade. Their industrialization drive was based on a particular model of development – a noncapitalist economy focused on heavy industry (mining, metallurgy, and machine building). Stalin and his fellow leaders abolished the NEP free market and took control of all economic resources. A state-run economy suited both Party leaders' anticapitalist ideology and their desire to channel materials and labor into building steel mills quickly. The crash industrialization drive that followed involved a great deal of waste, upheaval, and human suffering, but it resulted in the construction of hundreds of new factories. For all the pain it inflicted, the state-run economy transformed the Soviet Union from an underdeveloped, agrarian country into an industrial and military power.

Stalin provided a rationale for rapid industrialization. In a 1931 speech he stated that industrialization was necessary to overcome Russia's backwardness:

One feature of the history of old Russia was the continual beatings she suffered because of her backwardness. She was beaten by the Mongol khans. She was beaten by the Turkish beys. She was beaten by the Swedish feudal rulers. She was beaten by the Polish and Lithuanian gentry. She was beaten by British and French capitalists. She was beaten by Japanese barons. All beat her – because of her backwardness ... We are fifty or a hundred years behind the advanced countries. We must make good this distance in ten years. Either we do it or we shall go under.[14]

Stalin's words proved to be prophetic. Ten years later, Nazi Germany launched a massive invasion of the Soviet Union. Without steel mills, tanks, artillery, and guns, the Soviet Union never would have survived.

Given the hostile international environment, there were rational reasons to industrialize quickly. But that is not to say that Stalinist industrialization was carried out in a rational manner. Stalin and his fellow leaders displayed a certain fanaticism in their drive to modernize the country. They continually raised production targets and exhorted managers and workers to over-fulfill their quotas. The First Five-Year Plan of Economic Development called for coal, iron, and steel production to triple – what would have been an astonishing jump. Stalinist planning reflected a Promethean desire to make a great leap forward, to transcend the boundaries of time itself – "Fulfill the Five-Year Plan in Four Years!" became the slogan.

Industrialization in western Europe had taken a century. What made Party leaders think they could industrialize their country in a decade? First of all, their confidence stemmed from a cult of willpower. In the same speech quoted earlier, Stalin proclaimed, "There are no fortresses that Bolsheviks cannot storm." Recalling the heroic days of the Civil War, when the Communists had triumphed against all odds, Stalin and his fellow leaders believed that no obstacles could stop them from reaching their goal – the creation of a modern, militarily powerful, socialist state. They also believed in the superiority of a socialist economy. In their view, Soviet workers had been freed from the shackles of capitalist exploitation and would dramatically raise labor productivity. Moreover, Party leaders thought that a state-run, socialist economy could be more efficient than capitalism. Unlike capitalist economies, which suffered from unemployment, business failures, competition, and greed, the Soviet economy was going to be characterized by the purposeful deployment of materials and labor, all working together for the common good.

To accomplish this task, Party leaders established a planned economy. The idea of economic planning was not uniquely Soviet, nor even necessarily socialist. All major combatant countries during World War I had increased state economic controls to plan wartime production. Soviet state planning was based on the German wartime economic model. Already in the 1920s the Soviet government formed the State Planning Agency (Gosplan).[15] Gosplan drew up the Five-Year Plans, which allocated raw materials and set production targets for all industrial enterprises around the country. Many progressive economists in western Europe and the United States shared Soviet officials' enthusiasm for state planning. Americans Stuart Chase and Rexford Tugwell, the latter a future member of Franklin Roosevelt's New Deal brain trust, traveled to Moscow in 1927 and praised the Soviet planned economy.[16] After the onset of the Great Depression, even more observers saw the Soviet system as an appealing alternative. At a time when capitalist countries suffered economic stagnation and high unemployment, the Soviet Union experienced remarkable economic growth and full employment. It seemed that the Soviet model might indeed provide for more efficient and equitable industrial production.

In practice, the Soviet economy proved far from efficient. Waste, shortages, and breakdowns became the rule.[17] The rational designs of Gosplan economists were supplanted by wildly unrealistic goals that were more political exhortation than economic plan. Labor productivity actually decreased in the rush to hire new workers and train them on the job. Factory managers scrambled for raw materials to fulfill production quotas. State planners were supposed to allocate needed materials, but the inadequate Soviet railway network resulted in transportation bottlenecks. Industrial commissariats, and branches within these commissariats, competed with one another for scarce resources. Factory managers resorted to deceit and even outright theft to get the raw materials they needed. Some managers sent agents to intercept deliveries bound for other industrial plants, bribing transport workers to get these supplies for themselves. Far from the ideal of a smoothly functioning bureaucratic machine, the Soviet state in the 1930s was characterized by infighting, corruption, and inefficiency.

Despite staggering problems, the Soviet economy grew tremendously. New metallurgical complexes were constructed in the Urals and western Siberia. Coal and iron ore mining operations expanded in tandem with new steel mills, and the oil fields of Baku and Grozny grew as well. Huge new tractor factories were built in Stalingrad, Cheliabinsk, Kharkhiv, and Rostov. A giant hydroelectric plant was erected on the Dniepr River. A sprawling new automobile factory opened in Gorky. Existing machine building plants in Moscow and Leningrad grew dramatically in size.

The total number of industrial enterprises in the country increased from 9,000 in 1929 to 64,000 in 1938. Steel production doubled during the First Five-Year Plan alone, and for the entire decade, total industrial output tripled. Armaments and defense production during the 1930s increased twenty-eight times. Stalinist industrialization produced growth rates rarely matched before or since.[18]

What accounted for this incredible industrial growth? The key to the Stalinist economy's success was not efficiency but rather mobilization. Party leaders channeled the country's labor and raw materials into building new steel mills and factories. Collectivization gave them control over grain supplies. The elimination of private shops and enterprises gave them control over urban goods and materials. A completely state-run economy allowed officials to pursue their industrial priorities at the expense of consumerism. The channeling of resources into heavy industry caused a sharp drop in living standards. Food was rationed in cities, while in the countryside peasants starved. Workers lived in overcrowded barracks and people struggled to find basic clothing. But hundreds of new factories were built, and the Soviet Union became a modern industrial power.

To accelerate industrialization, Soviet leaders also imported technology from the West. They paid for these imports by exporting grain. As a late-industrializing country, the Soviet Union could progress more quickly using the industrial equipment already developed in more advanced countries.[19] By neglecting consumption, Soviet planners were also able to create a closed production cycle in heavy industry – the steel being produced was used to build more steel mills and machine building plants – allowing this sector of the economy to grow geometrically. In addition, the Soviet government hired hundreds of foreign specialists, especially German and American engineers, to help oversee the construction of new factories.[20] That the Soviet industrialization drive coincided with the Great Depression meant that there were many unemployed technical specialists in western Europe and the United States who were willing to work in the Soviet Union. Their expertise proved especially valuable in constructing new plants and installing imported technology.

Urbanization

Stalinist industrialization was accompanied by rapid urbanization. New factories required millions of new workers; the number of industrial workers in the Soviet Union doubled during the First Five-Year Plan alone. The great majority of these new workers were former peasants, some 23 million of whom moved to Soviet cities during the 1930s – a rate of urbanization unprecedented in world history. Existing cities grew extremely rapidly. Moscow's population increased from 2 million to 4 million in the span of a decade. Leningrad also doubled in size, to 3 million, while Gorky (formerly Nizhny Novgorod) and Sverdlovsk tripled in size. In addition, entirely new cities were built. The largest of these, Karaganda in northern Kazakhstan, did not exist in 1930 and had a population of 166,000 people by 1939. Other brand-new cities included Magnitogorsk in the Urals, Stalinsk in western Siberia, and Komsomolsk in the Far East.[21]

Collectivization, dekulakization, and new job opportunities in industry prompted millions of peasants to leave their villages and settle permanently in urban areas. Peasants who were dispossessed as kulaks but not deported had little choice but to seek employment in cities. Other peasants fled falling living standards and hunger in the countryside to move to urban areas. Many young adult peasants had long wished to try their luck in the city but had been deterred by high urban unemployment during the 1920s. With the industrialization drive, these peasants took advantage of new factory jobs and left their villages for good. Soviet managers were desperate for workers to build and staff their new factories, so they hired anyone they could, regardless of their inexperience.

To prepare new workers, the Soviet government expanded training programs, though not nearly enough to accommodate the millions of former peasants now entering the workforce. Most new workers simply learned on the job, despite the hazards this entailed. Ivan Gudov, a peasant turned worker, later described the fright he felt when he first entered a Moscow machine-building plant.

The ground shook from the rumble of machinery. On the equipment I was walking past there poured an unending stream of water and milk (soon I learned it wasn't milk but emulsions) ... I was trying not to bother anyone, and not to catch on some sort of flywheel. It seemed as if one careless movement and I'd be hurled into a machine.[22]

The number of industrial accidents skyrocketed, both due to workers' lack of training and due to the rush to build factories and increase production (see Figure 2.2). In some cases, hastily built structures collapsed and in others misused machinery broke. Countless workers were injured or even killed in industrial and construction accidents during the First Five-Year Plan.[23]

Labor productivity fell sharply. Productivity was less important in the Soviet economy than in capitalist economies – Soviet managers were focused on fulfilling plan quotas, not on profitability. But Party officials nonetheless tried to boost productivity in order to increase overall output.

Figure 2.2 Expansion of the Leningrad Metal Works during the late
1920s.

In 1929, they endorsed an initiative called socialist competition, developed by members of the Komsomol (the Communist Youth League).
Socialist competition consisted of contests between worker brigades to
see which could produce the most. In some highly publicized cases, shock
workers set production records – the most cement poured in a 24-hour
period or the most steel produced in a week. Such contests led to short
bursts of activity, but not to long-term gains in productivity. Sometimes,
young workers worked intensively for two days and then missed the rest of
the week due to exhaustion. In other cases, machinery would break from
overuse.[24]

Factory managers generally disdained socialist competition, because it
disrupted work routines. But for young workers, socialist competition
provided an avenue to express both their enthusiasm and their personal
ambition. By calling themselves shock workers and participating in socialist competition, Komsomol members could circumvent established factory hierarchies. Shock workers received special status and bonuses.
The best shock workers at the Stalin automobile factory in Moscow
received new cars. More commonly, workers who participated in socialist
competition got pay increases or special rations.[25] Over time, socialist
competition became subsumed in factory routines. Managers, eager to

avoid disruptions, allowed workers to declare themselves shock workers or socialist competition participants without doing any additional work. Kaganovich soon complained that in some factories everyone was called a shock worker, so that the term had lost all meaning.[26]

From 1931 on, Party leaders began to emphasize wage differentials and piece rates – paying workers for the amount they produced. Stalin blamed wage leveling for high labor turnover, and he stated that paying higher wages to skilled workers would give new workers an incentive to stay put and raise their skill level. Industrial managers duly expanded wage differentials and the use of piece rates. While these measures smacked of capitalism (in that they increased wage disparities), workers did not necessarily oppose them. Wage differentials gave skilled workers the opportunity to earn higher wages. Even unskilled workers could earn more under piece rates, provided that they were willing to work overtime. While Soviet factories officially had a seven-hour day and restrictions on overtime, factory directors regularly ignored such strictures in their quest to fulfill production quotas. Workers often worked ten hours a day to increase their earnings, and in some cases put in double or even triple shifts.[27]

For the millions of former peasants who moved to cities, the transition to urban life was not always easy. When eighteen-year-old Evgeny Kostin stepped off a train in Moscow in 1931, he felt overwhelmed by the throngs of people. In his native village he had known everyone he saw, but now there was not a familiar face in sight. He was astonished at the height of the buildings and flustered by the screech of tramcars and general commotion of the city. But over time, his adjustment to urban life proved less difficult than expected. Relatives housed him, fellow villagers found him a job, and an acquaintance showed him around.[28] Like Kostin, most peasants who moved to Soviet cities in the 1930s received advice and aid from relatives and fellow villagers already living there. Even those dispossessed during dekulakization usually had urban relatives and friends who could help them. Village networks guided peasants from the same village to the same city and even to the same neighborhood. As a result, clusters of fellow villagers helped one another navigate the harsh urban environment.

Rapid urbanization caused severe housing shortages. As Party leaders prioritized the construction of steel mills and machine building plants, very little new housing was built. The millions of peasants arriving in cities lived in communal apartments, barracks, or their own makeshift dwellings, as shantytowns sprang up on the peripheries of large cities. An American who lived in Moscow during the 1930s described a workers' barracks as follows:

The room contained approximately 500 narrow beds, covered with mattresses filled with straw or dried leaves. There were no pillows or blankets. Coats and other garments were being utilized for covering. Some of the residents had no beds and slept on the floor or in wooden boxes ... I could not stay in the barracks very long. I could not stand the stench of kerosene and unwashed bodies. The only washing facility was a pump outside. The toilet was a rickety, unheated shanty, without seats.[29]

Even for former peasants, accustomed to living in overcrowded huts, the repulsive housing conditions posed a challenge. Food shortages also made life difficult. Compared to the countryside, where peasants were starving, cities were relatively well provisioned. But the Soviet government rationed food during the First Five-Year Plan, and often stores could not even provide workers with their full rations.

Given factory managers' desperate need for labor, however, workers had some degree of leverage. If conditions at their factory or construction site were too abysmal, they could always find a job elsewhere. Workers began to move from one construction site or factory to another in search of better food and housing. Labor turnover rates skyrocketed to 150 percent turnover nationwide in 1930, meaning that, on average, every industrial job turned over more than once a year. Party leaders and factory managers despaired at high turnover, as it disrupted industrial production. Commenting on the constant turnover of workers, Commissar of Heavy Industry Sergo Ordzhonikidze called one factory site "a nomadic gypsy camp."[30]

The directors of industrial enterprises soon realized that in order to keep their workers, they needed to provide them with housing and food. Factory directors constructed hundreds of new residences and barracks for their workers, hastily building on factory grounds or wherever they could find space. Even this spurt of housing construction could not keep pace with urban population growth, but managers at least attempted to house their workers. In 1930, factory directors also began to operate "closed workers' cooperatives" – stores open only to employees of the factory – through which they could guarantee their workers at least basic foodstuffs. Party leaders endorsed this system of food distribution, and factory managers created special departments to procure and distribute goods.[31] Some managers even established their own agricultural and livestock-raising ventures, including fishing and rabbit breeding operations, to supply their workers with food.[32] State enterprises, then, served not only as employers but as providers of workers' basic needs. In other countries too, during the twentieth century, the state's role in social welfare expanded, but largely remained limited to poor relief, disability aid, and old age pensions. The Soviet state took on these functions and more, as state responsibility for workers' provision became a permanent feature of the Soviet system.

The Stalinist industrialization drive transformed the Soviet Union from an agrarian country into an industrial power, from an overwhelmingly peasant society into an increasingly urban one. The way Party leaders accomplished this transformation – by creating an entirely state-run economy that focused on heavy industry – caused a sharp drop in living standards and a great deal of deprivation. Stalinist industrialization also permanently shaped the Soviet economy. For the remainder of its existence, the Soviet government operated a hyper-centralized, state-run economy that prioritized large industrial projects but failed to produce adequate consumer goods. In theory, the Soviet planned economy was to be rational and efficient, but in practice it caused upheavals, shortages, and hardship. Given the absence of a free market, state enterprises had to provide for workers' food and housing, albeit at substandard levels, and people became dependent on the Soviet state for social provision. In this sense, the Soviet Union became a type of authoritarian welfare state, though (ironically) a welfare state that did not safeguard people's wellbeing.

Cultural Revolution

Collectivization and state-directed industrialization were central to Party leaders' drive to build socialism. No longer were the means of production – factories, raw materials, agricultural equipment, and land – in private hands. But alongside these economic changes, Party leaders sought to establish new cultural norms as well. They envisioned a cultural revolution that would replace bourgeois values with new socialist ones. Merchants, with their decadence and greed, would be supplanted by a selfless collective of workers. Education would uplift workers and allow them to play a leading role in society. Peasants' ignorance, drunkenness, and filth would give way to enlightenment, sobriety, and hygiene. Superstition and religion would be succeeded by science and knowledge. Egotistical individualism would transform into self-sacrificing collectivism. The people who inhabited this new socialist world were to be qualitatively different from those who lived under capitalism.

After the 1917 Revolution, one group of Communist Party members had called for a cultural revolution that would create an entirely proletarian culture, with new art, literature, and ethics, as well as new cultural elites drawn from the working class.[33] As it turned out, Lenin and other

Communist leaders rejected the idea of a distinct proletarian culture and instead chose to preserve Russian high culture, including the classics of Russian art and literature. But they adopted the more general aims of cultural revolution – bringing culture to the masses and training workers to become a new elite.[34] Many non-Party specialists shared the goals of uplifting peasants and workers, and they played a crucial role in teaching the lower classes new norms of hygiene and literacy. The ideal of cultural revolution in fact became the vehicle by which many members of the non-Party intelligentsia found a role in the Soviet system.[35]

The Soviet government made literacy a top priority. Mandatory primary education ensured that children learned to read. In 1929, however, more than half of all adult peasants were still illiterate. By 1932, more than 14 million people were enrolled in adult literacy classes, and literacy rates increased dramatically – according to the 1939 census nearly 90 percent of the population of the Russian republic ages nine to forty-nine was literate.[36] Hygiene was another priority. Commissariat of Health officials instructed peasants and workers to bathe regularly, wash their clothes, and brush their teeth. Nadezhda Krupskaia, Lenin's widow and a leading Party member, stated, "To teach children and their parents to wash their hands more frequently – that is enormous revolutionary progress."[37] Using propaganda posters and inspections, cultural workers emphasized order and cleanliness in the home. Labor hygienists taught factory workers the importance of neatness, punctuality, and sobriety in the workplace.[38] For officials and specialists alike, the fostering of a healthy, productive population required the inculcation of new habits of everyday behavior.

Efforts to raise cultural standards were not unique to the Soviet Union. Beginning first in nineteenth-century Europe and later in countries around the world, government officials and social reformers sought to teach the lower classes habits of health and hygiene. Given the importance of corporeal labor in the industrial age, the bodily health of workers represented an important economic resource that officials and industrialists sought to safeguard. Many reformers were also motivated by an altruistic desire to improve the lives of the urban poor crowding the tenements of industrial cities. Productivity campaigns, housing inspections, temperance movements, and primary education served as the means "to civilize" the masses. In this light, Soviet values of literacy, efficiency, hygiene, and sobriety were part of broader international efforts to promote a rational and aesthetic ordering of everyday life.

Soviet values were nonetheless distinct in several ways. Whereas reformers in other countries often invoked religion in order to enforce temperance and obedience among the lower classes, Soviet officials attacked

Figure 2.3 Demolition of the Cathedral of Christ the Savior in Moscow, 1931.

religion as, in Marx's words, "the opiate of the masses." During collecti-vization, activists closed churches and arrested village priests. In cities, Soviet officials demolished a number of churches, including the Cathedral of Christ the Savior, the largest church in Moscow (see Figure 2.3). In Central Asia, mosques were closed and Muslim clergy arrested. In addition to repression, Soviet authorities used propaganda to disparage religion and promote atheism. The League of the Militant Godless conducted educational work to replace religiosity with faith in reason and science. The effectiveness of anti-religious work was limited, as many Soviet citizens retained religious beliefs, but the open practice of religion was largely prohibited.[39]

Soviet culture also derided values seen as bourgeois – individualism, acquisitiveness, and profit seeking. The violent dispossession of NEPmen and kulaks had already ended private ownership and the free market. But Soviet officials also made an effort to instill collectivism through educa-tion, propaganda, and youth groups. The Komsomol and Young Pioneers were the Communist organizations for young adults and teen-agers. In addition to regular meetings and activism, these groups partici-pated in physical fitness parades and summer camps. Young Pioneer activities were similar to the Boy Scouts and Girl Scouts, in that they taught hygiene, fitness, discipline, and patriotism. But Soviet ideologues drew distinctions, claiming that Boy Scouts were selfish individualists eager to accrue merit badges for themselves, while Young Pioneers worked for "a goal common to all participants."[40] In 1933, Kaganovich said to one Young Pioneer leader, "I am asking how much our children have progressed in truly human terms . . . with respect to getting rid of the mentality of the past, egotism, vanity, selfishness." Kaganovich went on to express doubt that the Soviet population had eliminated these "vestiges of the past," but he made clear the importance of instilling collectivist values.[41]

To promote collectivism, Soviet architects and urban planners sought to shape people's living environment. Some of their plans resembled urban renewal projects in other countries – they called for airy apartments, well-lit streets, and spacious parks. For them, as for urban planners around the world, the elimination of chaos and congestion would add efficiency and harmony to people's lives. But Soviet architects' designs differed in that they emphasized communal dining and living spaces that would instill a collectivist ethos among workers.[42] In the end, virtually none of Soviet architects' elaborate designs were ever built, due to a lack of government investment. Instead of modern, airy housing projects, Soviet workers experienced a different type of collective living – overcrowded communal apartments and filthy, lice-ridden barracks. Party leaders had limited capital, and they invested in factories, not housing. The bright new apartments that visionary urban planners hoped would instill collectivism were never constructed.

As part of its attack on bourgeois values, the Stalinist leadership also launched an assault on the country's intellectual and technical elite, so-called bourgeois specialists. In 1928, fifty-three mining engineers from Shakhty, a coal mining town in the northern Caucasus region, were put on trial for sabotage. The Shakhty trial received widespread publicity, and despite a lack of hard evidence, all but four engineers were found guilty – five were executed and forty-four were sent to prison. In 1930, another show trial was held – the Industrial Party trial. Economists who had worked at Gosplan and the Supreme Economic Council were accused of organizing a secret "Industrial Party" that conspired with Russian émigrés to aid France and the United Kingdom in planning to attack the Soviet Union. Several defendants were former Mensheviks who, as non-Communist specialists at Gosplan, had opposed the implausible tempos of the First Five-Year Plan. The defendants were found guilty and five were given death sentences, subsequently commuted to long prison terms.[43]

In the wake of the Shakhty trial, a wave of anti-specialist fervor swept the country. The secret police arrested several thousand bourgeois specialists – mostly engineers who had been trained under the tsarist regime. This older generation of technical elites was accused of sabotage and blamed for industrial accidents and slow production. Workers and Komsomol militants sometimes took matters into their own hands, denouncing or even assaulting engineers. The result was considerable disruption in factories. Although engineers were often forced to continue working (under guard) after their arrest, the Shakhty trial and its aftermath exacerbated a shortage of technical experts. Moreover, managerial authority was greatly undercut, as workers could readily disobey or denounce engineers and foremen. In an effort to restore hierarchy and order in the factories, Party leaders finally called a halt to persecution of specialists in 1931.

Why did the Stalinist leadership arrest economists and engineers at the very moment it needed them most? Given that technical expertise was essential to the industrialization drive, the persecution of engineers was highly detrimental to the country's progress. One reason for this persecution was Stalin's genuine distrust of bourgeois specialists. He felt that those who had been members of the prerevolutionary elite were not loyal to the Soviet Union, and he repeatedly called for their replacement with new specialists of working-class origin – something the Soviet government facilitated by training workers to become engineers. Stalin also believed that the old elite maintained ties with émigré capitalists who were allegedly plotting with western European governments to overthrow the Soviet regime. In 1928, he warned, "We have internal enemies. We have external enemies. We cannot forget this for a moment."[44] This statement in fact epitomized the mentality of Stalin and other Party leaders, and their constant fear of attacks by domestic and foreign foes.

The Shakhty trial and the Industrial Party trial also alerted technocrats that Stalin and his ruling circle would remain in charge. Economists and the old technical elite, some with ties to Bukharin and the right opposition, generally favored a more gradual pace of industrialization. Stalinist industrialization represented a rejection of a rational, technocratic approach to economic development. As discussed earlier, it had a Promethean character – an ambition to break the bounds of time and exceed what seemed rationally possible. Any questioning of Bolshevik tempos was regarded as treason. The trials made clear to non-Party specialists that complete devotion to the cause was required. As Gosplan chief Gleb Krzhizhanovsky declared at the time, "Whoever is not with us is against us."[45]

The attack on specialists spread to intellectual and cultural fields as well. Komsomol radicals, emboldened by the Shakhty trial, harassed non-Party bureaucrats in institutions around the country. The Komsomol "Light Cavalry" even raided government offices to condemn bureaucratism. Younger Marxist scholars seized the opportunity to dislodge entrenched senior scholars in universities and institutes. Militant groups such as the Russian Association of Proletarian Writers denounced established literary and artistic figures, including Maxim Gorky, whom Party leaders were trying to persuade to return to the Soviet Union from abroad. These acts constituted an iconoclastic youth movement that was not directed by the Communist Party. In some cases, Party officials used activists' initiatives to wrest control of cultural institutions from non-Party intellectuals, but they did not order, nor even always approve of, activists' actions.

In 1931, Party leaders reined in attacks on technical and cultural specialists. In part, their concern was to reestablish a sense of hierarchy in factories for the sake of industrial production. But Stalin also provided an ideological justification for restoring specialists' authority. He explained that with the elimination of capitalism, the old intelligentsia had reconciled itself to the Soviet order. And he went on to point out that new specialists of working-class origin – people with strong allegiance to the Soviet state – now played a leading role in industry. Arguing that "the working class must create its own industrial and technical intelligentsia," Stalin boasted that the Soviet government "has opened wide the doors of all the higher educational institutions ... to members of the working class."[46] Stalin's words were not empty rhetoric. During the First Five-Year Plan, hundreds of thousands of workers received training in technical institutes and became engineers or managers in the burgeoning Soviet industrial bureaucracy. At least 1.5 million workers moved into white-collar jobs during the First Five-Year Plan.[47] Party leaders' longstanding goal of creating a new technical elite, drawn from the ranks of the working class, had been attained.

The promotion of workers into managerial positions built social support for the Stalinist regime. Before the Revolution, workers could never dream of becoming engineers or factory managers. Now every year hundreds of thousands of workers were studying and advancing into positions of authority in Soviet industry.[48] Many of these workers also joined the Communist Party, and some even became high-ranking Party officials. They were loyal to the Soviet system because they benefitted from it. Indeed, for those who joined the industrial and Party bureaucracies, they became part of the system. The Stalinist regime did not rule only through coercion and fear. Its program of rapid industrial growth and working-class upward mobility fulfilled the ambitions of many workers. For those who were promoted, "building socialism" came to mean personal advancement as well as national pride in their country's progress.

Cultural revolution, then, was a broad concept of social and cultural transformation that was to accompany the economic transition from capitalism to socialism. Some cultural ideals promoted by Soviet officials included literacy, hygiene, and sobriety – values that were to uplift the masses. Non-Party professionals in Russia since before the Revolution had pursued this agenda, and many of them continued to serve as teachers, doctors, and cultural workers in the Soviet period. Efforts to cultivate a literate, healthy, and efficient population paralleled similar attempts by officials and professionals in countries around the world in the late nineteenth and twentieth centuries. But cultural transformation in the Soviet Union also had unique aspects. Official Soviet culture promoted atheism over religion and collectivism over individualism. Party leaders also persecuted old specialists and increasingly replaced them with newly trained engineers of working-class origin.

Soviet Nationality Policies

The large number of different nationalities and ethnic groups in the Soviet Union posed a special challenge for Party leaders. Many in the Stalinist leadership were themselves members of non-Russian nationalities – Stalin was Georgian, as was Ordzhonikidze; Mikoyan was Armenian; Krzhizhanovsky was Polish; Kaganovich was Jewish; Nikita Khrushchev was Ukrainian. Even ethnic Russian leaders such as Molotov, Voroshilov, and Kirov had held military or administrative positions in non-Russian regions of the country and were highly mindful that they ruled over an ethnically diverse population. As already discussed, the foundations of Soviet nationality policies were established under Lenin's leadership, when territorial units were assigned to major nationalities and a federal system established at the end of 1922. Throughout the 1920s and 1930s, Party leaders continued to enact nationality policies that had huge consequences for the non-Russian peoples of the Soviet Union.

Was the Soviet Union an empire? Historians have debated this question and most have concluded that it was. Officially the country was not an empire but rather a federation of sovereign national republics, the Union of Soviet Socialist Republics. Major nationalities had their own territorial units – union republics in the case of the largest nationalities, and autonomous republics or regions for some of the smaller national minorities. In theory, nationalities had the right to self-rule and even secession. In practice, non-Russian peoples had no real sovereignty or right to secede, as power remained in the hands of rulers in Moscow. In this sense, the Soviet Union was an empire. At the same time, the Soviet Union differed considerably from the tsarist empire as well as from western European colonial empires.[49] Unlike some tsarist administrators, Soviet officials did not try to Russify non-Russian subjects. And unlike British imperialists, they did not seek to subjugate the peoples they ruled. On the contrary, the Soviet government actually fostered the development of non-Russian languages and cultures and sought to integrate all nationalities into the Soviet polity.

The centerpiece of Soviet nationality policy was nativization – the recruitment of national minorities into the Communist Party and government bureaucracy. The territorial units of the major nationalities had local institutions staffed by indigenous elites. Each of these nationalities was granted a national flag, national anthem, and other symbols of nationhood. Nativization also entailed the development of non-Russian languages and cultures. Native languages were to be used in local government and taught in schools. Newspapers, journals, and literary publications were to appear in non-Russian languages as well. Some ethnic groups initially did not have a written language or well-defined sense of national identity. For these people, Party officials, with the help of non-Party linguists and ethnographers, developed written languages and cultures.[50]

On the surface, the fostering of national cultures by an avowedly socialist government seems odd. Given that Party leaders' ultimate goal was communism and the disappearance of national differences, why did they promote national identities among Soviet citizens? The reason was that Party leaders saw nationalism as a stage that all peoples had to progress through in order to move beyond it to socialism and communism. As Marxists, they thought people's sense of identity progressed along an evolutionary timeline that corresponded to economic stages of history (feudalism, capitalism, socialism, communism). Those ethnic groups in the Soviet Union that lacked national consciousness needed to develop it before they could move forward and transcend it. The objective of Soviet nationality policy among less developed peoples, then, was to consolidate feudal-era clans and tribes into nationalities, and then transform these nationalities into socialist-era nations that would all ultimately merge under communism.[51]

In practice, these policies meant assigning national designations to people who had no clear sense of national identity. The Caucasus region had a myriad of national, ethnic, and tribal groups. Georgians and Armenians were well-defined nationalities with national languages and cultures that had existed for centuries.[52] But the Muslim peoples of the south Caucasus constituted a number of disparate ethnic and linguistic groups that Soviet officials amalgamated into the Azerbaijani nationality. In the north Caucasus, ethnic fragmentation was even more extreme, with a range of mountain tribes and ethnic groups. Soviet authorities created a number of autonomous national regions within larger union republics. Even with numerous national designations, there was still no neat correspondence between Soviet administrative units and the complex ethnic reality of the region. In some cases, the Soviet government combined similar ethnic groups into one national territory, as with the Chechen-Ingush Autonomous Region. At other times, Soviet authorities combined peoples with different languages and cultures, as in the case of the Kabardino-Balkar Autonomous Republic.[53] Of course, Soviet officials' ultimate goal was the merging of all groups, though this goal was premised on the questionable assumption that over time peoples would naturally fuse into ever-larger nationalities and eventually transcend national identities altogether.

In Central Asia, ascribing national categories was also problematic, because most of the people there did not identify themselves in national terms. Throughout the 1920s, ethnographers in Central Asia found that those they questioned often had no ethnic identity or claimed several identities at once. Assigning people to national categories based on language and culture was not a clear-cut matter either. Ethnic and linguistic distinctions often did not coincide – for example, some "Uzbeks" were culturally Turkic but spoke Persian dialects. Drawing borders for national regions was even more complicated. Some people in Central Asia were nomadic, so officials could not pinpoint precisely where they lived. Even among sedentary populations, ethnic groups were intermixed. In the Fergana Valley, for example, those regarded as Uzbeks lived alongside neighboring villages of Kirgiz, and some Tajiks lived there as well.[54]

Soviet officials and ethnographers nonetheless proceeded to designate national categories and draw the borders of national republics. In Central Asia, they decreed five major nationalities – Kazakh, Kirgiz, Uzbek, Tajik, and Turkmen, and by the mid-1930s each of these nationalities had its own republic within the Soviet Union. In reality there was little to distinguish Kazakhs and Kirgiz, as they spoke virtually the same Turkic language and were different only in that Kazakhs were primarily nomads of the plains, while Kirgiz were mountain dwellers. The Uzbek national category absorbed many small Turkic peoples of the region. Tajiks were recognized as a distinct nationality because they spoke a Persian rather than Turkic language, but some of their communities were geographically intermingled with Uzbeks. As a result, Tajiks who ended up within the borders of Uzbekistan had to attend Uzbek-language schools. The various nomadic tribes who lived in the desert area east of the Caspian Sea were amalgamated into the Turkmen nationality and had to adopt common institutions and a single written language.[55] While seemingly arbitrary, Soviet authorities' designations of national identities and borders were in fact based on ethnographers' considerable study and expertise. The problem was that the complex ethnic reality of the Soviet population resisted the neat national categorizations that ethnographers and officials sought.

Despite the lack of clear national categories in Central Asia, Soviet officials' belief that people would come to identify themselves as members of a nationality turned out to be self-fulfilling. Because the Soviet administrative structure was delineated along national lines, people had to adopt a national identity in order to interact with the government. One ethnographer noted that following the creation of Uzbekistan as a Soviet republic in 1924, some people who had previously called themselves Sarts began to call themselves Uzbeks. When officials taking the 1926 census asked people in Uzbekistan their nationality, others still replied "Sart." The census questionnaire, however, did not include Sart as a nationality category, so census takers registered them as Uzbeks instead.[56] When Soviet authorities instituted an internal passport system in late 1932, every citizen who received a passport had their nationality inscribed in it, whether or not they identified themselves in national terms.

The categorization of people by nationality was not simply an academic exercise. The drawing of national borders for Soviet republics empowered members of the titular nationality in each republic and disempowered national minorities. Uzbeks in Uzbekistan could lay claim to water resources as well as educational and job opportunities, while Tajiks living there could not. People quickly learned to make appeals based on official national categories, and in this way they began to internalize national identities. Petitioners who identified themselves as Kazakhs living in Uzbekistan complained that Uzbek officials paid "insufficient attention" to their economic and cultural development and requested unification with Kazakhstan. For their part, Uzbek peasants in Kirgizia accused Kirgiz officials of "policies against Uzbek interests," including discrimination in school admissions. As one scholar concludes, "petitioners used the language of nationality in their interactions with the state, and in doing so helped to make official nationality categories real."[57]

Jews were treated like a nationality as well. Despite the fact that Judaism was a religion, Soviet authorities used Jewish as a national category, for example when people had to give their nationality for censuses or in a passport. The practice of Judaism as a religion was proscribed – most synagogues, like most churches and mosques, were closed by the Soviet government, and rabbis, like other clergy, were persecuted. But for administrative purposes, Jews were supposed to maintain a secular Jewish identity that would exist alongside other official Soviet national identities. Because Jews did not have a national territory, in 1934 the Soviet government created the Jewish Autonomous Region, popularly known by the name of its capital city, Birobidzhan. Located near the Chinese border in the sparsely populated Soviet Far East, this region was more than 5,000 miles from Moscow and other Jewish population centers in the European part of the Soviet Union. By 1939, only 18,000 Jews (out of a total Soviet Jewish population of 3 million) had moved to Birobidzhan. Despite the small numbers, Soviet authorities pushed ahead with plans to create a Jewish national territory. Hebrew, considered a religious language, was shunned, and Yiddish was decreed the official language of the region. Soviet officials established Yiddish newspapers, schools, and cultural institutions, including the Kaganovich Jewish Theater.[58]

In keeping with their Marxist evolutionary timeline, Party leaders expected the socialist offensive of the early 1930s to accelerate the development of national cultures. At the Sixteenth Party Congress in 1930, Stalin declared, "The period of the construction of socialism is the period of the flowering of national culture, socialist in content and national in form ... the development of national culture should unfold with new strength."[59] The Soviet government expanded educational opportunities for non-Russians, and in particular trained thousands of new teachers who were to spread literacy to national minorities in their native languages. Soviet linguists created more than forty written languages (sixteen in 1932–33 alone) for ethnic groups that had no written language of their own.[60] In 1931, Soviet officials heralded "the creation of new nationalities out of tribes which had earlier never dreamed of national existence ... [and] their transition in just six years through all the stages of development, which for other peoples required thousands of years."[61] Over time, the multitude of nationalities within the country was to be consolidated into ever-larger national groups that would eventually disappear under communism. But far from suppressing non-Russians, Soviet nationality policies actively promoted the identities of national minorities.[62]

National Cultures and Ethnic Conflict

Stalin's formula for nationalities' cultures was "national in form, socialist in content." The Soviet government encouraged certain forms of national expression, including language, literature, folklore, and costumes. The All-Union House of Folk Art in Moscow displayed the artwork and traditional costumes of different nationalities, while the government also sponsored folk singing competitions and festivals of national art through-out the country. Soviet folklore reflected nationalities' cultures not as they existed in everyday life but rather as colorful, superficial forms. Folk singers in bright national costumes sang upbeat songs about the bountiful harvest. Soviet Georgia, for example, was called "sunny socialist Georgia," and described as having fine weather that explained the "joy-ful" folk art produced there.[63] National minorities were presented as proud of their cultures but also as economically content and politically loyal (see Figure 2.4). New poems and folk songs were even composed in honor of Stalin and the Soviet government.

The political content of national cultures remained tightly controlled and "socialist." Some of the most significant national practices and beliefs, including economic traditions and religion, were abolished. Barter and trade customs were outlawed as capitalist, and nomadic herding was curtailed as backward. Soviet officials closed or even demol-ished most churches, synagogues, and mosques. Propaganda campaigns derided religious holidays, including Easter and Ramadan. Beginning in 1927, Soviet authorities in Uzbekistan sought to end the Muslim practice of the veiling and seclusion of women. Envisioned as a means to liberate women and modernize Uzbek society, the unveiling campaign led to violent confrontations between officials and Muslim Uzbeks who sought to defend veiling as their religious and cultural tradition.[64] The pilgrimage to Mecca, considered a religious duty for each able-bodied Muslim to undertake at least once in his or her lifetime, was prohibited by Soviet law in 1935.[65] Nationality cultures, while permitted and even fostered, thus remained tightly circumscribed.

Party leaders also guarded against "bourgeois nationalism," the label they gave to nationalist sentiments – including nationalist separatism – that privileged the interests of one nationality over those of the Soviet Union as a whole. Stalin in particular saw bourgeois nationalism as a danger to central control and a threat to the country's territorial integ-rity. When Ukrainian Party members objected to steep grain collection quotas in 1932, Stalin denounced them as anti-Communist Ukrainian nationalists and "agents of [Polish leader Jozef] Pilsudski," and he warned that the Soviet Union might lose Ukraine if these "rotten elements" were not rooted out.[66] The Soviet government carried out mass arrests and executions of nationalities in the late 1930s, but already in the early 1930s it arrested those Ukrainians, Poles, Finns, Tatars, Kazakhs, Tajiks, and so forth considered to be "bourgeois nationalists."[67] The Stalinist

Figure 2.4 Propaganda poster of Soviet nationalities by Vladimir Serov, 1934. The slogan reads, "Long live the unity and brotherhood of the laborers of all nationalities of the USSR!"

leadership, then, repressed any expression of nationalities' independent interests and subordinated national republics to the center.

Non-Russian peoples were affected not only by Soviet administrative and cultural policies but by economic policies as well. Industrialization and urbanization in particular had an impact on them. As thousands of national minority peasants migrated to the Soviet Union's cities and construction sites, their lives changed fundamentally – they became urban dwellers living alongside other nationalities. While Moscow's population remained overwhelmingly Russian, other nationalities such as Ukrainians, Tatars, and Bashkirs moved there in the 1930s. Ethnic violence erupted at several Moscow construction sites – in one instance a large-scale brawl between Russian and Tatar workers resulted in multiple arrests.[68] The ethnic balance in Ukrainian cities shifted dramatically during Stalinist industrialization. Whereas previously Russian and Jewish populations had predominated in many Ukrainian cities, this changed when large numbers of Ukrainian peasants moved to cities during the 1930s.[69]

In Kazakhstan, the Turkestano-Siberian railway employed thousands of Kazakhs who built the railroad. Heralded by Soviet officials as "the forge of the Kazakh proletariat," this construction project dramatically changed the lifestyle of many Kazakh herders, but it also sparked ethnic tensions. Some Russians mistreated Kazakhs working alongside them. One Russian foreman refused to train Kazakhs, saying, "Why should you Kazakhs be specialists? Riding bulls and pasturing sheep, that's your specialty." Russian workers insulted Kazakhs and, in some instances, smeared pig fat on their lips, in violation of Muslim strictures against eating pork. In other cases, groups of Russian workers assaulted new Kazakh recruits, resulting in mêlées and beatings.[70] Stalinist industrialization thus produced ethnic as well as social change, including a greater integration of different nationalities but also a rise in ethnic conflict.

Over time, Soviet nationality policies intended to supersede nationalism instead solidified national identities, even where none had previously existed. By requiring that all citizens be categorized by nationality, Soviet authorities reinforced the very national allegiances they hoped would gradually disappear. The federated system based on national territorial units also set the stage for the eventual breakup of the Soviet Union along national lines. Throughout the Soviet period, authority remained in the hands of Party leaders in Moscow, but with the fall of the Communist government in 1991 the Soviet Union became fifteen separate countries based on nationality. For non-Russians living under Soviet rule, nationality policies had far-reaching consequences. National minorities acquired educational and career opportunities, and some even joined the Communist Party and became Soviet officials within their republics. At the same time, non-Russians had many of their customs destroyed, as religious observances were prohibited and traditional modes of economic subsistence obliterated.[71] The collectivization of agriculture in particular devastated a number of Soviet nationalities, not least because it led to a deadly famine at the end of the First Five-Year Plan.

The Famine of 1932–1933

Collectivization had imposed a new political and economic order on peasants throughout the country. Authority in each village rested with the collective farm chairman, who took orders from the Communist Party. Peasants no longer privately owned land and livestock, which were now the property of collective farms. In theory, collectivized agriculture was to be more efficient, as individually owned strips of land were consolidated into large fields to be farmed with tractors rather than horse-drawn plows. In practice, Soviet officials failed to supply adequate farm machinery, so agriculture continued to require a great deal of manual labor. But the number of peasants and livestock left to work the land had fallen dramatically. More than 1.5 million peasants had been deported as kulaks, several million more had fled to the cities, and thousands of horses and cattle had been slaughtered by peasants unwilling to turn them over to collective farms.

Collectivization also caused severe disruption in the rural economy. Such a sudden and violent change produced widespread chaos. No longer guided by peasant traditions, planting and harvesting now fell under the purview of collective farm chairmen, who often lacked experience and expertise. Peasant letters to the Soviet government complained of "complete anarchy," "irresponsibility," and inept management on collective farms.[72] Moreover, peasants now had no incentive to work hard, as they no longer owned the crops they grew. Instead the grain and livestock belonged to state-run collective farms, and peasants simply received a payment in kind for their labor. Lacking incentives and deeply resentful that they had been coerced into joining collective farms, peasants put little effort into their labor. As a result, agricultural production dropped sharply. The harvest nationwide of 73 million metric tons of grain in 1930 fell to 57 million tons in 1931.[73]

While agricultural output fell, the amount of grain extracted by the government actually increased. Now that the harvest was in the hands of state-run collective farms rather than individual peasant households, it became much easier for Soviet authorities to take grain from the peasantry. Despite the lower harvest in 1931, Party leaders exported a record amount of grain – more than 5 million metric tons – and in exchange imported foreign technology for the industrialization drive. As a result of harsh grain requisitions, some peasants were left without adequate seed grain in the spring of 1932. This shortage, coupled with the overall disorder on collective farms, led to an even smaller harvest that autumn of 55 million tons of grain.[74]

Party leaders were aware of grain shortages and imminent famine in the countryside. After touring Ukraine in the summer of 1932, Molotov reported to the Politburo, "We are indeed faced with the specter of famine and in rich grain districts to boot."[75] The Stalinist leadership pushed ahead with grain requisitions and exports nonetheless, leaving millions of peasants with nothing to eat. Local officials who protested Party leaders' high requisition quotas were removed or even arrested. Peasants sought to hide grain, but grain collection brigades searched homes and took whatever they found. Lev Kopelev, then a young activist and later a Soviet dissident, recalled that he and other brigade members took the last grain from starving peasants. "With the others, I emptied out the old folks' storage chests, stopping my ears to the children's crying and women's wails … In the terrible spring of 1933, I saw people dying from hunger. I saw women and children with distended bellies, turning blue, still breathing but with vacant, lifeless eyes."[76]

A horrendous famine engulfed entire regions of the Soviet Union, particularly the primary grain growing areas – Ukraine, the lower and middle Volga regions, and the northern Caucasus. Government grain requisitions had been especially harsh in these areas. With no food left, peasants there began to starve. One government report described how people ate cats and dogs, as well as "carrion and garbage … and concoctions from weeds and potato peelings." There were even cases of cannibalism – people eating human flesh in order to survive. Millions starved to death. As another official report stated, "The sick die first … The children die, and barbarism has reached the point where the parents eat, and do not feed the children." Two leading scholars estimate that 5.7 million people died of starvation from 1930 to 1933, with the vast majority of these famine deaths occurring in 1932–33.[77]

Some historians have argued that the famine was a deliberate genocide of the Ukrainian people perpetrated by Stalin as a means to crush Ukrainian nationalism.[78] It is true that Stalin waged a fierce campaign against Ukrainian nationalists. It is also true that the famine killed several million Ukrainians. And Stalin and his fellow leaders undeniably bear responsibility for these deaths, as their policies caused the famine. But "genocide" denotes the intentional killing of an entire group of people, and the famine of 1932–33 was not genocide. As callous as they were, Party leaders found the famine highly undesirable, even alarming. Three times they curtailed grain procurement plans for Ukraine (in August 1932, October 1932, and January 1933), and they distributed small amounts of seed grain to famine regions beginning in April 1932. But these measures were far too little to save starving peasants. If Party leaders had halted grain exports and dispersed all grain reserves to famine regions, they could have saved millions of lives.[79] Instead their concern was pushing ahead with industrialization and using grain reserves for export or to feed workers in cities.

The Nazi genocide of the Jews was a massive state-sponsored operation aimed at annihilating all European Jews – literally an effort to wipe out the "Jewish genome" (genocide in the true sense of the word). By contrast, the death of millions of Ukrainians in the famine of 1932–33 was not the intention of Party leaders but rather the consequence of their reckless policies. In some Ukrainian villages, the results were nearly as catastrophic as genocide, with virtually the entire population starving to death. But Stalin and his fellow leaders did not seek to cause these deaths or annihilate all Ukrainians. Nor were Ukrainians the only ones who suffered in the famine. Members of other nationalities died as well, including Russians, Tatars, and Kazakhs. If we calculate famine deaths as a percentage of the population, Kazakhs suffered proportionally even more than Ukrainians. An estimated 1.5 million Kazakhs died during the famine, and the Kazakh population declined sharply.[80]

The famine in Kazakhstan was especially severe because Soviet officials there imposed sedentarization along with collectivization. Many Kazakhs were nomadic animal herders, and in addition to being forced to turn over their livestock to collective farms, they were required to settle in one place. The arid land of the Kazakh steppe meant that few locations had enough water to support permanent settlements with large livestock herds, precisely the reason for Kazakhs' nomadic lifestyle. But Party leaders in Moscow, with faint understanding of local circumstances, assumed that nomadism was a reflection of Kazakhs' backwardness. In their thinking, nomadism was a relic of feudal times and sedentarization would help Kazakhs progress. The Communist Party resolved that collectivization in Kazakhstan could only be achieved through the forced settlement of Kazakh nomads.

The consequences of forcing Kazakhs to settle on collective farms were disastrous. Some Kazakhs slaughtered their sheep and cattle rather than having them collectivized. Others assaulted Party activists, and were arrested and sent to Gulag labor camps. Many Kazakhs fled to other parts of Central Asia or across the border to China, taking their herds with them. Of the thousands of Kazakhs who set out for China, however, less than a quarter survived the journey. Even among those who joined collective farms, some had no way to feed themselves, as the new collective farms lacked the seed grain, equipment, animals, and water necessary to sustain agriculture. Nearly 80 percent of the Kazakhs' livestock died during this period, so Kazakhs' main food source was lost. Many Kazakhs fled hunger on collective farms only to wander the steppe with no means to feed themselves. The result was massive loss of life due to famine and related diseases.[81]

Collectivization similarly destroyed many livestock of the "small peoples of the north" – the Yakuts, Nenets, Komi, Chukchi, and other ethnic groups engaged in reindeer herding in the circumpolar region. Some herders slaughtered their animals, claiming "The reindeer will be taken away anyway, so it's better if we eat them ourselves." Other reindeer were not properly tended and died on collective farms. Roughly 35 percent of the total reindeer herd perished between 1930 and 1934. As in Kazakhstan, officials tried to settle nomadic herders and trappers in an effort to modernize them, though these efforts only further disrupted people's attempts to feed themselves. Unlike Ukrainians and Kazakhs, the inhabitants of the far northern regions of European Russia and Siberia did not suffer famine on a massive scale. But there too the destruction of their traditional lifestyle led to hunger, and in some cases starvation.[82]

One emergency measure Party leaders took to cope with the famine was the introduction of an internal passport system in late 1932. Some people assumed that the purpose of internal passports was to prevent starving peasants from flooding into cities. The passport system did hinder peasants' movement (peasants were denied passports), but Party leaders' primary objective was to purge major cities of what they called "superfluous people not involved in production or the work of institutions, as well as of kulak, criminal, and other antisocial elements hiding in the towns."[83] Their thinking was that, given worsening food shortages, only workers who contributed to socialist construction should remain in cities and be fed. "Persons not occupied in socially useful labor" did not receive passports or residency permits and were expelled from major cities. The passport system soon became an integral part of Soviet policing operations. A 1933 Politburo decree instructed the secret police to "establish order in the streets of Moscow and purge them of filth," and subsequently the police conducted sweeps of Moscow and other cities to arrest and exile those without passports.[84]

Despite these attempts to purge cities and guarantee industrial workers a steady food supply, severe shortages plagued Soviet cities in 1932–33. Unlike peasants, urban workers did not starve to death, but they experienced considerable hardship. Rations were reduced, and often stores did not even have food for those with ration coupons. In some localities, workers organized strikes and demonstrations. These protests were ultimately suppressed by authorities, but nonetheless took a political and economic toll.[85] The food supply crisis dragged down the entire economy. After spectacular economic growth during the First Five-Year Plan (1928–32), there was virtually no economic growth in 1933. Only after the famine abated in second half of 1933 did the Soviet economy recover and begin to grow again in 1934.

Collectivization, dekulakization, and the famine left deep scars on Soviet society. This was particularly true for families whose members died of starvation (and in hard-hit famine regions many families were wiped out entirely). Even among peasants who survived, resentments toward the Stalinist regime grew even greater. Peasants continued to leave their villages, particularly in the mid-1930s when employment opportunities in the cities began to rise once again. Those remaining on collective farms often focused on their own garden plots rather than on collectively farmed fields, and agricultural production stagnated. In addition, dekulakization meant that several million people in the Soviet Union were permanently alienated from the system. Not only were those deported as kulaks embittered, they were never reintegrated into Soviet society. Even after they served terms in special settlements, the Soviet government did not trust them and subsequently subjected them to discrimination and arrest.

The famine left a legacy of mistrust even within the Communist Party. Not surprisingly, some Party members began to question Stalin's leadership and policies. A group of high-ranking Party members even called for his removal. For his part, Stalin came to doubt the loyalty and commitment of Communist Party members. He and his fellow leaders sincerely believed that no material constraints could thwart their modernization drive. In the span of a few years they destroyed centuries-old peasant agricultural traditions and replaced them with collectivized agriculture. When agricultural output dropped and famine was imminent, they pushed ahead anyway. In their eyes, the failure to reach economic goals reflected either insufficient willpower or sabotage by internal enemies. Stalin in particular became convinced of the need to root out enemies, even within the Communist Party.

There were compelling reasons to modernize the Soviet Union – if Party leaders wanted to provide for their country's defense, they needed to industrialize rapidly. Party leaders also shared the longstanding desire of educated Russians to transform their country's overwhelmingly peasant population. But this goal of social modernization does not explain the violent methods of Stalinism. Why did Soviet authorities arrest engineers and productive peasants – people they needed for economic development? Why did they requisition grain to the point of famine – a famine that killed millions of people and impeded economic growth? Collectivization and industrialization reveal the ideological fanaticism of Stalin and his fellow leaders. They sought to drive the country forward toward their vision of socialism via state-directed, non-capitalist industrialization. And they assumed that peasants, national minorities, and other members of the population would be remade into productive, secular citizens. Believing the course of history to be on their side, Party leaders dismissed any resistance as "kulak sabotage" and sought to crush rather than accommodate those with opposing views.

Ideology, however, does not explain the forms of Stalinist state violence. These were shaped by total war practices inherited from World War I and the Civil War. Grain requisitions, deportations, and concentration camp incarcerations were used by Party leaders to pursue their ideological and economic goals. They carried out collectivization and industrialization as military operations, and they imposed state control over the entire economy. The state-run economy had the advantage of being able to mobilize resources for heavy industry, but it was highly detrimental to agriculture and the consumer sector. Shortages of food, clothing, and consumer goods came to characterize the Soviet system for the duration of its existence.

At one time, scholars attributed the Soviet regime's ability to enact this brutal economic and social transformation to its totalitarian character. According to this theory, the Soviet state was a well-oiled bureaucratic machine that exercised total control over the country and its population. But while the bureaucracy expanded enormously during the 1930s, Soviet governance was rather chaotic. State bureaucrats often worked at cross-purposes with one another, competing for raw materials and ignoring decrees. Economic plans crafted by Gosplan bureaucrats were regularly jettisoned in favor of higher production targets. The breakneck speed of industrialization produced mayhem on construction sites and in factories. The administrative structure in the countryside was relatively weak, so collectivization could only be accomplished by brigades of undisciplined activists backed by the secret police. Dekulakization was also disorganized – there was no clear definition of who was a kulak, but several million peasants were nonetheless dispossessed or deported. The deportees were sent to remote regions with no infrastructure, and thousands of them perished of exposure, disease, and starvation. In this sense, the Soviet government's lack of systematic control over its vast territory actually made Stalinist policies more lethal, as grand plans to remove and reeducate millions of "class enemies" led to appalling mortality rates.[86] Added to these deaths were millions of Ukrainians, Kazakhs, and others who starved to death during the 1932–33 famine – another consequence of the Stalinist regime's reckless drive to transform the country.

3   Socialism Attained (1934–1938)

In January 1934, Communist Party leaders and officials assembled at the Kremlin in Moscow for the Seventeenth Party Congress. They called it the Congress of Victors, celebrating their triumph in the battle to build socialism. One speaker after another heralded the fulfillment of the First Five-Year Plan and the collectivization of agriculture. Rapid industrialization had greatly increased the country's economic and military power, but for Party leaders, the planned economy meant even more than that. They saw it as evidence that their country had progressed along the Marxist timeline to socialism. The fact that they had eliminated the free market, expropriated the bourgeoisie, and replaced private ownership of the means of production with a state-run economy – all of this meant that capitalism had been abolished and the foundations of socialism had been built.

For Stalin and other Party leaders, the attainment of socialism amounted to nothing less than a new epoch in world history. While capitalist countries were mired in the Great Depression, the Soviet Union was surging ahead, leading the way toward the future. In his address to the congress, Stalin stated "the U.S.S.R. has become radically transformed and has cast off backwardness and medievalism. From an agrarian country it has become an industrial country. From a country of small individual agriculture, it has become a country of collective, large-scale mechanized agriculture. From a dark, illiterate and uncultured country it has become – or rather it is becoming – a literate and cultured country."[1]

As Stalin indicated, Party leaders saw economic accomplishments as a basis for social and cultural transformation. In Marxist terms, the new economic base would produce a new superstructure. Party leaders issued a new constitution in 1936, one that no longer disenfranchised class enemies, because bourgeois classes no longer existed.[2] The purported attainment of socialism also prompted changes in Soviet official culture. Whereas previously traditional institutions and culture were derided as bourgeois, now they could be used to support the new order. The family, long suspected of perpetuating capitalist beliefs, was now trusted to promote socialism among children. Monumentalist art and architecture, formerly instruments of the old order, now helped legitimate the new socialist order and symbolize its accomplishments. The iconoclastic, avant-garde culture of the 1920s gave way to more traditional cultural forms and socialist realism, enshrined in the mid-1930s as the officially sanctioned form of Soviet art and literature.

Paradoxically, the purported attainment of socialism also led to a further escalation of state violence. Party leaders found that despite their elimination of capitalism and its agents, not everyone abided by the Soviet norms and laws. Instead of being called "class enemies," these people were branded "enemies of the people" or "anti-Soviet elements," inveterate opponents of the state. With the rising international tensions of the late 1930s, Stalin unleashed a deadly wave of violence to eliminate these alleged enemies. Not only criminals and former kulaks but members of diaspora nationalities became targeted by the Soviet secret police as the Stalinist leadership sought to neutralize potential traitors in the event of war. Political and military elites were not safe either, as Stalin's Great Purges led to the arrest and execution of thousands of Party members and officers. Of the nearly 2,000 delegates at the Congress of Victors in 1934, more than half had been imprisoned or executed by 1938.

Socialist Realism

During the 1920s, avant-garde culture had flourished in the Soviet Union. Constructivist artists produced abstract paintings. Formalist writers experimented with new literary forms. Futurist poet Vladimir Mayakovsky proclaimed that all previous culture should be destroyed. He wanted museums demolished to liberate art from the past and to allow the creation of a culture that was entirely new. The 1917 Revolution greatly bolstered Russian avant-garde movements and unleashed a wave of cultural creativity. Many artists and writers supported the Soviet government and sought to create a new world under socialism. For this endeavor, experimental literature, theater, and art seemed essential. An artist using realist forms could only reflect the world as it was. To create a new world, abstract forms were needed to imagine something that did not yet exist (see Figure 3.1).

This blossoming of avant-garde culture, however, did not last. By 1930, Mayakovsky was disillusioned with the bureaucratism of the Soviet system. He became despondent and began to play Russian roulette with his life. On three occasions he placed a single bullet in a revolver,

Figure 3.1 Pavel Filonov, *Composition*, 1930.

spun the chamber, aimed the gun at his heart, and pulled the trigger. The third time, the gun fired and killed him. Mayakovsky's suicide is sometimes seen as the symbolic death of the Russian avant-garde. By the mid-1930s, avant-garde culture had been banned. It was replaced by socialist realism.

Socialist realism was a style of art and literature that used realistic (not abstract) forms to promote official Soviet values. Among those values were the glorification of manual labor, industrial progress, and collectivism. Fictional heroes in socialist realism embodied the qualities of the New Soviet Person – honesty, modesty, punctuality, sobriety, and self-sacrifice for the good of the collective. Intended to be accessible to the masses, socialist realist art provided straightforward depictions of peasants and workers laboring in clean, idyllic conditions (see Figure 3.2). Sunlight, orderly apartments, modern technology, and schools were all elements frequently used to represent the country's bright future under socialism. Socialist realism actually shared some traits with the avant-garde culture that preceded it. Both movements opposed the commercialization of art; both sought to erase the distinctions between high and low culture and pursued a totalistic artistic vision; both had explicitly political purposes, seeking to inculcate new ideas and values.[3] But whereas avant-garde art had been iconoclastic in an effort to destroy the old bourgeois

Figure 3.2 Sergey Gerasimov, *A Collective Farm Festival*, 1937.

world, socialist realism was a form of classicism that sought to preserve the new socialist order.

What precipitated this dramatic shift in official Soviet culture? Stalin told Soviet writers in 1932, "The artist ought to show life truthfully. And if he shows it truthfully, he cannot fail to show it moving to socialism. This is and will be socialist realism."[4] With the vestiges of capitalism eliminated, avant-garde iconoclasm was no longer needed to attack bourgeois culture. In a society no longer riven by class antagonisms, discordant art and music had no place. And abstract art was no longer needed to imagine the socialist future, because the foundations of socialism had already been achieved. Realistic art and literary forms were now appropriate to represent the new socialist order. Socialist realism showed life under Soviet socialism to be modern, orderly, pure, and harmonious.

Party officials established institutions that, in conjunction with government censors, enforced socialist realism as the only acceptable artistic genre. In 1932, the Central Committee decreed the establishment of the Union of Soviet Writers and the Union of Artists of the USSR. These organizations provided material benefits to members, ran publishing houses and journals, and operated institutes to train writers and artists. The Union of Soviet Composers and the Academy of Architecture of the USSR subsequently played similar roles in their respective fields. All independent cultural organizations were abolished. In effect, writers and artists became state employees who had to conform to official dictates on culture. Since the Civil War, government censorship had prevented the distribution of anti-Soviet art and literature. But within certain political parameters, artists and writers had previously been allowed to experiment with different forms. Now the Soviet government controlled culture completely and dictated its form and content.

The first congress of the Union of Soviet Writers opened in August 1934. Nearly 600 delegates attended, as well as a number of foreign guests. Maxim Gorky, who had returned from emigration in 1932, presided over the congress. His novel, *Mother*, served as a prototype for socialist realist literature. In his speech at the congress, Gorky urged writers "to participate directly in the construction of a new life." With the new socialist world coming into being, writers had a political duty to contribute to this heroic feat through their literature. Andrey Zhdanov, the Party leader in charge of cultural affairs, also addressed the congress and quoted Stalin's description of writers as "engineers of human souls." He asked rhetorically what this phrase meant and replied that writers must depict life "truthfully ... not simply as 'objective reality,' but to depict reality in its revolutionary development." He went on to say that writers should educate "the toiling people in the spirit of socialism."[5]

To some people, socialist realism seemed to have an internal contradiction – how could art and literature represent a future socialist utopia using realist forms, which by definition could only portray current reality? But as noted, Soviet leaders no longer thought of socialism as some future utopian stage. They believed that they were already achieving socialism, and socialist realism would show reality as it was becoming. Of course, paintings of prosperous peasants working contentedly on collective farms did not correspond to the real-life hardship in most villages. Rather than an absolute depiction of reality, socialist realism used realist forms to show the new world that was supposedly emerging since capitalism had been abolished – as Zhdanov had said, "reality in its revolutionary development."[6]

Russian National Culture

The eclipse of avant-garde culture led to a selective rediscovery of Russian national culture and the classics of Russian literature. Alexander Pushkin's work in particular received great attention. In December 1935, the Soviet government announced plans to commemorate the hundredth anniversary of Pushkin's death. It formed the All-Union Pushkin Committee to coordinate the 1937 celebration.

The Committee ordered that every school throughout the country incorporate Pushkin into the curriculum, obligated every theater to perform Pushkin's plays, and arranged for 19 million copies of Pushkin's works to be published. It also held contests for the design of Pushkin statues, organized Pushkin evenings where his works were read, and even mandated the sale of Pushkin cakes.[7]

The glorification of Pushkin reversed avant-garde criticism of him as a symbol of cultural conservatism. After the Revolution, Mayakovsky had declared, "We are shooting the old generals! Why not Pushkin?"[8] As a former aristocrat and serf owner, Pushkin was a somewhat unlikely emblem of revolutionary, socialist culture. But Soviet official culture of the 1930s remade Pushkin into a "people's poet," who was neglected by his noble parents and raised instead by a serf nanny who gave him a love for the common people. Pushkin was also heralded as an essential precursor to socialist realism, whose idealism and critical realism made the creation of socialist realism possible. At the same time that Soviet propaganda stressed Pushkin's eminence, it also emphasized his accessibility to all readers, including the former lower classes and national minorities.[9] The promotion of Pushkin as a cultural icon for all Soviet citizens fulfilled both a long-standing intelligentsia dream of bringing Russian high culture to the masses, and the Soviet goal of creating a common culture to be shared by all members of the population.[10]

The Soviet literary canon also incorporated some other prerevolutionary writers, including Lev Tolstoy. One article, "Lenin and Tolstoy," quoted Lenin proclaiming that Tolstoy's great works deserved the widest possible attention. It also claimed that the tsarist government had suppressed Tolstoy's writings, but that the Soviet government made them available to everyone.[11] Somewhat surprisingly, Mayakovsky's works also became part of the Soviet literary canon. Mayakovsky's iconoclastic statements and poetry did not fit the model of socialist realism, but his suicide helped make his elevation possible. Because he was no longer alive to stir up political controversy, he could safely be inducted into the pantheon of Russian writers. Many other contemporary Soviet writers ran afoul of the Party line in the 1930s and fell victim to the Great Purges. Of the 101 writers selected to lead the Union of Soviet Writers in 1934, thirty had been arrested by 1938.[12]

In the same way that Party leaders selectively incorporated prerevolutionary writers into official culture, they also rehabilitated political and military leaders from the Russian past. Historical heroes similarly provided a common heritage with which to unite the population. Prior to the mid-1930s, Party leaders had denigrated the tsarist era and suppressed expressions of Russian nationalism. They believed that any appearance of

Russian chauvinism would aggravate national minorities' resentment of past imperialism. In 1935, Stalin declared that this resentment and mistrust had been overcome, replaced by mutual friendship among Soviet peoples.[13] The "brotherhood of Soviet peoples" meant that official culture could now extol Russian national heroes without fear of antagonizing national minorities. The revival of tsarist heroes also promoted patriotism – an important requirement in the late 1930s with the threat posed by Nazi Germany and fascist Japan.

In the second half of the 1930s, the Soviet government produced a number of patriotic films. Sergey Eisenstein directed "Alexander Nevsky," a film that depicted an epic medieval battle in which the Russians defeated the Teutonic knights. For the film, Eisenstein received a Stalin Prize – the highest honor awarded to artists by the Soviet government. Other patriotic films about heroes of the tsarist era included "Minin and Pozharsky," depicting Russians who saved their country from Polish rule in the early seventeenth century, as well as "Peter I" about Tsar Peter the Great.[14] In a 1937 toast, Stalin explained the importance of honoring the tsars. He acknowledged that the tsars had "enslaved the people." But he praised them, because "they put together an enormous state [stretching] out to Kamchatka." And he proclaimed, "We Bolsheviks were the first to put together and strengthen this state not in the interests of the landowners and capitalists but for the toilers and for all the great peoples who make up this state."[15]

As is clear from Stalin's words, he did not see glorification of Russian national heroes as contrary to socialist ideology, as long as this past was promoted in the interests of workers and peasants. Indeed, now that Soviet society was no longer made up of antagonistic classes, "the people" could be depicted as a unified whole. This accorded with Marx's idea that violent proletarian revolution would ultimately restore the organic social unity that had been lost under capitalism. Whether violent expropriations and deportations could in fact unify the population is highly dubious, but in the minds of Party leaders, these measures had eliminated the bourgeoisie and class conflict. The Soviet people could now exist as one. A unified cultural canon, based on Russian high culture and the glorification of the Russian past, was promoted to further this social unity.

While Peter the Great might have inspired patriotism among ethnic Russians, however, he and other tsars had been conquerors of national minorities in the Soviet empire. Invoking these heroes fostered Russian nationalism at the expense of Soviet internationalism, and tended to alienate the country's national minorities.[16] Soviet cultural producers sought to mitigate this problem by also promoting national minority heroes from the past. For example, Bogdan Khmelnitsky was heralded as a great seventeenth-century Ukrainian leader, in part because his political union with Russia could serve as a symbol of the fraternal bond between Russians and Ukrainians.[17] Official culture also venerated leading poets of non-Russian nationalities – Taras Shevchenko of Ukraine, Shota Rustaveli of Georgia, and Ivan Kupala of Belorussia.[18] It is not clear that Ukrainians and other national minorities accepted such cultural propaganda or took it as a sign of their equality. Nonetheless, national heroes and writers of Soviet national minorities were also showcased in official culture of the late 1930s.

Some scholars have characterized the endorsement of Russian national culture as a sign of Soviet leaders' "Great Retreat" from communist ideology.[19] But Stalin and his fellow leaders remained committed Marxists, and they continued to view the world in terms of the Marxist historical timeline. In fact, it was their sense that they had progressed along this timeline to socialism that allowed them to use traditional culture to support the new socialist order. With capitalism and the bourgeois classes eliminated, traditional high culture and national heroes could now belong to Soviet peasants and workers, and could inspire their patriotic support of the Soviet state. Party leaders' sense of historical progress, then, proved crucial to changes in official Soviet culture and the promotion of literary and political figures from the tsarist past.

The Stalin Cult

The Stalin cult represented another official effort to unify the population behind the Party leadership. Beginning in the 1930s, Stalin portraits and statues became omnipresent in the Soviet Union. Newspapers lauded Stalin's genius, his leadership, and his concern for common people. In public writings and speeches, everyone was obliged to honor Stalin. On one occasion a Soviet writer concluded a speech with the words, "I thank you, Soviet power." Lev Mekhlis, one of Stalin's lieutenants and a chief architect of the Stalin cult, chided the writer for not thanking Stalin instead, claiming that "Soviet power is above all Stalin."[20] Stalin became an accessible symbol of the Soviet government, its personification. In reality, the Soviet government was a vast and impersonal bureaucracy that carried out brutal policies. But to attract people's loyalty, the cult gave the regime a human face, one that purportedly cared about the population.

The Stalin cult began with Stalin's fiftieth birthday in 1929. But at that time the Soviet press still emphasized the Politburo's collective leadership and depicted Stalin a strong but distant leader. It was only in 1934 that

Soviet propaganda began to present Stalin as a kind, paternalistic figure. The Stalin cult stressed not only his wisdom and benevolence, but also people's devotion to him. The lyrics of one official song went as follows:

> Now at last we do live well
> Comrade Stalin, we all agree
> That you have lifted us from hell
> And freed us from our poverty.[21]

To build a connection between the Stalinist leadership and the people, officials held highly publicized gatherings where Party leaders met with workers and peasants. Conferences at the Kremlin showed workers expressing their appreciation to Stalin. At the 1935 Conference of Leading Combine Drivers, Stalin, Molotov, and Voroshilov gave the peasant delegates words of encouragement and approval. One delegate, Comrade Petrova, became flustered giving her speech and said she was too scared to continue. Stalin encouraged her, saying, "We here are your family."[22] Similarly, a pilot invited to a 1937 Kremlin reception forgot what to say, but then, according to the account, Stalin "looked at him with a smile ... of such fatherly warmth" that his fear vanished.[23] The Stalin cult thus sought to create a symbolic family with Stalin as the father figure. The Soviet press began to refer to Stalin as "father," and frequently pictured him surrounded by children and smiling paternalistically. One front-page article in *Pravda*, for example, was entitled "Father Stalin," and showed Stalin with a smiling Tajik girl.[24]

The Stalin cult is often assumed to be a continuation of the mythology surrounding the tsars, who were also presented as paternalistic leaders. But placed in an international context, the Stalin cult emerges instead as a modern political phenomenon, akin to the personality cults of Mussolini and Hitler. Modern personality cults were the product of mass politics, and in particular of the need for mass mobilization that grew out of World War I. Using modern media – mass circulation newspapers, posters, radio, and newsreels – twentieth-century dictators could appeal to millions of people and inspire their allegiance. As noted, the Lenin cult was the first cult of a Soviet leader, though Party leaders established it only after Lenin's death in 1924. The Stalin cult, by contrast, deified Stalin while he was still alive, and followed the example of Mussolini's cult in Italy. Mussolini took power in 1922 and within a few years had consolidated his fascist dictatorship by portraying himself as *Il Duce* (the leader), who united the Italian masses into one powerful national body. The Stalin cult similarly presented Stalin as a transcendent, god-like figure who could unite the Soviet people behind him (see Figure 3.3).[25]

ДА ЗДРАВСТВУЕТ РАБОЧЕ-КРЕСТЬЯНСКАЯ КРАСНАЯ АРМИЯ—
ВЕРНЫЙ СТРАЖ СОВЕТСКИХ ГРАНИЦ!

Figure 3.3 Propaganda poster of Stalin and Kliment Voroshilov reviewing troops on Red Square by Gustav Klutsis, 1935. The slogan reads, "Long live the workers and peasants' Red Army – a faithful guardian of the Soviet borders!"

How did people respond to the Stalin cult? Some beneficiaries of the Soviet system, including Party members, newly promoted officials, and military officers, genuinely revered Stalin. In private letters intercepted by Soviet surveillance organs, some soldiers similarly expressed their gratitude and loyalty to Stalin.[26] Other people appealed to Stalin as a benefactor in the hope of winning material aid. One woman, who sought to receive a bonus of 2,000 rubles, wrote to local government officials expressing her "enormous thankfulness to our dear, beloved father and friend and teacher, Iosif Vissarionovich [Stalin]."[27] But in private, some people criticized Stalin and his cult. One worker remarked, "Is Stalin happy because there are many fools and they write 'the great Stalin' during his lifetime?" Another Soviet citizen, after observing an official parade, complained that "the portraits of Party leaders are now displayed the same way icons used to be" in religious processions. A third commented, "The radio only reports eulogistic speeches about the rulers ... I'm sick of it. Even illiterates are taught to read using phrases like 'dear comrade Stalin.'"[28] Many people grumbled that Stalin and other leaders lived well while common people suffered. The Stalin cult, then, had limited success in building a bond between the leadership and the people. It mobilized the support of some Soviet citizens behind the regime. But only during World War II did a greater proportion of the Soviet population internalize the official image of Stalin as their protector.

According to Stalin's adopted son, Artem Sergeev, Stalin once reprimanded his biological son Vasily for exploiting the Stalin name. "But I'm a Stalin too," implored Vasily. "No, you're not," replied Stalin. "You're not Stalin and I'm not Stalin. Stalin is Soviet power. Stalin is what he is in the newspapers and the portraits, not you, no not even me!"[29] The cult certainly swelled Stalin's own authority, and there is no question that he established the cult to elevate himself. But to see the cult solely as Stalin's means to amplify his personal power is to miss its larger role. In an era of mass politics, leader cults served a crucial mobilizational function. People's loyalty to the leader translated into support for the regime and its programs. And with war on the horizon, devotion to the leader could inspire patriotism and sacrifice as well.

Stakhanovites as the New Soviet Person

Aleksey Stakhanov was a miner at the Central Irmino coal mine in eastern Ukraine. Originally a peasant from Orel province, Stakhanov began mining in 1927, and by 1935 he had become one of the mine's leading pneumatic pick operators. In August of that year, he was approached by a local Party official and a supervisor who asked if he would be interested in setting a coal mining record. Stakhanov agreed, and the following night, aided by fellow workers who hauled away the coal, he hewed 102 tons of coal in a single six-hour shift. Upon hearing of this feat, Commissar of Heavy Industry Ordzhonikidze ordered widespread publicity to make Stakhanov a hero.[30] Workers in other branches of industry soon began setting production records too. Called "Stakhanovites," they were hailed as hero-workers whom others were to emulate.

From a practical perspective, Party leaders used Stakhanovite records to raise production norms, much to the resentment of workers. One former Soviet worker complained that factory administrators gave Stakhanovites special assistance that allowed them to set records. "After those fellows produced more than others, the trade union committee used to call a meeting and pointed out to the workers that we lagged in our efforts. Usually, the immediate motion was following, 'Let's increase the quotas.'"[31] Indeed, in 1936 the Commissariat of Heavy Industry averaged production figures by Stakhanovites and non-Stakhanovites to arrive at production quotas that were 30–60 percent higher than previous norms. Stakhanovism hence gave factory managers a lever with which to compel workers to produce more.

Stakhanovism, however, was more than an attempt to raise labor productivity. As model workers, Stakhanovites served as the incarnation of the New Soviet Person. Party theorists had long discussed the new qualities that people would develop under socialism. In contrast to the capitalist era, with its deceitful bourgeoisie and exploited workers, socialism was supposed to allow people to reach their highest human potential, both in labor and in life. Freed from capitalist exploitation, workers would become innovative and productive laborers – hence the record-setting productivity of Stakhanovites. Moreover, they would enjoy the fruits of their own labor with prosperous, cultured lives. Individualism and greed would be supplanted by collectivism and generosity. Degradation and conflict would be replaced by prosperity and social harmony. During the 1920s and early 1930s, the New Person had remained an abstract ideal, but with the purported attainment of socialism in 1934, it could become a reality.[32] Stakhanovites were held up as living proof that the New Soviet Person had come into being.

At the First All-Union Conference of Stakhanovites, Stalin called them "new people, people of a special type."[33] One Stakhanovite after another described his or her personal transformation. Many emphasized their humble roots and the exploitation they had previously suffered. Stakhanov himself explained that he came from a poor village where as a boy he worked from dawn to dusk hauling sacks of grain for a kulak mill owner. His "real life" began only after he became a Soviet coalminer and heroic worker. A. V. Dushenkov said that previously he had been "an inactive and unenlightened worker," but that as a Stakhanovite he was "astonished by the unexpected change that took place in me." A propagandist addressing the conference declared that the Stakhanovite movement had turned recalcitrant workers and drunkards into labor heroes, and he expressed pride at having contributed to "the great process of remaking people which is going on in our country."[34]

Stakhanovites also provided an example of how Soviet workers were to live. They were described as residing in new, spacious apartments that were clean and well-decorated. Their personal libraries, gramophones, and theater outings underscored their appreciation of high culture. Female Stakhanovites in particular were depicted as wearing elegant clothing. In her autobiography, Stakhanovite A. D. Generalova, a factory worker in Gorky, stated, "several years ago, I lived in barracks and had nothing to wear to go out for a stroll." But after becoming a Stakhanovite, she went on, "I have all the clothes I need, and I am a respectable, marriageable girl."[35] Stakhanovites' fine clothing and cultural activities symbolized their emergence as the New Soviet Person. They acted as living examples of the Soviet Union's progress toward a modern, prosperous, socialist society. As an iconic representation of the New Soviet Person, then, Stakhanovites were more than just hero workers. They had reached their full potential in all spheres, and their productive and cultured lives were to serve as an example of what people were becoming under socialism.

Did workers and peasants truly embrace the ideal of the New Soviet Person? Some did embrace the opportunity to advance in the Soviet system and participate in the building of socialism. A collective farm activist in the 1930s, Alexander Zhelezniakov, wrote in his diary,

There is not, was not, and will not be, in world history a generation more happy than ours. We are the participants in the creation of a new epoch! ... Had the October Revolution not taken place, could I really have understood life in this way, and could I really have exchanged my personal life for the struggle for common goals? No! I would have remained almost an animal, but now I am happy.[36]

It is clear that some people, particularly those like Zhelezniakov who had joined the Communist Party, internalized official Soviet values. And many Stakhanovites themselves may have felt genuine gratitude for their opportunities. There were also Soviet citizens who wrote letters expressing thanks for "the cultured, cheerful, and wealthy life" bestowed by the Soviet government, though it is not known whether these sentiments were sincere.[37]

Other workers did not internalize official values but nonetheless pursued the material rewards offered to Stakhanovites. At the First All-Union Conference of Stakhanovites in November 1935, Stalin made his famous pronouncement, "Life has become better, comrades. Life has become more joyous." He went on to stress that the Soviet system gave workers "material benefits and the opportunity for a rich and cultured life."[38] In conjunction with Stalin's slogan, the Politburo allocated more resources to housing and consumer goods, and ended rationing. But while these measures raised the standard of living slightly, they did not lift the general population out of poverty. In fact, a harvest failure in 1936 created new food shortages at the very moment when living standards were supposed to be improving.

While Stakhanovites enjoyed higher living standards, the vast majority of workers could only dream of the fashionable clothing, automobiles, and imported goods publicized by the Soviet media. Most of them struggled to obtain the bare necessities of food and clothing throughout the 1930s.[39] Following the Seventeenth Party Congress in 1934, when Stalin had defined socialism as "not poverty and deprivation, but the elimination of poverty and deprivation," some workers at factory meetings complained, "The speeches are good but there's no bread."[40] At a conference accompanying an exhibition of children's wares in 1936, members of the audience jeered, "Now we've seen that at the exhibition there are all imaginable things, and that's all very well, but they aren't in the stores and you won't find them." Others wrote anonymous letters complaining that life was becoming better only for the rich.[41] A number of workers expressed particular disillusionment regarding the slogan "Life Has Become More Joyous," explaining that they expected living standards to get better, which they had not. Soon people began to use the slogan "Life Has Become More Joyous" ironically, spouting it when something went wrong or when someone was experiencing hardship.[42]

The Stakhanovite movement illustrates that Soviet leaders took seriously their ideal of workers enjoying productive, prosperous lives under socialism. Stakhanovites' production records, new apartments, and fine clothing were to show workers how much they could attain, both in the factory and at home. The Soviet government thus rewarded a small number of hero-workers as a way to raise people's aspirations. But for the majority of Soviet citizens, prosperity remained far out of reach. Even as living standards improved slightly in the mid-1930s, average workers continued to reside in communal apartments or barracks, with only very basic food and clothing. Stories of Stakhanovites' "rich and cultured lives" often stirred not aspirations but resentments.

At the same time, worldwide economic conditions allowed Soviet workers to compare their economic prospects favorably with those of workers in other countries. The Great Depression meant that workers throughout the capitalist world faced unemployment and falling living standards. In the Soviet Union, by contrast, the economy was growing, living standards were improving (albeit slowly), and every worker had a job. Party leaders highlighted their country's full employment in contrast to high unemployment in capitalist countries. And many workers believed that, despite their hardships, Soviet socialism offered them a brighter future than did capitalism. In fact, as noted earlier, some Western economists agreed with them. At this historical moment, the Soviet planned economy seemed to be in ascendancy, poised (in the words of a Soviet slogan) "to catch up and surpass" the capitalist countries.

Gender Roles in the Workplace

Officially the Soviet government espoused the principle of women's equality. Under the Soviet system, women were to have a role equal to that of men in public life, including in the workplace. But most Party leaders did not give women's equality much priority, and throughout the 1920s unemployment among urban women remained high. Soviet officials recruited large numbers of women into the industrial workforce only during the 1930s, and they did so more to fulfill the industrialization drive's insatiable demand for labor than to pursue the goal of gender equality. On collective farms too, women received new opportunities, including as tractor drivers, though again the government's focus was on mobilizing women to overcome labor shortages.

Between 1929 and 1935, the number of women working in industry tripled to more than 2.6 million. By that time, women made up 42 percent of all industrial workers. If we include non-industrial sectors of the economy as well, the number of women working for wages increased by nearly 4 million in this period. By 1937, women made up slightly more than half of the industrial workforce in Moscow.[43] Many women entering the workforce took jobs traditionally held by female workers, such as in light industry and the service sector. For example, women became the overwhelming majority of workers in textile mills during the 1930s. But women also entered heavy industry jobs in large numbers at this time. They worked in the steel mills, automobile factories, and tractor plants that were at the center of the Soviet industrialization drive. To gain these jobs, they had to overcome substantial barriers to female employment.

When a twenty-year-old peasant named Vera Ivanova moved to Moscow in 1930, she went to a labor exchange and was offered a job in a textile mill. But she knew that workers in heavy industry received higher wages and rations. So she persuaded her father, who worked at a steel mill, to find her a job there. The factory manager, desperate for new workers, hired her, and she became the first woman ever to work as a crane operator in the plant's rolling shop. There, however, she endured the ridicule of male workers who called her "collective farm woman," denigrating her as both a peasant and a woman.[44] Other women who took jobs in traditionally male sectors of the economy also experienced discrimination and ridicule. Women who worked on the construction of the Moscow subway, for example, faced taunts of "show us your callouses" from male workers.[45]

Sexual harassment also increased as more women entered the workforce. In one instance, a female worker assigned to the night shift was repeatedly harassed by male co-workers. When she demanded to be switched to the day shift, her foreman fired her. In other cases women were subjected to obscene propositions, unwanted sexual advances, and even physical assaults. A male official with the Workers' Control Commission assigned to investigate women's complaints concluded, "They themselves are guilty. Where there are women, this always happens."[46] Sexual harassment was not new in Soviet factories, but the entrance of women into male-dominated sectors of the economy triggered an increase in the harassment of female workers – an increase that male officials and managers did little to prevent.

Not only did female workers face discrimination and harassment, they encountered continued wage inequality even as they received new employment opportunities. At large industrial plants, many foremen refused to hire women for more skilled jobs and instead assigned female workers to low-status, low-wage positions (see Figure 3.4). In steel mills, for example, most women worked in non-production departments, such as transportation and sorting, rather than in the forge. The Commissariat of Labor even drew up lists that designated certain positions, the less-skilled jobs, as those that were to be filled primarily by women. Soviet authorities thus reinforced the principle of a sexual division of labor even as they reordered that division. Low-wage positions in metalworking factories still paid more than jobs in textile mills, so women did benefit from new employment opportunities. But these opportunities did not lead to equality, as men continued to dominate both the managerial posts and the higher paying rank-and-file jobs.

In the countryside, women did not need to be recruited for jobs as they were already working on collective farms. Soviet officials, however, did

Figure 3.4 Women working as lathe operators in a Soviet factory, 1940.

seek to give them new roles in order to better utilize their labor. As millions of peasants migrated to cities in the 1930s, newly formed collective farms were often short of laborers. Soviet planners pushed for both the mechanization of agriculture and the promotion of women to meet labor needs. Gosplan projected that 600,000 women would become tractor drivers, and propaganda posters promoted the image of female peasants proudly driving tractors.[47] A number of peasant women responded to these appeals and took short training courses to become tractor drivers. Here too, however, they faced substantial opposition, particularly from male peasants, but even from older peasant women who did not see driving a tractor as women's work. While the number of female tractor drivers increased from just fourteen in 1926 to 18,000 in 1932, that still only constituted 6 percent of all tractor drivers nationwide. By 1937, the number had increased to 57,000, a substantial gain but still far short of official projections.[48] Women were also denied managerial positions, as in virtually all villages the collective farm chairperson was a man.

The delineation of gender roles in the Soviet workplace, then, kept female workers in subordinate positions. Nonetheless, recruitment campaigns raised aspirations among many women and gave them a sense that they had an active role to play in society. The Khetagurovite movement provides a good example. In 1937, a national newspaper published the article "Join Us in the Far East! Letter of Valentina Khetagurova to the Young Women of the Soviet Union." Seeking to bolster both the labor and defense capabilities of the sparsely populated Far East region, the letter made the following appeal:

Far in the east, in the Primor'e and Priamurskaia taiga, we women, together with our husbands and brothers, are reconstructing a marvelous land . . . And we need many more people to pacify nature, so that all of the region's riches can be exploited for socialism . . . We just need people – brave, decisive, and selfless . . . Wonderful work, wonderful people, and a wonderful future await.[49]

In response, nearly 300,000 young women wrote letters fired with enthusiasm to volunteer for the Khetagurovite movement. Some 25,000 of them were selected and sent to the Far East.

The Soviet system did provide opportunities for employment to women that they had previously lacked. And propaganda about women's equality, even when contradicted by actual policies, also instilled in many Soviet women a sense that they had an important role to play. Of course, given the food shortages of the 1930s, many women sought employment simply to help feed their families. But in contrast to the prerevolutionary period and also to most other countries at this time, women in the Soviet Union had unprecedented opportunities for education and employment. In other developing countries, women lived in deeply patriarchal societies where they had no political rights or economic opportunities. Even compared with their counterparts in Europe and North America, Soviet women had far greater employment opportunities, as well as the right to vote, which women in most southern European countries did not get until after World War II. So there is no question that the Soviet system provided opportunities to women. Measured against the Soviet government's stated goal of gender equality, however, women's actual position in society and in the workplace remained far short of that ideal.[50]

Family Policy and Motherhood

Soviet family policy also contributed to gender inequality. Early Bolshevik feminists denounced the family as a bourgeois institution and called for its elimination in the name of women's liberation. Aleksandra Kollontai proposed an alternative to the family – love freed from the confines of marriage and collective responsibility for child raising. Legislation in 1918 had in fact facilitated divorce and greatly weakened marriage. Kollontai and others predicted that the family would soon wither away. Yet by the 1930s, official Soviet culture endorsed strong families, glorified motherhood, and strove to raise the birthrate. The Soviet government also enacted legislation that made divorce more difficult and outlawed abortion.

Some commentators have cited Stalinist family policy as further evidence that the Soviet government retreated from revolutionary values in the mid-1930s.[51] A closer examination, however, illustrates that while officials touted the ideal of the family, they actually undermined family autonomy. The family became an institution to serve the state rather than a separate sphere safe from state intervention. In the eyes of Soviet leaders, stable families served the goal of increasing the population. Pro-family propaganda was part of the government's enormous pronatalist campaign, a campaign similar to those in virtually all European countries during the interwar period. Another factor was the purported attainment of socialism in 1934 and its influence on officials' thinking. During the 1920s, Soviet ideologists viewed the family as a bourgeois institution that might pass on bourgeois values to children. But following the elimination of capitalism and the bourgeoisie, Soviet leaders began to view the family as an institution that could instill socialist values and teach children to be loyal Soviet citizens.

As World War I had made clear, modern mass warfare required huge numbers of troops, and political leaders came to see the size of their countries' populations as crucial to military power. During the 1920s and 1930s, governments across Europe and indeed around the world sought to increase their countries' birthrates through pro-family propaganda and pronatalist policies. These policies included both incentives to have more children and restrictions on abortion. France, Italy, Germany, and Romania, for example, all criminalized abortion at this time.

The Soviet Union likewise outlawed abortion, issuing a decree in 1936 that prohibited abortion except for medical reasons. The decree stated that "abortion is not only harmful for a woman's health, but is also a serious social evil, the battle with which is the duty of every conscious citizen, most of all medical personnel."[52]

Alongside restrictions on abortion came incentives for people to have children. The governments of Italy, France, and Germany all adjusted their tax codes to reward families with children and punish people with none, and they also awarded monetary bonuses to women for having babies. The Soviet government also offered financial inducements; the same decree that outlawed abortion granted women a 2,000-ruble annual bonus for each child they had over six children, and a 5,000-ruble bonus for each child over ten children. Moreover, the Soviet government, like other governments at the time, promoted motherhood through propaganda. Articles in the Soviet press presented motherhood as a natural and fulfilling part of women's lives. One testimonial from a woman with five children described how much her children loved her, while another article claimed that children took care of each other, so that having many children was an advantage rather than a burden.[53]

In their efforts to raise the birthrate, policymakers across Europe glorified not only motherhood but also marriage. Marriage and the family were seen as institutions that, in an era of urbanization and rapid social change, would guarantee stability and a high birthrate. The Soviet government, like governments in other countries, sought to bolster marriage as a means to increase fertility. The 1936 decree that outlawed abortion also made divorce much more difficult. It largely reversed the 1918 and 1927 family codes that had deliberately weakened marriage. These previous codes had facilitated a quick divorce at the demand of either spouse. The new law required that both spouses appear in court to file for divorce. It also raised the fee for divorce from three to fifty rubles (with a fee of 150 rubles for a person's second divorce and 300 rubles for their third). Furthermore, this law reinforced paternal obligations; it increased the penalty for nonpayment of child support to two years in prison.[54]

The Soviet government's efforts to promote the (heterosexual) family coincided with its attacks upon same-sex sexuality. Already in March 1934, the government recriminalized male homosexuality. In 1936, the Commissar of Justice Nikolai Krylenko linked homosexuality to bourgeois decadence and counter-revolution, and stated that it had no place in a socialist society founded on healthy principles. He called homosexuals "declassed rabble, either from the dregs of society or from the remnants of the exploiting classes." Employing a heteronormative discourse, Krylenko declared that homosexuals were not needed "in the environment of workers taking the point of view of normal relations between the sexes, who are building their society on healthy principles."[55] The Soviet government at this time also took more coercive measures to combat prostitution, incarcerating women who engaged in it. Emphasis on the family should thus be seen as part of a larger effort by Soviet authorities to control sexuality and make heterosexuality and procreation compulsory in the interests of the state.[56]

Soviet family policy had a direct effect on the construction of gender. Pronatalism produced an essentialized view of women as mothers, and the ban on abortion sought to enforce obligatory motherhood. Accompanying this legislation was propaganda that depicted having children as women's "natural role." One article asserted, "There is no physically and morally healthy woman in [the Soviet Union] who does not want to have a child." Another article claimed, "A woman without children deserves our pity, because she does not know the full joy of life."[57] By defining motherhood as a necessary part of women's lives, and by outlawing women's terminations of unwanted pregnancies, the Soviet government restricted women's choices concerning their lives and their bodies. It also assigned them a social role distinct from that of men.

How did Soviet women react to the Soviet pronatalist campaign? Some women who received birth bonuses wrote letters to thank Soviet leaders and to promise to continue having children. But far more common were letters protesting the ban on abortion. One female student pointed out that she would have to drop out of medical school if she got pregnant and was not allowed to have an abortion. Several peasant women argued that pregnant women who were unmarried or who already had two or three children should be allowed to receive abortions. A woman engineer wrote that the abortion ban would mean "the compulsory birth of a child to a woman who does not want children," and she warned of increased deaths when women inevitably sought illegal abortions.[58]

In fact, the ban on abortion did lead to a huge number of illegal abortions. Commissariat of Health reports in October and November of 1936 cited thousands of cases of women hospitalized after poorly performed illegal abortions. Of the 356,200 abortions performed in hospitals in 1937, and 417,600 in 1938, only 10 percent had been authorized, and the rest were incomplete illegal abortions.[59] In response, the Soviet government stepped up efforts to identify those who performed illegal abortions, and in 1937 arrested and convicted 4,133 abortionists. As the law dictated, those found guilty of performing abortions were sentenced to a minimum of two years in prison.[60] But despite considerable efforts, Soviet authorities found it difficult to catch underground abortionists, because women who entered hospitals after botched abortions rarely cooperated with police.

The ban on abortion did result in a rise in the birthrate, but this rise was limited and temporary. The birthrate per thousand people rose from 30.1 in 1935, to 33.6 in 1936, to 39.6 in 1937. But in 1938 the birthrate began to decline again, and by 1940, marital fertility for European Russia was below the 1936 level.[61] The severe social disruption of the purges and mobilization for war in part accounted for the decline of the birthrate beginning in 1938. But even before these disruptions the birthrate had not approached pre-industrialization levels, and evidence on illegal abortions indicates that Soviet women as a whole did not abide by the government's abortion ban. As Soviet authorities had noted when they legalized abortion in 1920, but then chose to ignore in 1936, the outlawing of abortion only drove women to seek illegal abortions.

The glorification of motherhood and birth bonuses also failed to have much effect. The women who received the bonuses were primarily peasant women who already had many children prior to the introduction of monetary incentives. The resources allotted to expand maternity wards and child care were insufficient to improve markedly the lives of mothers. Government priorities continued to focus on heavy industry, while childcare systems and communal dining facilities remained woefully underfunded. And given the equally underfunded consumer sector, women had great difficulty obtaining basic necessities, including food and clothing for their children. There was no effort to restructure gender roles within the domestic sphere, so women were saddled with sole responsibility for shopping, cooking, cleaning, and child care. These hardships deterred women throughout the 1930s from having more children regardless of government exhortations.

One crucial difference between the Soviet gender order and that in other countries at the time was the place of Soviet women in the industrial workforce. Whereas pronatalist campaigns in France, Italy, and Germany defined women solely as mothers, Soviet propaganda assigned a dual societal role to women as both workers and mothers. At no time during the campaign to bolster the family did Soviet officials suggest that a woman's place was in the home. On the contrary, the Soviet government stressed women's obligation to make an economic contribution in the workplace, as well as to produce and raise children.

In sum, Soviet family policy emphasized women's reproductive capabilities and obligations, particularly during the pronatalist drive of the mid-to-late 1930s. The Soviet government outlawed abortion, recriminalized male homosexuality, and cracked down on prostitution – all measures to increase state control over sexuality and to make heterosexuality and procreation compulsory in the interests of the state. The pronatalist campaign promoted an essentialized view of women as mothers that accentuated gender differences, even as women continued to work in agriculture and industry. Moreover, Soviet leaders did not seek to restructure gender roles within the family. As a result, women ended up with the double burden of work outside the home and uncompensated domestic labor.

The Great Purges

The Great Purges represent one of the most bizarre and bloody episodes in all of Russian history. From 1936 to 1938, thousands of loyal Communist Party members – including such luminaries as Zinoviev, Kamenev, and Bukharin – were arrested and executed. Also targeted were top military leaders and some of the country's leading writers and artists. Especially puzzling were the absurd accusations against purge victims. Those arrested were accused not only of political opposition but of widespread treason, wrecking, and spying. Even more astounding is the fact that, both in public show trials and in secret police interrogations, purge victims confessed to these preposterous transgressions. Why did the Great Purges occur?

To explain the Great Purges, some historians have emphasized Stalin's personality – his alleged paranoid and bloodthirsty character. There is no doubt that Stalin was vindictive and ruthless. And there is no doubt that he was responsible for the purges – he initiated them and pushed fellow Politburo members to accept them; he oversaw arrests through his secret police chief, Nikolai Ezhov; and he signed execution orders for thousands of victims. But historical explanations that focus solely on Stalin's personality fail to address other key factors. The severe international threat faced by Stalin and his fellow leaders is crucial to understanding their siege mentality. Also significant is the Soviet surveillance system that continuously reported to Party leaders on disaffection among the population and on alleged conspiracies that threatened their power. Finally, the secret police as an institution both made possible and helped instigate Soviet state violence. The independent operation of the secret police allowed the arrest of high Party officials, and a leadership group within the secret police advocated for mass arrests and executions. All of these factors, in addition to Stalin's murderous drive to secure his power, explain how and why the Great Purges occurred.

Fear of foreign invasion was not new in the late 1930s. Soviet leaders certainly never forgot the foreign intervention that had occurred during the Civil War. Nor did they forget the invasion by Poland in 1920, which, while driven back, had allowed the White armies to regroup. This experience taught Soviet leaders the peril of foreign invasion combined with internal uprisings. Throughout the 1920s and 1930s, Party leaders remained cognizant of their country's vulnerability – the Soviet Union was the world's lone socialist state, and it was surrounded by hostile capitalist countries. Party leaders also understood that their coercive policies, such as dekulakization, had generated opposition within the country. They therefore maintained vigilance against both internal and external enemies.

The Nazis' rise to power in Germany in 1933 amplified the threat of foreign invasion. Hitler made no secret of his plans to conquer territory in the east. His aggressive actions in the late 1930s, combined with the unwillingness of the British and French to stand up to him, made war even more imminent. Simultaneously, Japanese aggression in East Asia (the invasion of Manchuria in 1931 and the invasion of China proper in 1937) meant that the Soviet Union faced the very real possibility of a two-front war. Beginning in 1936, Soviet leaders watched closely the unfolding of the Spanish Civil War, in which they aided the Republican forces while the Nazis aided General Francisco Franco and his rightwing troops. Franco surrounded Madrid with four columns of regular troops and then relied on a "fifth column" within the city to start an uprising and bring down the Republican government. Stalin and his fellow leaders concluded that, in the event of war, "fifth columnists" within their country could pose a similar danger.

The Stalinist leadership had in fact faced some opposition within the upper echelons of the Communist Party. In 1932, with famine looming in the countryside and industrial growth grinding to a halt, former Central Committee member Martemian Riutin circulated a document known as the Riutin Platform. The platform condemned Stalin's policies and called for his removal. Riutin was arrested and a number of his associates were expelled from the Party, so this challenge to Stalin was quickly quashed. But Stalin perceived that, at a moment of crisis, a small group within the Communist Party had sought to oust him. More generally, Stalin harbored a lingering mistrust of regional Party leaders ever since the debacles of collectivization. He blamed many problems in the countryside on their failure to fulfill central directives. Particularly during the famine, some Party officials had resisted grain requisitions and quietly criticized the Party leadership. Stalin viewed such criticism as disloyalty bordering on treason, and he was determined to purge the Party of potential traitors.

Then, on December 1, 1934, Leningrad Party Chief Sergey Kirov was assassinated. Not only was Kirov a Politburo member, he was Stalin's close friend and a member of his inner circle. The assassination alarmed Stalin and other Party leaders, particularly because Kirov was gunned down inside Leningrad Party headquarters by a Communist Party member. These facts seemed to indicate that security was inadequate, that Party members could not be trusted, and that the lives of all Party leaders were in danger. Kirov's assassin, Leonid Nikolaev, was a deranged Party member acting alone, but Stalin proclaimed that the assassination was the product of a broad conspiracy within the Communist Party.[62] The secret police interrogated Nikolaev and forced him to state that he had accomplices. Stalin in turn used the idea of a conspiracy to accuse his former rivals Zinoviev and Kamenev of complicity in Kirov's murder.

In 1936, Stalin orchestrated a show trial of Zinoviev, Kamenev, and several other alleged conspirators. Prosecutor Andrey Vyshinsky charged the defendants not only with Kirov's assassination but with plotting to kill Stalin, Voroshilov, Kaganovich, and other top leaders. He claimed the defendants took orders from Trotsky, Stalin's exiled rival who continued to criticize the Stalinist leadership from abroad. All of the defendants were found guilty and shot. In 1937 and 1938, two more show trials were held to condemn and execute other Communists who at one time had rivaled Stalin for power. At the third trial, Bukharin and his fellow defendants were charged not only with plotting to kill Party leaders but of working with Nazi Germany and Japan to dismember the Soviet Union.

Despite the absurdity of the accusations, the defendants at all show trials confessed their guilt. Some have speculated that these confessions reflected victims' willingness to sacrifice themselves for the good of the Party. In Arthur Koestler's novel, *Darkness at Noon*, the main character is modeled loosely on Bukharin. He has dedicated his entire life to Communist Party, and does not wish to blacken its name by challenging the Great Purges. After relentless interrogations, he finally confesses to false charges, knowing that he will be killed anyway and hoping to preserve the Party's image. While a few victims may have followed this logic, the vast majority were coerced into confessing. The secret police threatened people's families and tortured prisoners to make them confess. Signed confessions were often stained with victims' blood as a result of beatings from their interrogators. In some cases, purge victims were promised their lives would be spared if they did confess, though regardless most were shot anyway.[63]

The Great Purges quickly spread beyond the political elite to engulf military leaders as well. Stalin and Commissar of Defense Voroshilov had never trusted Soviet military commanders who had previously served as officers in the tsarist army. Since the time of the Civil War, the two of them had repeatedly sparred with these officers and such tensions continued during the 1930s. Ezhov and other secret police officials also suspected former tsarist officers of disloyalty and called for them to be purged.[64] In 1937, three of the country's five top commanders were arrested and executed as traitors and German spies. Among them was the Red Army's leading general, Mikhail Tukhachevsky. Tukhachevsky was a former member of the Russian nobility and had attended tsarist military academies prior to serving in World War I. After the Revolution, he had joined the Red Army and soon emerged as its most brilliant commander and theoretician. The execution of Tukhachevsky thus deprived the Soviet military of vital leadership. Following his arrest, several thousand other military officers were also imprisoned or shot.

The Great Purges soon spread to economic and cultural elites. Many high-ranking bureaucrats and factory directors were purged for alleged sabotage of industrial production. The frenetic pace of industrialization had resulted in many accidents, and rather than question unrealistic production targets, Stalin blamed managers and engineers for "wrecking." In some plants, scores of managerial personnel were denounced and arrested.[65] Prominent writers and artists were targeted as well. For privately reciting an anti-Stalin poem, Osip Mandelstam was sent to the Gulag, where he died. Writer Isaac Babel was executed for allegedly being a Trotskyist and foreign spy. Theater director Vsevolod Meierkhold, accused of spying for the United Kingdom and Japan, was arrested, tortured, and shot.

Rank-and-file Party members were also swept up in the Great Purges. A Central Committee directive in 1936 instructed local Party organizations to root out Trotskyists. This directive triggered a spiral of mutual recriminations, as some sought to protect themselves by denouncing others. When one member of a Party cell was "unmasked" as a Trotskyist, associates of that individual came under suspicion as well. Some Communists engaged in self-criticism, a longstanding Party practice, and professed their guilt in the hope that they might be spared. The Communist Party had a tradition of expelling members deemed unworthy, but previous purges had been bloodless. Now, however, denunciation and expulsion from the Party were quickly followed by arrest and interrogation by the secret police.

The secret police usually made arrests in the middle of the night. Ilya Slavin, a prominent Party member and jurist in Leningrad, was arrested in November 1937. His sixteen-year-old daughter Ida describes how secret police agents arrived at 1:00 a.m. to search their apartment and take her father away:

I was suddenly awoken by a bright light and strange voice, telling me to get dressed quickly. An NKVD [secret police] officer was standing at the door. He made half an effort to look away as I struggled to get dressed and then led me into Papa's office. There was Papa, sitting on a stool in the middle of the room, looking suddenly much older ... The house-search went on all night. From the office they went into the dining room and then into my brother's room. The floor was covered with pages ripped from books and manuscripts ... Many of these things they took away. They also took a camera, a pair of binoculars (evidence of 'espionage') and a typewriter ... It was morning when the search came to an end; everything was registered for confiscation, and father was led into the corridor.[66]

In the absence of any real evidence of treason, the secret police relied upon forced confessions to convict people. Eugenia Ginzburg was a Communist Party member who worked as a professor and journalist in the city of Kazan. Because she had had a co-worker arrested for "Trotskyist ideas," Ginzburg herself was arrested and interrogated for belonging to "a counter-revolutionary Trotskyist organization." As she describes in her memoirs, "I was put on the 'conveyor belt' – uninterrupted questioning by a changing team of examiners. Seven days without sleep or food, without even returning to my cell ... The object of the conveyor belt is to wear out the nerves, weaken the body, break resistance, and force the prisoner to sign whatever is required."[67] Ginzburg considered herself fortunate, for she was interrogated before the physical beatings of purge victims became the norm.

The Soviet government set up special tribunals to process the huge number of treason cases. Trials often lasted only fifteen minutes, as defendants were summarily convicted and sentenced. Those sentenced to death were generally shot the same day. Others received prison sentences and were sent to Gulag labor camps. One scholar estimates that 116,885 Party members were executed or imprisoned in 1937–38, while another has calculated that of the 767 members of the Red Army high command, 412 were shot.[68] High-ranking Party members, particularly Stalin's former rivals, were clearly targeted. As noted earlier, over half the delegates to the Seventeenth Party Congress were imprisoned or shot. The Great Purges eliminated almost all of the Old Bolsheviks – those who had been Party members since before the Revolution.[69]

Through the Great Purges, Stalin was able to consolidate his control over the Communist Party. Already by the end of the 1920s, Stalin had emerged as the Party's unquestioned leader, but decisions within the ruling Politburo were still debated and taken collectively. With the Great Purges, Stalin not only eliminated all possible rivals, but ensured that fellow Politburo members would not oppose his decisions. That is not to say that Stalin acted alone. Fellow Party leaders – Molotov, Voroshilov, Kaganovich, Zhdanov, as well as other Politburo members – played an active role in implementing the purges. But it was Stalin who orchestrated the Great Purges and overrode objections within the Party leadership. Ordzhonikidze tried to resist the arrests of his deputies at the Commissariat of Heavy Industry; when he could not reverse Stalin's purges, he committed suicide in despair.[70] Whereas previously one could speak of a Party leaders' oligarchy, after the purges Stalin enjoyed a personal dictatorship over the Party and the country.

The Mass Operations

While the Great Purges primarily affected the country's elites, Soviet state violence in the late 1930s also struck common people. Of the 800,000 death sentences handed down by Soviet extrajudicial organs between 1921 and 1953, 682,000 were in 1937–38. The number of Gulag prisoners increased from 965,000 in January 1935 to 1,930,000 by 1941, with an increase of 700,000 in 1937 alone.[71] The great majority of these victims were common people arrested during the mass operations and the national operations. The mass operations were an attempt by Party and secret police leaders to eradicate those they did not regard as loyal citizens, particularly former kulaks and recidivist criminals, as well as former White officers, priests, and others seen as untrustworthy.[72]

This period of Stalinist violence is often mislabeled "The Great Terror," which implies that the purpose of the arrests and executions was to terrorize the population.[73] According to this interpretation, the Soviet regime sought to keep the population in a state of fear and uncertainty through the random application of terror. Doubtlessly, Stalinist violence did terrorize victims and their families, and in fact Soviet leaders had no compunction about using terror, for they had carried out public executions during the Civil War. But the state violence of the late 1930s was not random, and it was not intended to terrorize the population. The arrests and executions of the mass operations were conducted in secret, and their purpose was to eliminate enemies, not to frighten people into submission. In other words, these actions were not exemplary violence aimed at terrorizing the population. Instead they were forms of excisionary violence intended to eliminate specific segments of the population – those deemed potential traitors in the event of war.

Why did the Stalinist leadership believe there were many potential fifth-columnists and why did it take violent measures against them? First of all, the Soviet Union had an extensive surveillance system whose very purpose was to detect political opposition. This system, based on agents, informants, perlustrated letters, and intelligence reports, was established during the Civil War and institutionalized as a permanent feature of Soviet governance. Secret police organs generated countless reports on anti-Soviet sentiments and warned of conspiracies against the government.[74] As part of the surveillance system, the secret police catalogued the population to keep tabs on potential enemies. Begun in the 1920s, police card catalogues were established throughout the country and contained thousands of names by the 1930s. Archivists had compiled, for example, a list of more than 600,000 former White army officers and administrators still living in the country. "Former kulaks," "representatives of the tsarist administration, nobles, landowners, and merchants," and former members of "anti-Soviet political parties" were also included in card files that in some localities included more than 10 percent of the population.[75] The cataloguing of the population provided both a justification for state violence and an instrument to enact it – lists of anti-Soviet elements seemed to prove the existence of internal enemies and provided the names and addresses of those to be arrested once the mass operations were underway.

Secondly, there were large numbers of people who deeply resented the Soviet government – a fact that seemed to legitimate calls for repression. Soviet authorities had dispossessed and persecuted former nobles, capitalists, priests, and kulaks. Even if these victims of Soviet oppression did not actively oppose the government, there was reason to believe they might. With collectivization and the creation of a state-run economy, Party leaders believed that bourgeois class enemies had been vanquished, but they now saw a new threat – the hidden enemy, in particular dekulakized peasants who were hiding their class origins. Stalin warned that former kulaks were infiltrating collective farms, factories, and even the Communist Party, where they engaged in theft and sabotage. While it was unfair to assume that dekulakized peasants were criminals and traitors, most of them did try to hide their background. More than 3 million peasants had been dispossessed but not deported during collectivization, and they had little choice but to hide their "kulak past" and seek work in the cities. In addition, of the more than 1.5 million peasants deported as kulaks, hundreds of thousands had escaped while others had been officially released by the mid-1930s. But these victims of dekulakization remained under suspicion and were not easily reintegrated into society. The "liquidation of the kulaks as a class," far from resolving social tensions, had left millions of people with broken lives. In their consternation about this mass of potentially treasonous former kulaks, Party leaders were facing a social crisis of their own making.

Thirdly, Party leaders had expected the attainment of socialism to eradicate crime and other social problems. During the 1920s, social ills had been attributed to NEP capitalism, but collectivization and the state-run economy of the 1930s meant the end of capitalist exploitation and unemployment. In theory, criminal behavior was to disappear as well, but far from vanishing, petty theft actually increased during the 1930s – a product of the dire shortages triggered by the industrialization drive. The Stalinist leadership viewed pilfering and black-market trade as a refusal on the part of some to abide by the socialist order. To them, deviant behavior represented not only crime but political opposition. At the 1933 Central Committee plenum, Stalin had stated that the theft of state or collective farm property was tantamount to "the undermining of the Soviet system."[76]

Finally, a core group within the secret police had long employed mass arrests and executions to counter perceived internal opposition during times of heightened external threat. This group, which included Efim Evdokimov, Mikhail Frinovsky, and several others, continuously advocated state violence to eliminate enemies. These secret police officials first carried out mass executions during the Civil War. Subsequently, during the 1927 war scare, Evdokimov stepped up extrajudicial executions of alleged internal oppositionists, claiming that it was "very important to destroy them," because they would be "a real force against us, in the event of an international conflict."[77] Evdokimov and his associates came to dominate the operational leadership of the secret police when their ally Ezhov was appointed secret police chief in 1936 – in fact, Frinovsky served as Ezhov's deputy. It was this secret police cohort that would carry out the arrests and executions of the mass operations.[78]

Stalin and his fellow Politburo members launched the mass operations in 1937. They were prompted by both rising international tensions and secret police reports in advance of elections to the Supreme Soviet – reports that revealed widespread political opposition among certain segments of the population. In July, the Politburo approved secret police order 00447. The order cited the presence of "former kulaks," "church officials and sectarians," "cadres of anti-Soviet political parties," "active members of bandit uprisings, Whites, members of punitive expeditions, repatriates," and "criminals," and it went on to state that "all of these anti-Soviet elements constitute the chief instigators of every kind of anti-Soviet crimes and sabotage." The order dictated the execution of 75,950 people and the sentencing of 193,000 (those classified as "less active, but still hostile") to 8–10 years in a labor camp. It provided arrest and execution quotas for each region of the country. The order concluded, "The organs of state security are faced with the task of mercilessly crushing this entire gang of anti-Soviet elements ... and, finally, of putting an end, once and for all, to their base undermining of the foundations of the Soviet state."[79]

The term "once and for all" indicates that Party and secret police leaders saw the mass operations as a final struggle to eliminate internal enemies and criminals. Indeed, later that year Stalin proposed the following toast at a private banquet: "Anyone who attempts to destroy the unity of the socialist state ... is a sworn enemy of the state and of the peoples of the USSR. And we shall destroy any such enemy ... To the final destruction of all enemies!"[80] The mass operations in fact resulted in far more death sentences than collectivization. Of the more than 5 million peasants dekulakized, less than 1 percent (some 30,000) were executed, while of the 767,400 people convicted during the mass operations, slightly more than half (386,800) were executed. Party leaders' fear of impending war accounts for the large number of death sentences, but the lethality of the mass operations also stemmed from their sense that those who continued to oppose the Soviet system, even after attainment of socialism, were inveterate enemies that had to be killed.

Most studies of Stalinist state violence have focused on Stalin's motivations for ordering these arrests and executions. But we should also consider what made the mass operations possible in both conceptual and practical terms. Rulers throughout history have used large-scale violence in dealing with their people. But only in the modern era have governments "scientifically" catalogued their populations and excised specific social groups. Soviet state violence was not the product of Russian backwardness. Instead it was based on a modern conception of society as an artifact to be categorized and sculpted through state intervention. Technologies of excisionary violence were another necessary precondition for the mass operations. Card files, surveillance systems, a secret police apparatus, and concentration camps provided the means to identify and remove those deemed socially harmful or politically disloyal (see Figure 3.5). European administrators first developed these technologies of social excision during colonial warfare and World War I, and Communist Party leaders institutionalized them during the Russian Civil War as permanent features of the Soviet system.

Of course, these instruments of state violence only provided the conditions of possibility. The direct cause of the mass operations was a decision taken by the Stalinist leadership. Stalin ordered and his fellow leaders approved the arrests, executions, and deportations that took place during the mass operations. Their Manichean worldview, their mentality of capitalist encirclement (heightened by threats from Germany and Japan), and their belief that the defense of socialism could only be

Figure 3.5 Gulag prison camp in Siberia, 1930s.

accomplished through the ruthless elimination of internal enemies – all of these features of Stalin and his ruling circle account for their use of state violence on a massive scale.[81]

The National Operations

Running concurrently with the mass operations were the national operations – secret police actions that targeted certain national minorities for deportations, arrests, and executions. Composed of several discrete police actions, the national operations singled out diaspora nationalities – nationalities with a homeland outside the Soviet Union – and were referred to as "the Polish operation," "the Latvian operation," and so forth. According to official statistics, from August 1937 to November 1938, the secret police arrested 335,500 people and executed 247,200 of them in the national operations.[82] Hence, the national operations were nearly half the size of the mass operations, and even more deadly in terms of the percentage of those arrested who were executed.

Party leaders suspected the diaspora nationalities of having allegiances to the country of their nationality rather than to the Soviet Union. The Soviet government was not fully in control of the cultures of diaspora nationalities. Stalin's prescription for national minority cultures – "national in form, socialist in content" – could be rigorously enforced within the country. But in capitalist countries, national culture could express opposition to socialism, and if spread to diaspora nationalities within the Soviet Union, "bourgeois nationalism" could undermine allegiance to the Soviet government. In Stalin's mind, national minorities' lack of allegiance could beget political hostility, sabotage, and espionage.

The growing threat of Nazi Germany made the problem of diaspora nationalities all the more urgent. Following Hitler's rise to power in 1933, a German campaign to send "Brothers in Need" (ethnic Germans in the Soviet Union) food packages and foreign currency seemed to indicate that hostile foreign governments could garner support among Soviet national minorities. More generally, the rising international tensions in the second half of the 1930s made Party leaders increasingly fearful that diaspora nationalities could be recruited as spies by the countries of their nationality. At the February–March 1937 Central Committee plenum, Stalin declared that "as long as there exists capitalist encirclement, we will have wreckers, spies, saboteurs, and murderers sent into our hinterland by the agents of foreign states."[83]

In July 1937, Ezhov ordered the secret police to arrest all German nationals working in military plants and on railroads. His order warned, "Recent operative and investigative materials have proven that the German General Staff and the Gestapo are organizing broadscale espionage and subversive work at the most important, primarily defense, industrial enterprises by utilizing German nationals who have taken root there."[84] The following month the Politburo approved secret police order 00485, entitled, "On the liquidation of Polish subversive espionage groups and organizations of the POV [Polish Military Organization]." The order called for the arrest of all Polish political émigrés and refugees, as well as "the most active part of local anti-Soviet nationalist elements from the Polish national districts."[85] Local secret police easily identified national minorities given that Soviet passports included each person's nationality, and once they had made arrests, the secret police prepared lists of the accused with summaries of the cases against them. Two-person tribunals, composed of the regional secret police chief and the local procurator, reviewed these lists and passed sentences of either incarceration or death. The sentences were then approved by Ezhov and Vyshinsky before being carried out.

The Polish operation became a model for similar actions directed against other diaspora nationalities. A series of secret police operations targeted, in addition to Poles and Germans, the following diaspora nationalities: Romanians, Latvians, Estonians, Finns, Greeks, Afghans, Iranians, Chinese, Bulgarians, and Macedonians. Large numbers of these national minorities were arrested and either incarcerated or executed.

The secret police also deported more than 200,000 ethnic Koreans from border regions of the Far East to Central Asia, a measure justified as preventing "the penetration of Japanese espionage."[86] In addition, the secret police conducted a special operation against the so-called Kharbinians – workers on the Chinese-Manchurian Railroad, headquartered in Kharbin, China but operated by the Soviet government. These workers were mostly ethnic Russians, and they returned to the Soviet Union after the railroad was sold to the Japanese-controlled government of Manchuria in 1935. Ezhov stated that the overwhelming majority of Kharbinians "belong to the Japanese secret service, which sent them to the Soviet Union over the last several years" to work as "spies, terrorists and saboteurs."[87]

Secret police documents referred to the national operations as directed against "nationalities of foreign governments."[88] This language makes clear that, despite the fact that these diaspora nationalities had resided in the Russian empire and Soviet Union for decades if not centuries, the secret police regarded them as loyal to the nation-state of their nationality rather than to the Soviet Union. At the same time, the fact that the national operations also targeted Kharbinians – ethnic Russians who had worked on the Chinese-Manchurian Railroad – indicates that these repressions were not a product of Russian chauvinism. In fact, the secret police in the late 1930s kept close tabs on anyone, including many ethnic Russians, who had connections with foreign countries.

The national operations did not seek to exterminate entire nationalities. Soviet authorities executed only those ethnic Germans, Poles, and so forth whom they (summarily) convicted of espionage and sabotage. For Soviet leaders, unity did not mean racial purity or ethnic homogeneity. As discussed earlier, Soviet nationality policy even promoted the development of national minority cultures. Soviet officials moreover praised the intermarriage and intermixing of ethnic groups, as opposed to authorities in many countries (Germany, the United States, the United Kingdom, France, and so forth) who warned against miscegenation. In contrast to the Nazi project, which was only for Germans or Aryans, the Soviet project was to include everyone.[89] Victims of the national operations were targeted not based on racial or national ideology, but rather because, in Stalin's eyes, they were potential spies and saboteurs.

Soviet leaders had some basis to suspect the presence of spies within their borders. Germany, Japan, and Poland, for example, engaged in espionage within the Soviet Union, just as Soviet spies operated in those countries.[90] These three countries also shared intelligence information about Soviet military capabilities with one another. But the scale of espionage was quite limited and in no way justified the arrest and execution of hundreds of thousands of people. German foreign ministry records show that of the roughly 1,100 German nationals arrested by the Soviet secret police in the late 1930s, only two were involved in espionage. And of the roughly 100,000 ethnic Poles arrested in the national operations, few if any were actually spies, for by that time Polish intelligence agencies had ceased even trying to recruit Soviet Poles.[91] The approach taken by Stalin and Ezhov was to arrest huge numbers of people in order to catch any possible spies or opponents of the regime. Ezhov even instructed secret police agents to err on the side of excess when making arrests.

The massive number of arrests and executions in 1937–38 sharply undercut normal societal and economic functioning. Fear and mistrust prevented Party officials from working together. Industrial managers and collective farm chairmen ceased to take initiative out of fear they would be denounced for sabotage if something went wrong. Labor discipline deteriorated and economic growth was disrupted. Eventually, Stalin called a halt to this wave of state violence. A November 1938 government resolution sharply criticized the secret police for excesses and abolished the secret police tribunals. Despite the fact that Ezhov had acted under Stalin's meticulous supervision, Stalin made him a scapegoat and removed him from power. The following year Ezhov was arrested, and in 1940 he was executed. Hundreds of other secret police officials were shot as well.[92]

Stalin apparently believed that the enormous number of arrests and executions of the late 1930s had eliminated internal enemies and strengthened the Soviet state. At the Eighteenth Party Congress in 1939, Stalin proclaimed "that in case of war, our front and home front will be stronger than in any other country, due to our uniformity and internal unity."[93] Decades later Molotov made a similar case, using "1937" as shorthand for the arrests and executions of the period. He stated, "Nineteen thirty-seven was necessary. If you consider that after the revolution . . . enemies of different sorts remained, and in the face of impending danger of fascist aggression they might unite. We owe the fact that we did not have a fifth column during the war to '37."[94] It is true that the Stalinist leadership did not face any serious internal opposition during World War II. However, this was due not to preemptive arrests, but rather to a patriotic surge of support in the face of the Nazi onslaught.

Far from preparing the country for war, the Great Purges, mass operations, and national operations greatly weakened it. Hundreds of thousands of innocent people were executed. Nearly 2 million citizens languished in the Gulag. Thousands of capable Party administrators and economic managers were imprisoned or killed. Particularly harmful was the loss of military leaders. At the outset of the war, the Red Army suffered horrendous casualties due to its lack of experienced commanders. In fact, the Stalinist regime barely survived the Nazi invasion – the German army reached the outskirts of Moscow before being stopped in late 1941. As we will see, the Soviet Union won World War II in spite of Stalinist state violence, not because of it.

4   World War II (1939–1945)

For the Soviet Union, World War II represented a cataclysm of immense proportions. Nazi Germany's invasion destroyed Soviet cities, killed millions of people, and nearly conquered the country. Vast territories fell under Nazi occupation, where the population was subjected to brutal treatment – expropriations, enslavement, and genocidal massacres. Within months of the June 1941 invasion the German army had reached the outskirts of Moscow, where the Red Army finally stopped its advance and saved the capital. But the following year, German forces drove all the way to the Volga River. There, at the city of Stalingrad, the largest battle in all human history took place. While the Red Army ultimately won this battle and the war, much of the country was left in ruins and 27 million Soviet citizens were dead.

In some respects, the Soviet system was well-geared for warfare. The Stalinist planned economy was essentially a wartime economy even prior to the war. The Soviet government proved successful at mobilizing the country's population, and victory in the war seemed to vindicate both the prewar industrialization drive and the Stalinist system itself. Yet victory was won at a frightful cost. The figure of 27 million dead in itself leads historians to question the effectiveness of the system and of Stalin's leadership in particular. Stalin himself was to blame for catastrophic losses suffered at the beginning of the war, when, despite intelligence warnings about the German invasion, he failed to place Soviet troops on alert. On the first day of the war, the Soviet air force was decimated while the Red Army had thousands of soldiers killed or captured. Only after four years of suffering and bloodshed did the Soviet Union finally defeat Nazi Germany, thanks largely to the heroism and sacrifices of Soviet soldiers and civilians.

Analysis of the war must begin with the prewar diplomacy that shaped the course of the war. Rather than concluding an alliance with the United Kingdom and France against Nazi Germany, Party leaders signed the Nazi-Soviet Pact in 1939, a treaty Germany breached when it invaded the

Soviet Union in 1941. How the country rallied from calamitous defeats at the outset of the war to stop and ultimately defeat the German army is a central question of this chapter. The Red Army's military triumphs at the battles of Moscow, Stalingrad, and Kursk were key in winning the war, but civilians' contributions to the war effort were also crucial to the victory. Brutal Nazi occupation policies provoked resistance from partisans fighting behind the lines. In addition, the herculean efforts of industrial workers proved vital to supplying tanks, planes, and guns for the war effort. Gender roles during wartime shifted as women provided most of the labor in factories and collective farms, and large numbers of women served in a military capacity as well. The war deeply affected Soviet society, and victory in the war changed the course of world history itself.

Prewar Diplomacy

The rise of Nazi Germany in the 1930s posed an existential threat to the Soviet Union and to other European countries as well. Hitler had made no secret of his plans to conquer the Slavic peoples to the east and establish a German empire on territory that included the Soviet Union. After taking power in 1933, he began a huge military buildup that violated the Versailles Treaty and provoked alarm across Europe. It certainly would have made sense for the Soviet Union to form a military alliance with other countries to counter the Nazi threat. But instead the Soviet government shocked the entire world by signing a non-aggression treaty with Nazi Germany, its arch enemy. The Nazi-Soviet Pact led to the German invasion of Poland and the beginning of World War II in Europe. Why did the Soviet Union fail to form an anti-German alliance? And why did it make a pact with Nazi Germany instead?

First, we should note that Soviet leaders believed war with capitalist countries was inevitable. While some commentators have claimed that Hitler duped Stalin into thinking he could avoid war by signing the Nazi-Soviet Pact, neither Stalin nor any other Soviet leader had the illusion that they could forestall military conflict indefinitely.[1] Indeed, their preparations for war were evident throughout the 1930s as Soviet defense production dramatically increased, and the size of the Red Army had roughly quadrupled by the end of the decade.[2] To give themselves more time for military preparations, Soviet leaders hoped to postpone the coming war, in part through the Nazi-Soviet Pact. According to Molotov's recollections, "Stalin reckoned before the war that only in 1943 would we be able to meet the Germans as equals."[3]

Second, we must keep in mind the daunting geopolitical situation faced by Soviet leaders in the late 1930s. The Soviet Union had to defend the longest borders of any country in the world, and Nazi Germany was not the only country that posed a threat.[4] On the western border, the Baltic countries, Poland, and Romania all had hostile relations with the Soviet Union. In the east, Japanese aggression imperiled Siberia, particularly after Japan invaded Manchuria in 1931 and China proper in 1937. Japanese forces repeatedly tested Soviet border defenses and fought major border battles with Soviet troops, first at the Battle of Lake Khasan in 1938 and then at the Battle of Khalkhin Gol in the summer of 1939. A decisive Soviet victory in the second battle helped deter further Japanese aggression, but the Soviet military faced the very real possibility of fighting a two-front war. Indeed, Molotov signed the Nazi-Soviet Pact in August 1939, during the Battle of Khalkhin Gol. In addition to forestalling a clash with Germany, the pact prompted the Japanese to abandon their thoughts of allying with Germany against the Soviet Union and seizing eastern Siberia. Japan instead turned its expansionist ambitions to southeast Asia, and the Soviet Union avoided a two-front war.

Third, Party leaders did not trust the United Kingdom, France, or Poland, despite the fact that Nazi Germany was their common enemy. They saw the United Kingdom and France as hostile capitalist powers. Even in the late 1930s, when Nazi Germany clearly posed a greater menace, they suspected the United Kingdom and France of trying to turn Hitler to the east instead of opposing him. The Munich Conference in 1938 seemed to confirm this view, as the United Kingdom and France sought to appease Hitler by allowing him to seize part of Czechoslovakia. The Stalinist leadership did not trust Poland either, viewing it more as an enemy than a potential ally. After the 1920 Soviet–Polish war, relations between the two countries had remained tense. During the 1930s, Party leaders labelled Poland and its right-wing government "a fascist state."

For their part, British, French, and Polish leaders were not eager to ally with the Soviet Union. They saw the Communist government as hostile, and they also doubted that the Soviet military would contribute much in a war against Germany. Soviet foreign minister Maxim Litvinov sought collective security against Nazi Germany, but trilateral negotiations with the United Kingdom and France went nowhere. The United Kingdom and France wanted the Soviet Union to join them in guaranteeing Poland's security against German aggression, but proved unwilling to provide security guarantees to the Soviet Union in return. And in any case, Poland refused to sign any agreement with the Soviet Union, partly for fear of provoking Germany. Stalin eventually abandoned the goal of collective security and replaced Litvinov with Molotov, who was more inclined to strike a deal with Germany (see Figure 4.1).[5]

Figure 4.1 Viacheslav Molotov signing the Nazi-Soviet Pact in Moscow, 1939. German foreign minister Joachim von Ribbentrop is standing behind him (to the left), next to Stalin.

The Nazi-Soviet Pact gave Soviet leaders hope that they could postpone any confrontation with Hitler, and that Germany would become embroiled fighting France and the United Kingdom. Such a conflict could weaken all three countries and buy the Soviet Union valuable time to continue industrializing and strengthening militarily. The pact also contained secret protocols that designated "spheres of influence," granting Germany the right to seize most of Poland and giving the Soviet Union control over eastern Poland, the Baltic countries, part of Finland, and Bessarabia, a region of Romania. After Germany quickly conquered most of Poland in early September 1939, the Soviet Union invaded and occupied eastern Poland. It then forced Estonia, Latvia, and Lithuania to allow Soviet troops to be stationed on their soil, followed by the forcible annexation of the Baltic countries the next summer. In late November 1939, the Red Army invaded Finland, only to suffer substantial casualties fighting against the much smaller Finnish army.

Military debacles in the so-called Winter War revealed weaknesses within the Red Army, but in the end, Finland was forced to cede some territory. The Nazi-Soviet Pact thus resulted in the Soviet Union's expansion along its western border. The acquisition of eastern Poland allowed Soviet authorities to incorporate western Belorussian and Ukrainian populations, seeming to eliminate the danger of cross-border agitation. There and in the Baltic countries, the Soviet military began the construction of new border defenses, while the secret police carried out mass arrests of nationalists and others who opposed Sovietization.[6] The German invasion of Poland, and the resulting declaration of war on Germany by the United Kingdom and France, also seemed to serve Soviet interests. Stalin remarked to Comintern leader Georgy Dimitrov that the elimination of Poland meant "one fewer bourgeois fascist state to contend with," and he also approved of the capitalist countries "having a good hard fight and weakening each other."[7]

In hindsight, however, the Nazi-Soviet Pact was clearly a colossal blunder. The failure of the Soviet Union and other countries to forge an anti-German alliance gave Hitler a tremendous strategic advantage. In conquering first Poland, then France, and then attacking the Soviet Union, he was able to avoid a two-front war. Nor did the pact buy Soviet leaders much time. Instead of a four-year stalemate on the western front, as had occurred in World War I, Germany defeated France in just six weeks in 1940. Though the United Kingdom did not surrender, it could not threaten Germany on the continent, leaving the German army free to turn east in 1941 and invade the Soviet Union. The Soviet military had insufficient time to construct new border defenses, making it more vulnerable than before it seized eastern Poland, the Baltic countries, part of Finland, and Bessarabia. The populations there remained bitterly anti-Soviet, and some, such as the Finns and Romanians, joined Nazi Germany in fighting against the Soviet Union. Finally, the Nazi-Soviet Pact badly damaged the Soviet Union's international reputation. Previously a harsh critic of fascism, the Soviet government had now signed a treaty with Nazi Germany and joined it in invading smaller countries. Observers around the world condemned Soviet aggression, and foreign communists tore up their party cards in disgust.

Stalin committed an even greater blunder by failing to put Soviet troops on alert prior to the Nazi invasion. British intelligence officers warned that Hitler was preparing an attack and even pinpointed the likely date of the invasion. But Stalin refused to believe them, suspecting the United Kingdom of trying to draw the Soviet Union into a war with Germany. Soviet intelligence also notified Stalin that a German attack was imminent, but he disregarded these warnings as well, believing that Germany would never launch a war in the east without first defeating the United Kingdom in the west. Stalin deluded himself into thinking that Hitler would use his recent troop buildup to issue an ultimatum demanding territory, not to invade. Here the hyper-centralization of power in the Stalinist system proved to be a liability, because Stalin's misjudgments could not be challenged and the Soviet armed forces were left unprepared.[8] Stalin's error cost millions of Soviet lives, and it nearly cost the country its very existence.

The German Invasion and the Battle of Moscow

Just before dawn on the morning of June 22, 1941, Germany launched a massive invasion of the Soviet Union. With more than 3 three million soldiers, 3,600 tanks, and 2,700 aircraft, the German military smashed through Soviet border defenses. The offensive orientation of Soviet military doctrine meant that many troops, planes, and tanks were stationed in forward positions and thus vulnerable to the surprise attack. Thousands of Red Army soldiers were surrounded and captured even before they knew the war had begun. German bombers destroyed much of the Soviet air force on the ground during the first day of war. Even after they had learned of the invasion, Stalin and Commissar of War Semyon Timoshenko initially believed it was just a provocation and ordered Soviet troops to hold their fire.

General Ivan Boldin, deputy commander of the Western Military District, later recounted a phone call he received from the Kremlin in the first hours of the war. Timoshenko told him, "Comrade Boldin, remember that no action is to be taken against the Germans without our knowledge ... Comrade Stalin has forbidden to open artillery fire against the Germans." Boldin expressed disbelief and yelled back, "Our troops are in full retreat. Whole towns are in flames, people are being killed all over the place." Still not comprehending the situation, Timoshenko authorized only limited air reconnaissance, which Boldin explained would be impossible anyway, "since the Nazis had knocked out practically all our front-line air force."[9] When Stalin and Timoshenko finally recognized that it was a full-scale German invasion, they ordered a counter-offensive, resulting in even greater casualties at a moment when the Red Army should have made a strategic retreat.

As the German air force bombed towns near the border, civilians began to flee eastward. Refugees clogged the roads and were left vulnerable to German planes strafing from overhead. Many soldiers fled as well. The head of the Belorussian Communist Party reported, "The retreat has caused blind panic ... At the first bombardment, the formations collapse, many just run away to the woods, the whole area of woodland in the front-line region is full of refugees like this. Many throw away their

Map 4.1 Europe and the Soviet Union during World War II.

weapons and go home. They regard the possibility of being surrounded with extreme anxiety."[10] Red Army soldiers had good reason to fear encirclement, as the German blitzkrieg tactics employed columns of tanks that broke through Soviet lines and then encircled massive numbers of troops. Some 2 million Red Army soldiers were captured during the first few months of the war.

Taking advantage of the disarray, the German army drove 200 miles into Soviet territory in the first week. By the beginning of August, it had captured Smolensk, and in early October it was approaching Moscow (see Map 4.1). The German air force began nightly air raids on the capital. Residents had to sleep in the Moscow Metro, using it as a bomb shelter. When the Germans renewed their offensive, Party leaders were uncertain they could hold the city. They ordered the evacuation of government offices, foreign embassies, the university, theaters, museums, and armaments factories. Some buildings were mined and government documents were burned. Declaring "Moscow is in danger," Moscow Party chief Alexander Shcherbakov called for civilian volunteers to fight alongside the Red Army. Thousands joined volunteer battalions and were thrown into battle with little or no training.[11]

The evacuations sparked a panic among the population in mid-October. Believing the fall of Moscow to be imminent, thousands of officials and civilians fled. People jammed railway stations, seeking to board trains to the east, while officials with cars drove away, with or without a government permit. Those who remained in the city began to hoard food, and there were cases of looting as well. But on October 17, Shcherbakov announced that Stalin was still in the Kremlin and that Moscow would be defended to the last drop of blood. As factory worker Olga Sapozhnikova explained, the announcement that Stalin had not abandoned the city "made an enormous difference to morale; it now seemed certain that Moscow would not be lost."[12] Muscovites rallied to the cause – they dug trenches, built fortifications, worked overtime in factories, and stood guard on rooftops to watch for incendiary bombs.

On November 7, 1941, Soviet leaders held the annual Revolution Day parade in Red Square. Overcast skies diminished the chance of an air raid, and in defiance of the German troops fighting just west of the city, Politburo members stood on Lenin's mausoleum and reviewed Red Army soldiers as they marched through the square. With the sound of artillery booming in the distance, Stalin addressed the troops. He acknowledged that they were celebrating the anniversary of the October Revolution under "very hard conditions," but he reminded them that throughout history Russia had always defended itself against foreign invasions. He concluded his speech with the words, "Death to the German invaders! Long live our glorious country, its freedom and independence! Under the banner of Lenin – onward to victory!"[13] Troops in the parade marched directly from there to the front.

The Battle of Moscow raged for several months, and by late November, German troops neared the outskirts of the city. But in such a concentrated battle, the mechanization and superior mobility of the German army no longer held sway. Though Soviet soldiers still suffered dire shortages of tanks and aircraft, they fought ferociously. Some even carried clusters of grenades and threw themselves under German tanks to stop them. Entire divisions of soldiers were transferred from Siberia to the Moscow front, giving commander Georgy Zhukov fresh troops to use as reinforcements. Despite horrendous casualties, the Red Army succeeded in halting the German advance. Hitler, expecting a quick victory, had neglected to order winter uniforms for his troops. With supply lines stretched thin and the bitter cold of the Russian winter setting in, morale among the German soldiers faltered. Then, in December, Zhukov ordered a counter-attack. Soviet troops went on the offensive and pushed the Germans back 100 miles. Moscow had been saved.[14]

The importance of the Battle of Moscow is hard to overstate. The Germans came very close to capturing the capital and perhaps winning the war. But the Soviet victory denied them a knockout blow, and it meant that the war would continue for several more years. In a long conflict, the Soviet Union's greater population would prove decisive against Germany. The Battle of Moscow also marked the first time in World War II that the German army had been defeated. It shattered the myth of Nazi invincibility, and bolstered Soviet citizens' confidence that they could win the war. Years of sacrifice and suffering still lay ahead, but victory now seemed possible.

The Siege of Leningrad

Nazi war plans foresaw conquest of the Soviet Union within a few months. The conquered territory of Ukraine, Belorussia, and European Russia would then become a vast German colony, part of the thousand-year empire that Hitler planned to create. In his vision, Jews would be exterminated, Slavic peoples would be enslaved or allowed to starve, and vast new territories would be opened up for German settlement. Accordingly, Nazi occupation policies were ruthless and murderous. The German army's advance through Belorussia and Ukraine left large Jewish populations under its control. Nazi leaders created special forces within the army to carry out mass executions of Jews. In occupied towns and villages, these special forces routinely separated all Communist Party members and Jews from the rest of the population and shot them. Following the fall of Kiev in September 1941, the Nazi security police and special forces marched tens of thousands of Jewish men, women, and children to Babi Yar, a ravine outside the city, and machine-gunned them to death. Of the roughly 6 million Jews killed in the Holocaust, at least 1.3 million were Soviet citizens.[15]

While the Nazis did not systematically murder non-Jewish Soviet civilians, they directly or indirectly killed millions of them. Anyone resisting the occupation was executed. When partisans fought back in occupied territory, German troops publicly hanged them and carried out vicious reprisals, burning homes and massacring entire village populations. Four million Soviet citizens were deported to Germany for slave labor, where some were literally worked to death. In accordance with Nazi plans, the German military expropriated available food. Nazi leaders expected 30 million civilians in the Soviet Union to starve to death during the first winter of the war – a prospect they welcomed as a means to depopulate the region and make room for future German colonists. Many civilians did starve, as did captured Soviet soldiers, roughly 3 million of whom died in German prison camps during the war.

The siege of Leningrad epitomized the suffering of the Soviet population at the hands of the Germans. The country's second largest city, Leningrad, had slightly more than 3 million inhabitants at the beginning of the war. By early September 1941, the German army along with their Finnish allies had virtually surrounded the city, cutting off all supply routes. Hitler ordered his troops to lay siege to the city and let the population starve to death. To hasten the starvation, the German air force dropped incendiary bombs on the city's main food warehouses and burned them to the ground. With dwindling food reserves and virtually no way to supply the city, Leningrad authorities reduced the daily bread ration to just 250 grams (about eight ounces) for factory workers, and to half that for everyone else. To extend meager flour supplies, bakeries made bread from a mixture of flour and sawdust. Malnutrition became widespread, and the city's residents soon began to die of starvation.

Anna Likhacheva, a doctor at the clinic of a Leningrad factory, described in her diary the winter of 1941–42.

The darkness, the deadly cold, the hunger, the lack of strength to stand nights in line to receive the daily ticket for the food that was supposed to be given to us – it did me and my whole family in, and led to the loss of my husband and my son. The fatalities began in December, when the lack of food was coupled with the cold and loss of public transportation. Cold starving people, faithfully carrying out their duties before the besieged city, trudged tens of kilometers, often on only 125 grams of ersatz bread per day and soured cabbage leaves or yeast soup for dinner.[16]

The starving people of Leningrad became obsessed with food, thinking and talking about nothing else. They ate whatever they could – cats, dogs, dead crows, wallpaper paste, and boiled leather. Instances of cannibalism were also reported.

Compounding the suffering was the city's lack of fuel and electricity. Apartment buildings went unheated, and some residents froze to death. Water pipes burst, and people had to chop through the ice in the Neva

Figure 4.2 Bodies to be buried at the Volkovo Cemetery during the Siege of Leningrad, 1942.

River for drinking water. Without electricity, trams could not run and, as described earlier, people had to walk long distances through the bitter cold. Some residents collapsed in the streets and died. Others were killed by German artillery bombardments, which continued throughout the siege. With the death rate mounting, even the burial of siege victims became difficult. Lacking transportation, some people had to pull the bodies of deceased family members on sleds to the cemetery. Workers there dumped the bodies into mass graves (see Figure 4.2).

The only supplies to reach Leningrad during the siege were transported across Lake Ladoga, which lies to the east. When the lake froze solid in the winter, authorities made a road across the ice that became known as the "Road of Life." Truck convoys transported aid to the city and evacuated children and other non-working civilians. Even this route proved perilous, as the German air force repeatedly bombed the convoys, killing people and blasting craters in the ice. The Siege of Leningrad lasted almost 900 days and was fully lifted only in January 1944, as the

German army was driven back. Nearly 1 million civilians died in the siege – a single-city death toll unmatched in the entire history of human warfare.[17]

The Siege of Leningrad and other atrocities exposed the inhumane, indeed genocidal, character of the Nazi regime. At the outbreak of the war, Soviet citizens who had suffered under Stalinism might have welcomed a change of government. But they quickly learned that the German occupation was far worse. Expropriations, starvation, slave labor, and the massacre of civilians transformed the war into a struggle for national survival. Surrender meant enslavement or death for the vast majority of the population. And the suffering of the Soviet people only strengthened their resolve to fight. The partisan movement began as a small-scale resistance effort, carried out mostly by Communist Party members caught behind the German lines. But as the war went on, increasing numbers of civilians joined the partisans in waging guerrilla warfare against the Germans. And even during the darkest days of the siege, Leningrad workers continued to manufacture guns to supply the Red Army in its fight against the fascists. The Soviet population's willingness to persevere despite tremendous hardships proved crucial to the war effort.

Propaganda, Repression, Industrial Mobilization

Even before the brutality of the Nazi regime became apparent, a surge of patriotism swept the Soviet Union. On the first day of the invasion, thousands of men and women jammed recruiting centers to join the army. Others began working extra shifts in factories to produce tanks and artillery. Writers volunteered to serve as war correspondents at the front. Despite defeatist talk in some quarters, the Soviet population as a whole demonstrated strong support for the war effort.[18] This support partly stemmed from prewar propaganda that had emphasized citizens' patriotic duty to defend the socialist motherland. But beyond that, people were motivated by a sense of outrage at the German invasion and by a basic instinct to defend their homeland, regardless of their loyalty to government.

Soviet wartime propaganda sought to promote these feelings of patriotism. Building on themes already initiated in the late 1930s, propagandists invoked Russian tsars who had led the country to military victories. Peter the Great was heralded for his leadership, and Sergey Eisenstein's epic film "Ivan the Terrible" (part 1, 1944) glorified Ivan IV for making Russia powerful. In a speech on November 7, 1941, Stalin invoked the memory of past Russian leaders and generals, stating, "Let the manly images of our great ancestors – Alexander Nevsky, Dmitry Donskoy, Kusma Minin, Dmitry Pozharsky, Alexander Suvorov, Mikhail Kutuzov – inspire you in this war!"[19] Soviet writers also made more general appeals to defend the motherland. Poet Viktor Gusev wrote, "Motherland Russia is immortal. Immortal are the endless Russian fields which have seen storms and misfortune. Immortal are the towers of the Kremlin. Immortal is the force of the Russian nation."[20]

Seemingly connected with these nationalist appeals was a revival of the Russian Orthodox Church during the war. Previously the Soviet government had closed churches and persecuted religious leaders. But in 1943, the government relaxed its persecution of Church leaders and allowed them to elect a Patriarch, a post that had been vacant since 1925. After the newly elected Patriarch Sergey died in 1944, a grand gathering of more than 200 Church dignitaries, including leaders of Orthodox Churches in eastern Europe, installed Metropolitan Aleksey as the new Patriarch in January 1945. The timing of these events casts doubt as to whether these concessions to the Russian Orthodox Church were in fact an appeal to nationalist sentiment. The Church's revival did not coincide with the need to mobilize popular support early in the war, but rather occurred when the Red Army was recapturing territory and advancing into eastern Europe. One scholar has shown that the revival of the Church actually served two other objectives. It allowed Soviet authorities to place churches that had been reopened in occupied territories under the Moscow patriarchate, and thus reassert central control over Belorussia and Ukraine. It also served foreign policy purposes of building links with Orthodox Christian communities in eastern Europe and placating American and British allies, who criticized the lack of religious freedom in the Soviet Union.[21]

One other major theme of Soviet propaganda was hatred of the enemy. As the war progressed, writers began to describe German atrocities and characterize enemy soldiers as "barbarians" and "Huns." Ilya Ehrenburg emerged as the most virulent anti-German propagandist. His columns in the Red Army newspaper included passages such as this one from 1942:

Russia's heart is bleeding. The enemy is trampling underfoot the rich fields of the Kuban ... One feeling unites every man and woman of our people: hatred ... Today there is nothing except this one thought: kill the Germans. Kill them all, and dig them into the earth.[22]

Extremely popular among soldiers, Ehrenburg's columns were credited with hardening their resolve to stop the German advance. Given the brutality of Nazi occupation policies, his vilification of the Germans resonated strongly within the Red Army. One Red Army captain said that his soldiers were "thirsting for revenge," and that he had a hard time preventing them from killing German prisoners.[23]

The themes of Soviet propaganda paralleled wartime appeals in other countries. In this era of mass warfare, all countries sought to maintain morale, both within the military and among civilians. Warfare was no longer the province of professional armies, and during World War II the lines between the battlefield and home front blurred more than ever. Most immediately, military leaders needed soldiers who were inspired to fight. But almost as important were civil defense volunteers who built fortifications, and factory workers who worked overtime producing munitions. Emotional propaganda, emphasizing patriotism or vilifying the enemy, was used by every country in the war. New technologies, particularly film and radio, helped disseminate propaganda. Films and newsreels were even shown to soldiers at the front. And Stalin, like his counterparts in other countries, was able to address the entire population in radio broadcasts. Hand-in-hand with propaganda efforts went government censorship to silence defeatist sentiments – another technique common to all combatant countries.

What distinguished Soviet propaganda was neither its themes nor its technologies but rather the Communist Party's preexisting propaganda apparatus. Since before the Revolution, the Bolsheviks had engaged in propaganda to rally workers to their cause. Once in power, Lenin and other Party leaders continued to utilize propaganda to garner support for their regime. They built up a vast network of propagandists, both within the Party organization and the Red Army. When the German invasion came, the Party leadership relied on this network to convey wartime appeals. Writers, artists, and filmmakers also helped promote patriotism by emphasizing the defense of the motherland and hatred of Germans. And the Soviet Union's equally extensive censorship apparatus meant that censors could oversee the content of all publications and films. Other countries during World War II had to create or expand government agencies to control and disseminate information, but the Soviet Union already had such bureaucracies in place.

Repression, another central feature of the Stalinist system, also continued to be widely deployed. As we have seen, Party and secret police leaders had remained on guard against enemies, real and imagined, since the time of the Civil War. With the German invasion, they became even more vigilant to safeguard against possible internal uprisings. As it turned out, there were no anti-Soviet revolts during World War II. On the contrary, widespread patriotism meant the great majority of the population supported the regime, even despite the disastrous reversals in 1941. But the secret police and its extensive surveillance network continued to detect opposition and, under Party orders, act accordingly.

On the first day of the German invasion, special secret police detachments were mobilized for the war. They arrested those suspected of espionage, including large numbers of ethnic Germans. In addition, they began to patrol defense factories and railway stations to guard against sabotage. Secret police detachments also operated within the Red Army to ensure that soldiers would fight. Party leaders took the large number of surrenders early in the war as a sign of soldiers' disloyalty. Most who surrendered had been encircled, due to no fault of their own. But suspecting treason, Party leaders ordered secret police forces to be stationed behind Red Army lines to prevent unauthorized retreats. Soldiers who deserted their posts could be summarily shot, though some were instead assigned to penal battalions. These units were given the most dangerous missions, such as frontal assaults and the clearing of minefields, and death rates within them were extremely high.

Of course, other countries also took harsh wartime measures, including the execution of deserters and the incarceration of those whose loyalty was questioned. But no other country repressed its own citizens to such an extent, just as no other country (with the exception of Germany) had such an extensive secret police force or prison camp network. Party leaders apparently believed that massive repression was necessary to ensure their regime's survival at this moment of crisis. But instead it meant a further waste of lives at a time when the war effort demanded all the support the country could muster. Repression also undercut local initiative, as officials in regions under attack urgently needed to take action, but instead, fearful of arrest, waited for orders from above. And given the population's support of the war effort, widespread repression was by no means necessary. It only added to the suffering that the Soviet people endured during the war.

In addition to repression, Soviet leaders banked on another hallmark of the Stalinist system – the planned economy. Since the beginning of the industrialization drive in the late 1920s, the Soviet government had controlled all economic assets through Gosplan, the state planning agency. Even before the war, Gosplan had channeled labor and raw materials to defense-related industries. Particularly in the late 1930s, it had emphasized the manufacture of armaments. With the outbreak of the war, Gosplan chief Nikolai Voznesensky took charge of military production and prioritized the making of guns, tanks, and aircraft. Consumer goods, already a low priority in the Soviet economy, were further curtailed and distributed via a rationing system that also predated the war. Whereas other countries had to establish state economic controls and rationing, the Soviet Union already had these in place.

Voznesensky's first task was planning the evacuation of industry from the western part of the country. The rapid German advance meant that hundreds of factories were soon to be overrun, and on the third day of the war Party leaders created a Gosplan council to oversee industrial evacuation. Equipment from more than 2,500 factories, along with many workers and engineers, was shipped by rail to the east – the Volga region, the Urals, Siberia, and Central Asia.[24] There, makeshift structures housed new plants that, despite enormous disruption, began producing armaments. The loss of airplanes and tanks at the beginning of the war made it all the more essential that Soviet industry rearm the military as fast as possible. In addition to overseeing the relocation of factories, Voznesensky and Gosplan bureaucrats directed the conversion of nonmilitary industry to defense production. Automobile plants were converted to tank production, machine building plants manufactured artillery, while smaller factories began making rifles and ammunition.[25]

Throughout the first year and a half of the war, the Red Army suffered an acute deficit of weaponry compared with the German Wehrmacht. Indeed, the horrendous casualty rates among Soviet soldiers were largely due to the fact that they were fighting German tanks and bombers with little more than rifles and hand grenades. But by 1943, Soviet industry was outproducing German industry. That year alone Soviet factories built 30,000 tanks, and by the following year they were producing 2,000–3,000 aircraft every month. Aid from the United States, through the Lend-Lease program, added trucks and ammunition to the growing Soviet arsenal. In battles from 1943 to 1945, the Red Army was able first to match and then to overwhelm the German military in terms of firepower. Given the importance of mechanized combat during World War II, Soviet industrial production was crucial to the war effort.

In some ways, then, the Stalinist system was well geared for warfare. As noted earlier, the Soviet state was born at a moment of total war. Accordingly, it was a mobilizational state that could marshal the country's forces. The Soviet government already had a large propaganda apparatus, secret police force, and economic planning organization long before World War II began. Whereas other countries had to create or expand government agencies to enact wartime measures, the Soviet government already had these bureaucracies in place. At the same time, the hypercentralized Soviet system had its liabilities. Soviet authorities' distrust of the population and excessive use of coercion hampered local initiative. People had to wait for orders from above or risk arrest. Particularly at the outset of the war, this lack of initiative in the face of the German invasion had proven disastrous.

Gender Roles in Wartime

The recruitment of women into heavy industry factory jobs during the 1930s had already caused flux in gender roles, even though it did not lead to women's equality. The war presented another moment when women were given new responsibilities, including military service, that might have lessened gender differences. Instead, gender distinctions hardened during the war, as men were identified as soldiers and women were depicted as martyrs or as the mothers of soldiers. Virtually all young men had to serve in the military during the war, and masculinity became increasingly defined in terms of bravery in battle. And notwithstanding the fact that more than 800,000 women served in the armed forces, including 120,000 in combat positions, official propaganda largely portrayed women as passive victims of the war rather than as combatants.

Military service was required for young men, and in 1939, the Soviet government extended conscripts' service from two to three years and restricted exemptions from service. At the time, Politburo member Mikhail Kalinin described military heroism as "the rejection of life and death in the name of life, in the name of the motherland. In this is the greatness of a real man."[26] He thus defined masculinity in terms of military service and a willingness to die for the sake of the country. Propaganda following the German invasion stressed male soldiers' duty to defend their motherland and families. One article described how German soldiers smashed a child's head in front of his mother and then raped and killed her, while another listed the rapes of several Soviet women and concluded, "The honor of women, sisters, mothers, and daughters – what is more valuable for a man, a defender of his motherland, of his family?"[27] Masculinity became tied to combat duty to protect women and children.

At the time of the German invasion, the Red Army had about 300 divisions with 6.8 million troops. Despite the loss of 46 divisions of soldiers killed or captured during the first month of the war, additional mobilizations brought the number of divisions to roughly 400 by August 1941.[28] Mortality rates in the Red Army continued to be very high throughout the war. Particularly during the first year of the war, Soviet commanders often sent unprepared troops into battle in their desperation to stem the German advance. Officially, 8.7 million Soviet soldiers died in the course of the war, and this figure does not even include losses among partisans and militia groups. High casualty rates required more recruits, and, with the exception of specialists working in defense-related industries, men ages 18–51 were conscripted into the military.

As most men left for the front, women became the country's main labor force in factories and on collective farms. The fact that already in the 1930s large numbers of women had joined the industrial workforce facilitated this process. Unlike in the United States, for example, there was no need for a "Rosie the Riveter" campaign to shift definitions of femininity from the domestic sphere to the industrial sphere. The departure of many male workers meant that even more positions opened for women in heavy industry, where they produced steel and armaments crucial for the war effort. Women also made up virtually the entire remaining labor force on collective farms. Moreover, women joined civilian militias and civil defense organizations throughout the country. In these capacities they guarded supplies, served as lookouts and search-light operators, drove transport trucks, and worked in fire brigades.

Women also played an important role in the Soviet military itself. During the 1930s, the government had made no definitive pronounce-ment about whether women could take on combat roles, but the Komsomol included young women in combat-related training, and some Soviet war films featured military heroines. In contrast to Nazi ideology, which consigned women to the domestic sphere, Soviet propa-ganda always emphasized the important public roles women were to play in building and defending socialism. In 1939, a government decree clar-ified that only men would be soldiers and women in the military would serve in auxiliary roles. But when the German invasion came, thousands of young Soviet women nonetheless volunteered to fight. Recruiting centers generally turned them away or assigned them to nursing, but some women persisted and were sent to the front. Rita Kogan, who served in the Red Army as a frontline radio operator, recalled her own enlistment.

I had no idea what war was really like, but I wanted to take part in it, because that was what a hero did ... I did not think of it as 'patriotism' – I saw it as my duty – that I could and should do everything in my power to defeat the enemy ... I did not think of death and was not afraid of it, because, like my Soviet heroes, I was fighting for the motherland.[29]

As the war progressed, the Soviet government reversed itself and began to recruit women for combat. In October 1941, it authorized the forma-tion of three women's air combat regiments that enlisted around 300 women to train as fighter pilots and bombers.[30] Then, in 1942, Party leaders ordered the military to accept thousands of women for both combat and non-combat positions. More than 300,000 female volunteers

Figure 4.3 Red Army sniper Liudmila Pavlichenko during World War II.

joined the Red Army directly or through civilian militia units that were incorporated into the army. Nearly 500,000 more women were recruited through the Komsomol for military service. Women served as snipers, machine gunners, and antiaircraft troops, as well as combat medics, doctors, supply workers, and radio operators. Some even became war heroes, such as sniper Liudmila Pavlichenko, who was widely heralded for having more than 300 kills (see Figure 4.3).[31]

The women who served in the Red Army were overwhelmingly ethnic Russians from urban areas. Most were either workers or university students, and were between the ages of 18 and 25. While military recruiters accepted almost all male volunteers and conscripts (turning away only those with serious health problems), they proved much more selective with female recruits. Women were only accepted if they had high levels of education, including complete literacy in Russian – a requirement that limited the number of national minority women in the Red Army. Female recruits also had to meet certain requirements for health and physical strength, and almost all were unmarried and did not have children. Because the Komsomol played a large role in recruitment, most female soldiers were also Komsomol members.[32]

Despite the increasing role that women played in the army, Soviet military propaganda continued to portray the front as masculinized space. Articles in the Red Army newspaper emphasized comradeship among male soldiers and neglected to mention the contributions of female soldiers. Women were still primarily presented as victims.

The most publicized Soviet woman during the war was Zoya Kosmodemyanskaya, a partisan who was caught trying to set fire to a village where Germans soldiers were billeted. Tortured and hanged by her German captors, Zoya received widespread publicity in newspapers and in a wartime film about her. But she was not depicted as a heroine who helped defeat the Nazis by her actions. Articles reported that Zoya had failed in her sabotage mission, but highlighted the fact that with her final words she called for vengeance. Her story was reported to have prompted a brigade of male soldiers to vow "to destroy mercilessly the German aggressors in revenge for the torment of Zoya."[33] In this way, she was presented as a martyr – a woman whose death could inspire male soldiers to defeat the Germans.

The other dominant depiction of women in Soviet propaganda was as mothers. One article contended that a mother's greatest contribution to the war effort was sending her son to fight. "Let him fight for the two of them, for her too, with twice the strength, twice the hatred."[34] Here again, despite the large number of female soldiers in the Red Army, women were overlooked as combatants and relegated instead to a secondary role. A renewed pronatalist push begun in 1944 further emphasized women's roles as mothers. The government awarded medals to women with five or more children and the title of Mother-Heroine to women with ten or more children. It also extended monetary assistance to single mothers and doubled rations of supplementary food for pregnant women and nursing mothers.[35] Soviet newspapers at this time glorified motherhood as contributing to the war effort. An article lauded one woman not only for having twelve children, but also because "she gave the Red Army eight manly warriors."[36]

Partly because the front continued to be regarded as a masculinized space, women at the front had difficulty being regarded as legitimate soldiers. Some male officers refused to accept women into their units. One battalion commander later sought to justify his rejection of two female platoon leaders.

I considered it unnecessary for women to go to the front line. There were enough men for that. I also knew their presence would cause no end of trouble with my men ... For them to be giving orders would have involved a lot of problems, because they were girls.[37]

Female soldiers fought to overcome the sexism of male officers and soldiers. As Maria Kaliberda stated:

We wanted to be equal – we didn't want the men saying, "Oh, those women!" about us. And we tried harder than the men. Apart from everything else we had to prove that we were as good as them. For a long time we had to put up with a very patronizing, superior attitude.[38]

Some men viewed women at the front not as combatants but as sexual objects.[39] Stories circulated of female soldiers and military nurses who had sex with male officers. Male soldiers expressed resentment that female soldiers received special treatment from male officers, some of whom took "campaign wives" at the front. After the war, female veterans insisted that they had maintained high moral standards. Nonetheless, the popular perception and memory of women at the front emphasized their sexuality rather than their combat achievements. Many of these women were scorned rather than honored for serving in the Red Army. So, despite the fact that Soviet women made an enormous contribution to the war effort, both at the front lines and on the home front, their efforts did not lead to women's equality. While men were honored for their military achievements, women were primarily recognized as victims of the war or as the mothers of soldiers.

The Battle of Stalingrad

In the spring of 1942, Stalin and his generals expected the German army to make another thrust at Moscow. Accordingly, they concentrated many of their troops there to defend the capital. But Hitler and his generals had a different plan. They instead launched an offensive to the south, with the oilfields on the Caspian Sea as their ultimate objective. Caught off guard, the Red Army suffered another round of catastrophic losses. Both Voronezh and Rostov fell to the Germans, and Soviet forces had to retreat. While some German divisions drove farther south toward the Caucasus Mountains and Caspian Sea, others proceeded eastward toward the Volga River and Stalingrad (see Map 4.1). It was here that a decisive battle was fought, one that proved to be the turning point of the entire war.

The Battle of Stalingrad was the largest battle in all human history. An epic struggle with more than 2 million combatants, it lasted from late August 1942 to early February 1943. The German assault began with intense bombing that reduced the city to rubble. More than 300,000 German soldiers backed by tanks and artillery then invaded the city. General Vasily Chuikov, commander of the Soviet 62nd Army at Stalingrad, recalled the attack:

The main blow was aimed at the Central [Train] Station. This was an attack of exceptional strength. Despite enormous losses, the Germans were now crashing ahead. Whole columns of tanks and motorized infantry were breaking into the

Figure 4.4 Soviet troops during the Battle of Stalingrad, 1942.

center of the city . . . Our soldiers – snipers, anti-tank gunners, artillery men [were] lying in wait in houses, cellars and firing points.[40]

Red Army soldiers fought back from bombed out buildings and slowed German progress to a crawl. The Central Train Station and Mamaev Kurgan (a strategic hill in the city) changed hands multiple times, as German and Soviet troops attacked and counterattacked. Both sides suffered enormous casualties.

The Germans had substantial superiority in terms of tanks and aircraft. In fact, the German air force dominated the skies throughout the battle and bombed Soviet positions mercilessly. The Red Army had to withdraw its artillery to the east bank of the Volga River and from there continue firing in support of troops on the west bank. Moreover, all ammunition and reinforcements had to be ferried across the river, mainly at night due to constant German bombardment during the day. Air superiority gave the Germans an advantage, but the Soviet tactic of "hugging the enemy" – digging in as close to enemy lines as possible – limited its effectiveness. German tanks were also hampered, due to limited maneuverability amidst piles of rubble throughout the city. The battle was fought street by street and building by building, with machine guns, grenades, and hand-to-hand combat (see Figure 4.4). There were firefights in the city's sewers and within buildings themselves, with Soviet soldiers in one room firing at German soldiers in another.

By late September, the Germans had captured most of central Stalingrad and began their offensive on the industrial district just north of the center. Here, several large factories became the focus of fighting. In mid-October the Germans launched what was to be a final thrust toward the river. Chuikov described the attack as the most intense of the entire battle.

There were three thousand German air sorties that day. They bombed and stormed our troops without a moment's respite ... It was a sunny day, but owing to the smoke and soot, visibility was reduced to 100 yards. Our dugouts were shaking and crumbling up like a house of cards ... By midnight it was clear that the invaders had surrounded the Stalingrad Tractor Plant, and fighting was going on in the workshops.[41]

The Germans captured the tractor plant and at one place reached the riverbank, cutting the Soviet forces in two. But Soviet troops refused to surrender. Clinging only to a narrow strip of land along the Volga River, they continued to fight. Many units were virtually wiped out, but new regiments were ferried across the river to replace them.[42]

With the German army's offensive stalled and its supply lines badly overextended, Soviet generals planned a counter-attack. Code-named Uranus, this operation massed Soviet troops north and south of the city and took aim at Romanian and Hungarian forces guarding the flanks of the German army. Launched in mid-November, Operation Uranus smashed through the Axis forces and encircled the German Sixth Army in Stalingrad. German units attempted to break through and relieve their encircled troops, but the Red Army repelled this effort and tightened the "noose" around the Sixth Army. Able to receive supplies only by air, the trapped German soldiers soon ran short of fuel, ammunition, and food. The battle continued into the winter as Soviet troops closed in on German soldiers huddled in the basements of ruined buildings. Hitler ordered his soldiers to fight to the death, but by February the roughly 90,000 still alive finally surrendered.

The Battle of Stalingrad marked the pivotal moment of World War II. The very best units of the German army were lost at Stalingrad, and Hitler never again launched a successful large-scale offensive. Though the Red Army suffered more than a million casualties in the battle, it won a tremendous victory. The Normandy invasion by Allied forces was still a year and a half away – the Soviet military had defeated the Axis forces virtually on its own. Confidence among the Soviet people soared, and despite the hardships still ahead, many began to believe that the war would be won. The Nazi leadership, on the other hand, became pessimistic about its chances, and the mood in Germany plummeted.

From Kursk to Berlin

In the summer of 1943, another massive engagement between Soviet and German troops took place at the Battle of Kursk. Here for the first time the Red Army was able to thwart German blitzkrieg tactics. Previous German assaults using columns of tanks had succeeded in penetrating battle lines and encircling enemy troops. In this battle, General Zhukhov ordered multiple lines of Soviet defenses with large numbers of tanks, mines, and anti-tank artillery. Even when German tanks broke through the first or second lines of defense, they still came under fire from Soviet troops and could not advance. Soviet industrial production proved crucial for this battle. The fact that factories had produced large quantities of heavy tanks and artillery meant that the Red Army could finally match German tanks on the battlefield. Increased production of aircraft also ensured that, for the first time since the German invasion, the Soviet air force could contest control of the skies.

With the Soviet military now evenly equipped in terms of airplanes and tanks, warfare became more mechanized. The clash of tanks lasted for several weeks, and the battlefields around Kursk were soon littered with smoldering wreckage from both sides. One combat medic, Olga Omelchenko, described the constant shelling: "The sky throbs, the ground throbs, your heart seems about to burst, your skin feels ready to split ... Everything crackled, everything rumbled ... The ground heaved."[43] Both sides suffered heavy casualties, but greater reserves allowed Red Army commanders to replenish their ranks. Increased partisan activity behind the German lines also undercut the Nazi offensive by disrupting supplies and communications.[44] Once the Red Army had blunted the German assault, it launched its own offensive. Deploying tanks backed by infantry, the Soviet military seized the initiative and drove the German army back. The German army, now fighting Allied forces in Italy as well, suffered troop shortages and had to retreat. For the remainder of the war they were on the defensive.

In 1944, Soviet soldiers continued to advance, breaking the blockade around Leningrad, liberating Belorussia and the rest of Ukraine, and finally advancing into the Baltic countries, Romania, Poland, Czechoslovakia, and Hungary.[45] The Normandy invasion in June of that year meant that Germany had to divert more troops away from the eastern front, leaving the Soviet military with an even greater numerical advantage. As the Red Army approached Warsaw, Polish resistance fighters staged an uprising against German occupiers. Soviet troops, however, did not press forward to aid the Poles, and the German army crushed this revolt and destroyed much of the city. The commander of Soviet forces outside Warsaw, Konstantin Rokossovsky, later claimed that his troops paused to fend off German counterattacks, but the Poles felt that the Soviets had deliberately withheld support to deprive them of the chance to liberate their own capital.[46] The Red Army subsequently resumed its advance, driving the Germans out of Poland and, after bitter fighting, capturing Prague and Budapest as well.

By early 1945, Soviet troops were marching through Germany itself. There they engaged in looting and atrocities, including widespread sexual violence. In some cases, troops burned down buildings or even entire towns, just because they were German. Other Soviet soldiers robbed civilians and committed acts of indiscriminate violence. Thousands of German women were raped, many multiple times. One female communications officer in the Red Army recalled that upon entering towns, male soldiers seeking vengeance would loot homes, drink any alcohol they found, and gang rape German women and girls.[47] Soldiers could be disciplined and even shot for these crimes, but in practice officers generally overlooked looting and sexual violence.

Soviet soldiers engaged in violence toward civilians as acts of revenge. They had witnessed German brutality on Soviet soil – massacres, rapes, forced starvation, destruction of cities and villages. Moreover, wartime propaganda had harped on German atrocities, including the rapes of Soviet women. Even as the Red Army entered Germany, Soviet propagandist Ilya Ehrenburg continued to publish his anti-German diatribes, proclaiming "The hour of revenge has struck!"[48] Soldiers took earlier German crimes as license for their own barbarities, including the sexual violence they perpetrated against German women. Belatedly, Soviet political and military leaders attempted to restrain this behavior. They stopped publication of Ehrenburg's hate propaganda, and the Red Army newspaper declared, "If the Germans marauded, and publicly raped our women, it does not mean that we must do the same ... Our soldiers will not allow anything like that to happen – not because of pity for the enemy, but out of a sense of their own personal dignity."[49] However, many Soviet soldiers continued to commit atrocities nonetheless.[50]

In mid-April, the Soviet military began its final assault on Berlin (see Figure 4.5). Under Zhukov's command, some 2.5 million Red Army soldiers massed outside the German capital. Following a devastating artillery bombardment, Soviet soldiers fought their way through the city in house-to-house fighting reminiscent of Stalingrad. Casualties were

Figure 4.5 Red Army soldiers raise the Soviet flag over the Reichstag
building in Berlin, 1945.

extremely heavy, as roughly 300,000 Soviet and 200,000 German soldiers
were killed. As Red Army troops approached the center of Berlin,
on April 30, Hitler committed suicide in his bunker. Eight days later the
German military high command unconditionally surrendered, and the
war in Europe came to an end.[51]

The Legacy of the War

News of the victory arrived in Moscow on May 9, 1945, and it set off a euphoric celebration. People flooded into the streets to rejoice that the war was finally over. British journalist Alexander Werth wrote:

The spontaneous joy of the two or three million people who thronged the Red Square that evening ... was of a quality and a depth I had never yet seen in Moscow before. They danced and sang in the streets; every soldier and officer was hugged and kissed ... They were so happy, they did not even have to get drunk.[52]

That night a spectacular fireworks display capped the celebration. And in June, the Soviet government held a victory parade in Red Square, where soldiers piled captured German standards at the feet of Stalin and other Communist leaders. The Soviet people had fought the largest armed conflict in world history, and after years of suffering and sacrifice, they had won.

The triumphant celebration, however, could not mask the terrible price the country had paid. The 27 million Soviet soldiers and civilians dead dwarfed the roughly 7 million Germans killed in the war. By way of comparison, about 450,000 Britons and 400,000 Americans died in the war. Whole regions of the Soviet Union had been destroyed, entire cities reduced to rubble, and an estimated 20 million people were left homeless. Wartime destruction had set back the country's economic progress by years if not decades. Armaments production was the only economic sector that had grown, but it did nothing to raise living standards. Most Soviet people looked forward to a time after the war when they could enjoy life, but instead the need to rebuild the country demanded more sacrifice. And the horrible wartime casualties – millions permanently disabled in addition to those killed – meant fewer workers to accomplish the task of rebuilding.

In some ways the wartime struggle against a common enemy had been a unifying experience for the Soviet Union. Even people hostile to the government felt that for once they were on the same side as Communist leaders. There was a surge in Communist Party membership, as many soldiers in particular joined. And old class differences faded, as even some former kulaks had become military heroes.[53] But unity did not extend to everyone – those who had surrendered during the war were ostracized. Many Soviet prisoners of war returned from German prison camps only to be arrested and sent to the Gulag, suspected of having given up without a fight. People who had been under occupation and collaborated with the Germans were also liable to be denounced and arrested.

In a similar way, the war had been a moment of either unity or ostracism for Soviet nationalities. The Stalinist leadership had sought to mobilize all national and ethnic groups for the war effort, and propaganda depicted Soviet nationalities as a "brotherhood" fighting together to defeat the fascist invaders.[54] The proportion of national minorities in the Red Army had grown throughout the war, particularly given high casualty rates among Russian soldiers and the mobilization of recruits from the Caucasus and Central Asia. Late in the war, as the Soviet military liberated the western part of the country, additional Belorussian and Ukrainian troops were added to the Red Army as well. But Party leaders branded some nationalities as traitors. Crimean Tatars, Kalmyks, Chechens, Ingush, Balkars, Karachays, and Meshketian Turks were all accused of having collaborated when the Germans occupied Crimea and the northern Caucasus. While there were indeed some collaborators, as was true in every region the Nazis occupied, other members of these nationalities had served loyally in the Red Army. But at the urging of secret police chief Lavrenti Beria, Stalin ordered the wholesale deportations of these peoples in 1944. Close to 200,000 Crimean Tatars, the largest of these national groups, were forcibly removed from their homes and transported in cattle cars to Central Asia.[55]

The Baltic peoples – Estonians, Latvians, and Lithuanians – were also persecuted late in the war, as their countries were once again forcibly incorporated into the Soviet Union.[56] Those who resisted, as well as those suspected of having aided the Germans, were subject to incarceration in the Gulag. Members of the Ukrainian Insurgent Army were also arrested or killed at the end of the war. This Ukrainian nationalist organization initially fought as partisans against Nazi rule, but then also fought for independence against the Red Army when it reconquered Ukrainian territory. Soviet authorities arrested not only Ukrainian Insurgent Army members but their relatives and supporters as well, several hundred thousand people in all.[57] So despite postwar propaganda that commemorated the collective struggle of Soviet nationalities, the war was not necessarily a catalyst for ethnic unity. For some nationalities, it instead became a time of exclusion and persecution.

Another important legacy of the war was its lasting effect on those who fought. Particularly for soldiers who had gone directly from school into the military, their only adult experiences were the regimentation of the army and the brutality of war. Millions of veterans felt alienated when they returned to a civilian life they hardly knew. In addition, many suffered under the burdens of post-traumatic stress disorder and unprocessed grief for comrades who died during the war. In contrast to the prior ideal of the New Soviet Person – a cultured, productive laborer – these veterans were not workers but warriors. Stakhanovites, the personification of the New Person in the 1930s, had distinguished themselves by their heroic labor. But during World War II, heroism instead became associated with killing Germans. Zhdanov even praised those who exterminated "the fascist reptiles" as "Stakhanovites on the military front."[58] The New Soviet Person was supposed to build a harmonious world under socialism, but Soviet war heroes had been decorated for killing.

Finally, the war vindicated and even reinforced the Stalinist system. All of the repressive elements of Stalinism – collectivization, the planned economy, state violence – were credited for the great victory. Government control of land, factories, and materials seemed justified to mobilize for war. Censorship and repression were seen as necessary to maintain a unified front. Even the Great Purges were excused by some as having eliminated potential traitors within the country. In reality, mass executions of innocent people had greatly weakened the country on the eve of the war. The purge of military officers in particular left the army completely unprepared for the Nazi onslaught. But in the glow of victory, this fact was forgotten. Propaganda credited Stalin personally for leading the country through the war, and the Stalin cult swelled to huge proportions. Patriotism came to mean loyalty to Stalin and the Soviet government. As Stalin's prestige soared to new heights, his authority and the Stalinist system could in no way be challenged.

5   The Postwar Years (1946–1953)

After the war, the Soviet Union confronted many of the same issues as did other countries – the demobilization of soldiers, the reconstruction of cities, the transition to a peacetime economy, and coming to terms with the wartime past. In some areas, the Soviet case mirrored the experiences of other European countries. Millions of soldiers were demobilized and, although welcomed as heroes, they faced a difficult transition to civilian life. Hundreds of cities and towns had been leveled during the war and had to be rebuilt. But in other spheres the Soviet case was distinctive. In particular, the Stalinist economy had always been a wartime economy, so there was no consumer-oriented economy to which the country could return. And while collaborators were punished in the postwar era, a complete coming to terms with the wartime past, including acknowledging Stalin's mistakes, would have to wait until after his death in 1953.

The major element that shaped Soviet foreign and domestic policies – and indeed dominated world politics for the entire postwar era – was the Cold War. The wartime alliance between the Soviet Union and the United States soon gave way to a bitter rivalry for world domination. In eastern Europe, the Stalinist leadership installed socialist governments under its control, while in western Europe the United States sought to bolster capitalism and liberal democracy. This Cold War rivalry soon spread to Asia, with the Chinese Communist Revolution and the Korean War. The Soviet Union was no longer a lone socialist state facing capitalist encirclement. It was now a superpower – the leader of an entire socialist bloc that seemed to be in ascendancy.

This leadership role, along with the prestige gained by having defeated Nazi Germany, gave the Soviet Union new prominence on the world stage. But its rise did not go uncontested. The United States and its allies viewed the spread of communism as a grave danger and sought to contain Soviet power. With heightened tensions, both sides maintained vigilance and clamped down on internal dissent. And both countries engaged in an arms race that, over the coming decades, would cost several trillion dollars. In the Soviet case, the enormous sums spent on weaponry drained resources that might have been used to develop other sectors of the economy. People's living standards remained low, and Soviet economic planners continued to prioritize military production.

The Origins of the Cold War

The seeds of the Cold War may be found in prior Soviet-American relations. In 1917, the United States had refused to recognize the legitimacy of the Soviet government – indeed, it had sent a contingent of soldiers to aid anti-Communist forces in the Russian Civil War. It was not until 1933 that the US government finally established diplomatic relations with the Soviet Union. Following the German invasion of the Soviet Union in 1941, the United States only reluctantly supported the Soviets. The US State Department called the Communist Party dictatorship just as intolerable as the Nazi dictatorship, but stated that it should be helped since the Nazis posed a greater threat. Harry Truman, a senator at the time, declared, "If we see that Germany is winning the war, we ought to help Russia, and if Russia is winning we ought to help Germany and that way let them kill as many as possible."[1]

When the United States entered the war six months later, after the Japanese bombing of Pearl Harbor, it became military allies with the Soviet Union. This alliance, however, was based not on shared values or even a formal treaty, but instead on the fact that Nazi Germany was their common enemy. Mutual suspicion between the two countries continued during the war. While the United States sent large amounts of aid to help the Soviets fight Nazi Germany, what Stalin and Molotov sought most urgently was the opening of a second front in France. (American diplomats noted that Molotov seemed to know only four words in English: "yes," "no," and "second front.") A British-American invasion of German-occupied France in 1942 would have drawn German troops away from Stalingrad where the Red Army was barely hanging on. President Franklin Roosevelt first promised to open a second front in 1942, and then in 1943. But it was not until June 1944 that the Normandy invasion finally occurred, and in the meantime the Soviet Union had suffered horrendous casualties. While a lack of landing craft forced repeated delays of the Normandy invasion, to Communist Party leaders it seemed that Roosevelt and British Prime Minister Winston Churchill were indeed letting the Soviets and Germans kill as many of one another as possible.

In February 1945, as the war was nearing an end, Stalin met Roosevelt and Churchill at the Yalta Conference to discuss plans for postwar

Figure 5.1 The Yalta Conference, 1945. Seated (from left) are Churchill, Roosevelt, and Stalin.

Europe (see Figure 5.1). Vehement arguments broke out between them over the future of eastern European countries, Poland in particular. Roosevelt and Churchill wanted the London-based Polish government-in-exile to assume power after the war. Stalin saw these Polish leaders as anti-Soviet and put forward instead a group of Polish leftists. With the Red Army occupying Poland, Stalin had all of the leverage in these negotiations, and he permitted the London Poles only token representation in the new Polish cabinet. Roosevelt got Stalin to agree to the vaguely worded Declaration of Liberated Europe that promised countries self-determination. But this declaration did not prevent the Soviets from subsequently holding rigged elections in eastern European countries and installing Communist governments.

Roosevelt died in April 1945, so it was his successor Harry Truman who met Stalin and Churchill (and Churchill's successor Clement Atlee) at the Potsdam Conference after the war ended. Tensions between the nominal allies continued to rise as they argued over the fate of Germany as well as of eastern Europe. Germany was divided into four zones of occupation, with the American, British, and French zones in the west and the Soviet zone in the east. The leaders made no plans to divide Germany permanently, but they could not agree on the country's future. Soviet leaders wanted a weakened, deindustrialized Germany that would pose no threat to their country. American and British leaders saw a need to revive the German economy, believing that capitalism and trade with other countries was the best guarantee against a return to fascism or a turn to communism.

In 1946, the brewing Cold War became public when, at Truman's invitation, Churchill delivered his Iron Curtain speech in Fulton, Missouri. Churchill warned that Soviet-backed Communist parties in eastern European countries were seeking "totalitarian control." He declared,

From Stettin in the Baltic to Trieste in the Adriatic, an iron curtain has descended across the continent. Behind that line lie all the capitals of the ancient states of central and eastern Europe . . . all these famous cities and the populations around them lie in the Soviet sphere and all are subject in one form or another, not only to Soviet influence, but to a very high and increasing measure of control from Moscow.[2]

The following year, in what became known as the Truman Doctrine, Truman declared that the United States should aid Greece and Turkey to resist the spread of communism. "Containment" of Soviet expansionism – a term coined by US diplomat George Kennan – became the guiding spirit of American foreign policy.

Could the Cold War have been avoided? Had the Soviet-American alliance continued, the world might have been spared the division of Europe, international conflicts such as the Korean War, and a costly arms race that lasted for decades. But this alliance had been a wartime necessity rather than a stable partnership. The United States and Soviet Union had radically different ideologies and interests. Both were seeking security in the postwar world, but they had opposing ideas of how to achieve it. American leaders wanted European countries to have self-determination, liberal democracy, capitalism, and free markets. Soviet leaders desired socialist economic and political systems, and at a minimum wanted to guarantee that the countries on their borders were not antagonistic. Both sides came to view the other as a mortal enemy, virtually equivalent to Nazi Germany in the threat they posed. With this mentality, and the fate of the world seemingly at stake, Soviet and American leaders proved unable to avoid the decades-long confrontation known as the Cold War.[3]

Soviet Domination in Eastern Europe

Though Stalin secured Soviet territorial gains and envisaged eastern European governments that were "friendly" with the Soviet Union, he had no masterplan for imposing the Stalinist system on eastern Europe. In the aftermath of a devastating war, his primary concern was his own country's security, which he viewed as tantamount to socialism's future. Western commentators who saw Soviet expansionism as driven by revolutionary ideology fundamentally misunderstood Stalin's motives. Nonetheless, with the rising tensions of the Cold War, Stalin sought ever greater control over eastern Europe. What began as leftist coalition governments in eastern European countries soon became Communist Party monopolies. Soviet domination in eastern Europe in turn worsened the Cold War, as it remained a major point of contention with the United States and its allies.

At the end of World War II, the Soviet government reincorporated the territory it had seized in 1939–40, along with some additional territory. The Baltic countries (Estonia, Latvia, Lithuania), eastern Poland, Bessarabia and Bukovina from Romania, sub-Carpathian Ruthenia from Czechoslovakia, part of Karelia in eastern Finland, and Königsberg in East Prussia all became part of the Soviet Union (see Map 5.1). The transfer of territory was accompanied by population transfers, including the deportation of Poles from what was now western Ukraine and Belorussia, and the deportation of several million Germans from East Prussia, where the Polish-German border was moved to the west. These population transfers resolved, in a brutal manner, disputes over territory that Hitler had used to justify his invasion of Poland at the start of World War II. They also enforced ethnic homogeneity in the western borderlands of the Soviet Union and thus eliminated Stalin's concern with the presence of Polish minorities within the country.[4]

Beyond gaining territory, the Soviet government exercised control in eastern European countries occupied by the Red Army. It built up Communist parties in Poland, Hungary, Romania, and Bulgaria, as well as in Czechoslovakia, where the Communist Party was already strong. Initially it had local Communists rule in coalitions with democratic and socialist parties. From 1947 on, however, the Soviet government used strong-arm tactics to eliminate coalition governments. Rigged elections combined with the arrest of opposition politicians ensured that Communist parties gained monopolies on power. Aside from protesting, British and American leaders had few options. Most countries of eastern Europe were still occupied by Red Army units, and short of military action, nothing could challenge Soviet control. At the direction of Moscow, Communist governments in eastern European countries gradually imposed

Map 5.1 The Soviet Union and Europe after World War II.

the Stalinist model on their societies – the abolition of capitalism, collectivized agriculture (with the exception of Poland), and state-run economies.[5]

Yugoslavia was distinctive in that Communist partisans there, under Josip Broz Tito, had liberated the country from German and Italian occupiers without the aid of the Red Army. After the war, they voluntarily followed the Stalinist model, collectivizing agriculture and writing a constitution patterned on the Soviet one. But Tito proved too independent for Stalin's liking. Among other things, he aided Greek Communists in their struggle to take power. Stalin had agreed with Churchill that Greece would remain in the Anglo-American sphere of influence, and he refused to support the Communist insurgency (which was subsequently crushed by the Greek government with British and American aid). Stalin punished Tito for his independence by expelling Yugoslavia from the Cominform – the Communist Information Bureau, a Moscow-based organization that coordinated international Communist activity.[6] Western observers had assumed that the Communist bloc in eastern Europe was monolithic, as the Soviet government would have preferred, but the Soviet-Yugoslav split showed this was not entirely the case.

Soviet leaders saw Communist regimes in eastern Europe as a necessary buffer between their country and Germany. They were fearful that within a generation Germany might rebuild and launch another invasion, perhaps supported by Hungary, Romania, and Bulgaria, which had all fought on the German side in World War II. In retrospect it is clear there was no resurgence of German militarism, but at the time many feared that, just as after World War I, Germany would soon threaten neighboring countries once again. The Soviets were joined by politicians in France and throughout Europe in worrying about German revanchism. Indeed, Czechoslovakia and Poland appeared to need Soviet support to guarantee that Germany would not seize territory from them in the future.

Because the Red Army occupied only the eastern part of Germany, Soviet leaders could not impose their will on the entire country. Their preference was for a united but weak Germany. As war reparations, they shipped large quantities of German industrial equipment back to the Soviet Union. American, British, and French leaders controlled the western part of Germany as well as the western part of Berlin (which was located within the eastern zone). Opposed to Soviet designs for Germany, they announced in June 1948 that they would create a separate West German state. Later that month they introduced a new currency that began circulating in West Germany.

The Soviet Union took aggressive action to try and block the new currency and the new state. It introduced a separate East German currency and cut off rail and road links between West Germany and West Berlin, seeking to make the population there economically dependent on

Figure 5.2 Residents of West Berlin watch a US cargo plane arrive during the Berlin Airlift, 1948.

East Germany. By threatening to incorporate West Berlin into East Germany, the Soviet leadership tried to force the British and Americans to give up either West Berlin or their plans for West German statehood. But they did neither, countering the land blockade with the Berlin Airlift – a massive operation to supply West Berlin by airplane. Flying more than 1,500 flights per day, American and British cargo plane crews transported several thousand tons of food, coal, and other supplies daily to provide for the needs of the population (see Figure 5.2). The airlift proved successful, and after eleven months the Soviets relented and reopened land routes to West Berlin.

Following the Berlin Airlift, two German states were formally established – the Federal Republic of Germany in the west, and the Soviet-controlled German Democratic Republic in the east. By 1949, Berlin, Germany, and Europe itself were all clearly divided between the western and Soviet blocs. Soviet leaders had control of most of eastern Europe, including East Germany, and had installed Communist regimes and state-run socialist economies in those countries. Simultaneously, the

American presence in western Europe was strengthened. Through the Marshal Plan, the United States was providing billions of dollars in aid and loans to rebuild capitalist economies in western Europe. The division of Europe into antagonistic capitalist and socialist spheres epitomized the Cold War rivalry between the United States and Soviet Union.

Nuclear Weapons and Environmental Contamination

The Cold War also had important nuclear and environmental dimensions. The atomic bombing of Hiroshima and Nagasaki, Japan, by the United States at the end of World War II shocked people throughout the world, including Soviet leaders. The Americans' possession of atomic weapons radically altered the balance of military power at the expense of the Soviet Union. While the Red Army was still the world's most powerful conventional army, it had nothing that could match the destructive capacity of an atomic bomb. Stalin privately stated, "No doubt Washington and London are hoping we won't be able to develop the bomb ourselves for some time. And meanwhile, using America's monopoly ... they want to force us to accept their plans on questions affecting Europe and the world. Well, that's not going to happen."[7]

Despite Stalin's tough stance, he and other Soviet leaders knew that their country was vulnerable to an American attack. Truman in fact told his advisers that he was fully prepared to drop an atomic bomb on Moscow if he deemed such action necessary. At the time of the Berlin Airlift in 1948, Truman transferred B-29 bombers to the United Kingdom, and the American military drew up contingency plans to drop atomic bombs on Soviet cities.[8] The following year, the United States formed NATO (the North Atlantic Treaty Organization) – a military alliance to counter the Soviet threat to western Europe. The now permanent American military presence in Europe, along with its growing arsenal of weapons, appeared increasingly threatening to Soviet leaders. In the early years of the Cold War they gave top priority to developing an atomic bomb of their own.

In a 1946 speech at the Bolshoi Theater in Moscow, Stalin predicted that, given "proper assistance," Soviet scientists would soon "not only overtake but even outstrip the achievements of science beyond the borders of our country."[9] Secret police chief Beria was in charge of the Soviet bomb project. He allocated immense resources to it under the direction of physicist Igor Kurchatov. Kurchatov assembled an elite group of Soviet physicists and engineers at Arzamas-16, a secret nuclear weapons facility near the city of Gorky. He also had a reactor constructed at the newly founded town of Ozersk in the Ural Mountains, and by 1948 it was producing plutonium. Aided by information from British and American scientists spying for the Soviets, Kurchatov and his team were able to complete work the following year. In August 1949, the Soviet Union successfully detonated an atomic bomb at a test site in Kazakhstan.[10]

The end of the American nuclear monopoly did not end the arms race – on the contrary, it accelerated it. In an effort to gain a strategic advantage, both countries sought to build more and bigger bombs. By 1952, the United States exploded a hydrogen bomb, a thermonuclear weapon far more powerful than atomic bombs. The Soviet Union had its own thermonuclear weapons program led by physicist Andrey Sakharov, and it successfully tested a small-scale H-bomb in 1953 and a larger model two years later. Soviet physicists were wholeheartedly devoted to the development of nuclear weapons. They felt it was their patriotic duty to create atomic and thermonuclear bombs for national defense in the face of the American nuclear monopoly. Sakharov later wrote that he felt "committed to the goal which I assumed was Stalin's as well: after a devastating war, to make the country strong enough to ensure peace."[11]

In the race to produce atomic and nuclear weapons, neither the United States nor the Soviet Union paid adequate attention to the dangers of radioactive contamination. When the Ozersk reactor first began producing plutonium, its uranium fuel rods overheated and cracked, releasing radioactive isotopes. After a brief shutdown, Kurchatov restarted the plant, exposing himself and workers there to high levels of radiation. Once Soviet scientists had produced enough plutonium for one bomb, they closed the reactor for repairs. But instead of the one year needed, Beria gave them only two months to get the reactor running again. In their rush to replace cracked fuel rods, technicians entered the reactor's center and extracted radioactive uranium slugs by hand. Rather than fully cooling the uranium to reduce radioactive isotopes, they then quickly reprocessed it, releasing radioactive gases into the atmosphere. To make matters worse, subsequent accidents leaked additional radioactive waste into surrounding lakes and streams.[12]

Over time, hundreds of square miles around the plutonium plant became contaminated. Residents of the region were not notified of the dangers, because the entire project was secret. Workers at the plant in particular, but other Urals residents as well, later suffered extremely high rates of cancer due to radioactive exposure. A similar environmental and health disaster simultaneously unfolded in the United States. Just after the Soviet Union's successful atomic test in 1949, American scientists at the plutonium plant near Richland, Washington experimented with the rapid reprocessing of uranium. This technique discharged a radioactive plume that spread across the Columbia River basin. Over the next four decades, the Richland plant and the Ozersk plant each released at least 200 million curies of radioactivity into the environment.[13] In the context of the Cold War, both countries brushed aside safety concerns in order to produce nuclear weapons as quickly as possible.

Radioactive contamination was just part of the overall environmental degradation caused by the Stalinist regime. Already during the 1930s, rapid industrialization had entailed destructive mining and logging operations, along with new factories that increased air and water pollution. Contrary to the conventional wisdom, the Soviet approach to resource utilization was not crudely utilitarian. Soviet conservation scientists stressed both the efficient use of resources and the importance of preserving the country's natural environment. New research has shown that their ideas influenced Soviet political leaders and their policies.[14] But during the industrialization drive, the frenzy to fulfill economic plans often overrode environmental concerns. And following the war, Gosplan once again sought to build up heavy industry at any cost, often resulting in waste, pollution, and environmental devastation.[15]

The Cold War provided the context for both nuclear and industrial contamination in the postwar period. The race to build up military capabilities outweighed concerns with resource conservation and public health. Soviet political leaders and scientists alike spoke of the urgent need for a "nuclear shield" – Soviet nuclear weapons that would deter an American attack. These security concerns took precedence over environmentalism, particularly as Cold War tensions grew. As noted, the same mentality led American leaders to jeopardize their citizens' health and their natural environment's purity for the sake of military strength. Mutual fear and hostility prompted both countries to develop nuclear weapons rapidly, at horrific environmental cost.

The Cold War in Asia

The Cold War soon spread to Asia. During World War II, Chinese Communists under Mao Zedong had fought both the Japanese army and the Chinese Nationalists under Chiang Kai-shek. After Japan's defeat, Stalin advised Mao to negotiate with Chiang rather than seizing power. Here again Stalin placed Soviet security ahead of communist revolution abroad, as he strove to maintain relations with the Nationalists and avoid possible American intervention in China. In addition, Stalin distrusted Mao, seeing him as an unorthodox Marxist who relied more on the peasantry than the working class. He also worried that, like Tito in Yugoslavia, Mao might not faithfully take orders from Moscow.

Despite the lack of Soviet encouragement, the Chinese Communists defeated the Nationalists in 1949 and established the People's Republic of China. Mao then traveled to Moscow where he met with Stalin and other Soviet leaders. Their talks were characterized by continuing mistrust, but in early 1950 they nonetheless signed the Sino-Soviet Treaty of Friendship, Alliance, and Mutual Assistance. A military alliance, this treaty also provided Soviet financial aid to the Chinese government. American political leaders, already alarmed by the Communist takeover in China, viewed the Sino-Soviet alliance as evidence that the Soviet bloc had expanded to Asia. With international communism seemingly on the march, they stiffened their resolve to resist its spread anywhere in the world.

This resolve was soon tested during the Korean War. When Korea was liberated from Japan at the end of World War II, Soviet troops occupied the northern half of the country, while American forces occupied the southern half. In 1948, Communists established a government in North Korea, and a pro-Western government was elected in South Korea. Soviet and American military forces subsequently withdrew. But North Korean leader Kim Il-Sung hoped to unify the entire peninsula under the Communist regime, and he believed that a North Korean invasion would be welcomed by much of the population in South Korea. Stalin hesitated to approve such an invasion. Eventually he agreed to it in the spring of 1950, though he promised no military involvement and told Kim that he must rely on Chinese troops instead.[16]

In June 1950, the North Korean army invaded South Korea. Equipped with Soviet tanks and heavy artillery, it quickly overwhelmed South Korean troops and within days captured Seoul, the South Korean capital. Anxious to stop the spread of communism, the Truman administration obtained United Nations resolutions first condemning the attack and then pledging forces to repel it. North Korean troops occupied most of South Korea, but an American-led UN military force intervened and drove the North Korean army back. After retaking South Korea, American troops advanced into North Korea nearly all the way to the Chinese border.

Stalin was alarmed by American intervention and carefully sought to avoid any direct Soviet-American military clash.[17] Providing only limited air support, he urged Mao to commit Chinese forces to the conflict. Once Mao and the Chinese leadership agreed, they sent in 200,000 soldiers who decisively swung momentum the other way. Driving the American-led forces out of North Korea, the Chinese army then advanced into South Korea. American counteroffensives eventually led to a stalemate near the 38th parallel, the original border between North and South

Korea. Though no peace treaty was signed, negotiations resulted in an armistice in 1953, and the war came to an end. In territorial terms, then, the war produced no real change, but it caused more than 2 million military and civilian casualties.[18]

The Korean War also had repercussions beyond Asia, heightening Cold War tensions around the world. Superficially, the Soviet Union benefitted from the war's long-term damage to Sino-American relations. Given American antagonism, Chinese leaders had to remain within the Soviet sphere for their own country's security. But privately, their distrust of the Soviet Union grew, since Stalin had urged them to fight but proved unwilling to commit his own troops. For their part, American leaders saw the invasion of South Korea as a possible prelude to an invasion of West Germany. Together with their NATO allies they dramatically increased defense spending to counter the Communist threat. Soviet leaders monitored NATO's buildup, apprehensive that the United States might be preparing an attack on eastern Europe. The Korean War left both sides increasingly fearful and belligerent.

Within the Soviet Union, the Cold War reinforced the militarization of society that had occurred during World War II. As tensions with the United States intensified in both Europe and Asia, not only Stalin but Soviet officials at all levels felt the need to maintain military preparedness. They never forgot how close their country had come to losing World War II, and they were determined to remain vigilant in case of an American attack. Soviet authorities sacrificed improved living standards for the sake of military production. They perpetuated compulsory military service for young men and civil defense training for male and female students. They also expanded surveillance and counterespionage measures that led to more arrests and repression. Due to the Cold War, the Stalinist system continued to emphasize military preparedness and state control even in peacetime.

Economic Reconstruction

After years of deprivation, the Soviet people looked forward to living well after the war. They hoped that shortages and rationing were in the past, and that victory would usher in a bright future for their society. But the extent of wartime devastation, as well as the Cold War, dashed these hopes. Food shortages continued and indeed got worse. A harvest failure in 1946 caused a famine in which up to 2 million people died. Cities from Kiev to Stalingrad lay in rubble. Reconstruction proceeded slowly and prioritized industrial needs over housing. Millions lived in barracks, shanties, and dugouts. No clothing was available in stores, and many people dressed in rags.

Other European countries also needed to rebuild after the war. Those in the Soviet bloc established planned economies geared toward heavy industry, and living standards remained low. By contrast, countries in western Europe benefitted from billions of dollars in Marshall Plan aid. The immediate postwar years included material hardship there as well, but these countries' capitalist economies were oriented toward consumption, and living standards began to rise. Furthermore, the construction of standardized mass housing in West Germany, Italy, France, and the United Kingdom alleviated overcrowding. In the Soviet Union, efforts to increase housing and consumer goods did not occur until the 1960s. The Stalinist planned economy, with no free market, was not set up to meet consumer demand. During the war it had become even more closely tied to defense production, which Soviet leaders prioritized anyway due to the Cold War.

The story of one family helps illustrate the hardships people faced in the postwar years. Zinaida Bushueva and her three children lived in a communal apartment in the city of Perm. They shared a room with Zinaida's mother and brother, as well as his wife and two children – nine people in one small room, with three or four people per bed. Perm lies well east of Moscow and had not been bombed in the war, but nonetheless its buildings were dilapidated. Zinaida's apartment block had gone without repairs since the beginning of the war; it had no running water or electricity and part of the roof had caved in. Zinaida could not feed her children on just one ration card, so her twelve-year-old daughter had to work as well. Zinaida patched up secondhand clothes for her children to wear, though one of her daughters later recalled, "We could not go to the theatre, we were too ashamed. All I had to wear was a three-ruble pair of lace-up canvas sandals."[19]

Throughout the country living standards remained abysmally low. In war-torn regions, many people lived in bomb-damaged apartment buildings or even in underground hovels. Some workers protested their miserable conditions. In a letter to authorities, one worker wrote:

So this is what we have come to! This is what you call the state's concern for the material needs of the working people in the Fourth Stalinist Five Year Plan! Now we understand why there are no meetings to discuss these concerns – they might turn into revolts and uprisings. The workers will say: "What did we fight for?"[20]

At several factories in the Urals and Siberia, workers did hold strikes and demonstrations, demanding better living conditions and, in the case of those evacuated there during the war, the right to return to their home cities.[21] Where protests occurred, Soviet officials generally arrested strike leaders while, at least temporarily, improving the food supply to mollify other workers.

Conditions in the countryside were equally grim. So many peasant soldiers had been killed or disabled that collective farms lost almost two-thirds of their able-bodied men. In some villages no young men returned, because they all had either died or settled in cities after the war. Much of the livestock had been lost as well, particularly horses used for transport during the war. Nor had any new tractors been manufactured, given the emphasis on tank production. Peasant women were left to do almost all the agricultural labor, and they had to do it by hand. Harvest yields naturally decreased, while the government directed much of the grain to cities or for export abroad. Peasants therefore went hungry, particularly during the famine of 1946–47, but also throughout the postwar years. One peasant complained, "We work on the collective farm as we used to work for the landlords in the days of serfdom. They drive us to work and they neither feed us nor pay us."[22]

The gender imbalance, especially severe in the countryside, affected the entire society. Three-quarters of those killed in the war were men between the ages of 18 and 45. After the war there were twice as many women as men in this age group. Women therefore continued to fill many factory jobs. Unlike in the United States during the postwar period, there was no propaganda campaign declaring "a woman's place is in the home." Not only was this slogan counter to Soviet gender ideals, but so many men did not return that women's factory labor continued to be essential. This imbalance also meant that a high proportion of women were either widowed or never had the chance to marry. Single motherhood became common, and it further added to women's burdens. Given the economic scarcity of these years, child care and communal dining facilities remained underfunded, providing little help to Soviet women.[23]

Soviet economic struggles were not well known internationally. Censors hid the extent of wartime devastation, not wishing to reveal any weakness during the Cold War. Nor were the consumer sector deficiencies of the planned economy immediately clear. The postwar economic boom in western Europe did not begin until the late 1950s, and only then did the relative affluence of the West become increasingly apparent. What international observers did know was that economic planning had modernized the Soviet Union and equipped the most powerful land army in the world. For many developing countries, therefore, the Soviet system offered an appealing model of rapid industrialization. Thrust onto the world stage by its wartime victory, Soviet socialism might well have attracted more adherents had its leaders carried out the liberalizing reforms for which their people longed.

Political Repression and the Lack of Reform

Many Soviet citizens hoped not only for material well-being but for political liberalization. Given their immense wartime sacrifices, they felt entitled to the government's trust. Surely, they thought, Stalin and the Party elite would reward them for their victory. Instead, during the post-war years, the Stalinist leadership rejected any reforms and continued political repression. Stalin demoted or purged military commanders and other potential rivals. The secret police rounded up suspected collaborators and dissidents. Party control and censorship were tightened. Rather than share the glory of victory, Stalin and the Communist Party claimed it all for themselves, and the Soviet system became more authoritarian than ever.

One reason for people's misplaced hopes was that during the war they had become accustomed to a greater civic role. Soldiers, partisans, medics, civil defense volunteers, armaments workers – all had contributed directly to the war effort. They were defending their homeland, and for once it felt like the country belonged to them. In her poem "1941," Julia Neiman later recalled what the war meant to her generation.

> Those Moscow days ... The avalanche of war ...
> Uncounted losses! Setbacks and defeats!
> Yet, comrades of that year, tell the whole truth:
> Bright as a torch it flamed, that shining year! ...
> The dubious yardsticks that we measured by –
> Forms, questionnaires, long service, rank and age –
> Were cast aside and now we measured true:
> Our yardsticks in that year were valor, faith ...
> For then at last seemed real
> Our pride as citizens, pure-shining pride.[24]

After the war, this pride lingered, and Soviet citizens hoped to have a voice in their country's future.

Veterans felt this sense of entitlement most of all. They had earned enormous prestige from their military victory, and they also had gained greater resourcefulness during the war (see Figure 5.3). In the heat of battle, they had been forced to take the initiative. When they returned home, they were more apt to question the existing system. One officer who had seen Nazi concentration camps wrote Party leaders to demand the end of arbitrary arrests and imprisonments in the Soviet Union.[25] Other veterans called for the disbanding of collective farms.

Figure 5.3 Red Army soldiers welcomed home as heroes after World
War II, Moscow, 1945.

A government report explained that demobilized soldiers were spreading
anti-collectivization sentiments based on what they had seen abroad.
"A lot of comrades have been in Romania, Hungary, Austria, and the
Baltic countries, and they have seen the system of private farming."[26]
More generally, veterans had observed that living standards were higher
in those countries – a fact that contradicted Soviet propaganda and led
them to question the Stalinist system.

Soviet leaders feared that returning veterans would be a destabilizing,
perhaps even revolutionary force. But for several reasons, this challenge to
the regime soon dissipated. First of all, veterans were coopted by the
government. They received accolades, medals, and, in the case of disabled veterans, pensions.[27] During the war, many soldiers had been
recruited into the Communist Party, and they continued to hold this
status after the war. Some were appointed to positions of authority, as
managers of institutes, factories, and collective farms. Not all veterans

had the expertise or experience to merit these posts, but wartime service outweighed everything else.[28] Of course, the transition to civilian life was not easy. The return of 8.5 million demobilized soldiers meant that many initially had difficulty finding jobs and reintegrating into society. A number took refuge in taverns where they could drink with fellow veterans and reminisce about the war. Compared with most of the population, however, veterans held a privileged position.

Second, as noted earlier, the wartime victory seemed to vindicate the Stalinist system. Whatever discontents veterans and other citizens harbored, they were loath to challenge a regime that had guided them through the war. Connected with this sentiment was a third factor – the Cold War and the threat of a new conflict. Given the challenge posed by the United States, it seemed there could be no relaxation of vigilance. Rumors circulated that war was imminent. In 1946, Party officials in Novosibirsk Province reported, "in a number of collective farms after Churchill's speech in Fulton [Missouri] people long expected English and American military moves again the USSR at any time."[29] With the outbreak of the Korean War, residents of the Soviet Far East began to hoard salt, soap, and kerosene in anticipation of the war spreading to Soviet territory. With this siege mentality, most people put off hopes for reform.

Viacheslav Kondratiev later recalled the malaise that overtook him and his fellow veterans after the war:

We had beaten the Fascists and liberated Europe, but we did not return feeling like victors, or rather, we felt that way for a very short time, while we still had hopes for change. When those hopes did not come true, the disappointment and the apathy, which we had at first explained to ourselves as physical exhaustion from the war, seized hold of us completely.[30]

Despite the prestige of returning soldiers, they did not emerge as a political force that challenged the Stalinist regime in the postwar period.

Those who had not fought often found themselves subordinated to veterans after the war. Within the Komsomol, for example, civilian leaders were replaced by returning veterans. While the cohort of young veterans was small due to wartime casualties, this group lorded over the generation that came of age after the war. Postwar youth lived in the shadow of veterans, exhorted to emulate them but unable to replicate their heroic deeds. Consequently, some young people became disaffected with the Soviet system. They continued to march in parades and mouth official slogans, but these performative behaviors masked their growing alienation and resentment. Many of them pursued their own self-interests rather than sacrificing for the collective. Some urban youth also became enamored with Western popular culture and privately scorned socialist realism.[31]

For its part, the Stalinist leadership followed well-established practices – secret police surveillance and the repression of potential rivals – to ensure there were no rebellions.[32] Military leaders were the first to be demoted or purged. Zhukov, who enjoyed huge popularity, was denounced by Politburo members and removed as commander of the Red Army in 1946. He along with other leading generals, such as Rokossovsky and Aleksey Antonov, were transferred to lower-level positions away from Moscow. Their names were also written out of official accounts of the war. Henceforth, history textbooks gave Stalin and the Communist Party sole credit for commanding the military and leading the country.[33]

In 1949, the so-called Leningrad Affair saw the arrest of some 2,000 Party members. Zhdanov, head of the Leningrad Party organization, had died the previous year, and his protégés now fell victim to a purge directed by his rivals within the Politburo. Georgy Malenkov, supported by secret police chief Beria, led the purge that included the execution of Gosplan director Nikolai Voznesensky and his fellow Leningrader Aleksey Kuznetsov. In addition to eliminating political rivals, the Leningrad Affair curbed the autonomy of the country's second largest city, one that had by necessity functioned independently during the siege. Leading technical and cultural figures in Leningrad, in addition to Party functionaries, fell victim to the purge and were arrested. In this manner, Party leaders in the Kremlin reasserted centralized control.[34]

The size of the Gulag ballooned even beyond what it had been in the late 1930s. The total number of prisoners reached roughly 2.5 million by the early 1950s.[35] In addition to victims of political purges, this figure included wartime collaborators and former Soviet POWs suspected of having surrendered too readily during the war. Moreover, it comprised members of national minority groups – particularly Estonians, Latvians, Lithuanians, and western Ukrainians, who had resisted forcible incorporation into the Soviet Union at the end of the war. Soviet labor camps also held German prisoners of war up until 1956. The total number of Gulag prisoners does not even count those national minorities from Crimea and the northern Caucasus (Crimean Tatars, Kalmyks, Chechens, Ingush, Balkars, Karachays, and Meshketian Turks) who were deported to Central Asia. These deportees were not held in formal prison camps, though they were not allowed to return home either. The Soviet state, then, continued to use mass incarcerations and deportations to repress any opposition.

A limited number of Gulag inmates were released at the end of the war. Maria Ilina, formerly the director of a factory in Kiev, had been arrested during the purges in 1937. She served an eight-year term in a Gulag labor camp and was released in 1945. She then went in search of her daughter, Marina, who was only two years old at the time of her mother's arrest. Maria finally found her daughter at an orphanage in Ukraine. Marina, by that time ten years old, later recounted their awkward reunion.

"Someone's come for you," everyone was telling me ... I came out. There was a strange woman there. I did not know what to do ... No one had told me that the woman was my mother. And I didn't know it was her, because I had never seen her, not even in a photograph. She was no longer young ... She did not look like a mother, not as I had pictured her.[36]

Because the government prohibited former Gulag inmates from living in large cities, Maria and Marina could not return to Kiev. Instead they moved to the Ukrainian town of Cherkassy and found a small room in a hostel. They lived there together for the next twelve years, but they never became close. Their story illustrates the emotional scars that Stalinist coercion left even on those who survived the Gulag.

Alongside coercion, the Stalin cult continued to strengthen not only Stalin's personal authority but the power of the Stalinist regime. The adulation of Stalin made it difficult to question anything about the system that he led. The cult assumed even greater proportions in the postwar years. World War II films of this period, such as "The Fall of Berlin" (1950), depicted Stalin as single-handedly leading the country to victory. Soviet propaganda heralded Stalin not only as a great political leader but as a military genius, a brilliant philosopher, and as a benevolent father figure of the Soviet people. In 1949, foreign Communist Party leaders, including Mao Zedong, lavished praise on Stalin at his 70th birthday celebration at the Bolshoi Theater in Moscow.

Not all Soviet citizens believed propaganda glorifying Stalin, but evidence indicates that many did. People blamed shortages on local authorities rather than on Stalin. According to surveillance reports, complaints about rationing were followed by the comment, "Stalin knows nothing about it." Instead, people claimed that every official "is stuffing himself, filling his own belly, sitting around and deceiving Stalin."[37] Those who embraced the image of Stalin as a father figure thought that if only he knew of their suffering, he would help them. Popular anger was instead directed at the local officials who implemented Stalinist policies. Thus, despite the hardships and discontent of the postwar years, there emerged no serious political threat to the Stalinist regime.

Zhdanovism in Culture

Party leaders enacted repressive policies in the cultural sphere as well. During the war, government censors had loosened restrictions, for example allowing the publication of poetry that did not conform to the strictures of socialist realism, as long as it was patriotic. But during the postwar years, Soviet officials exerted stringent control over culture and condemned artists and intellectuals seen as "bourgeois" or pro-Western. As the Politburo's leading ideologist, Zhdanov imposed this cultural clampdown, which continued even after his death in 1948. It became known as Zhdanovism – a cultural policy that enforced rigid ideological and anti-Western standards in the arts, literature, theater, cinema, and music, as well as in academic fields.

Zhdanov initiated this policy by denouncing two prominent writers – poet Anna Akhmatova and satirist Mikhail Zoshchenko. He criticized both for bourgeois, apolitical writings and even derided Akhmatova as a "harlot-nun whose sin is mixed with prayer."[38] Akhmatova and Zoshchenko were expelled from the Union of Soviet Writers, and two literary journals that had published their work were closed. Zhdanov thereby made an example of these two writers whose work was artistically brilliant, but who did not take a political stance in support of the Stalinist regime. Party leaders intended Zhdanov's condemnation as a signal to the entire intelligentsia that apolitical work was impermissible and that once again they had to toe the Party line. For writers and artists this meant adherence to the genre of socialist realism; their work had to illustrate the superiority of Soviet socialism.

Even Alexander Fadeev, head of the Union of Soviet Writers, was harshly criticized under Zhdanovism. His 1945 novel, *The Young Guard*, told the story of a band of young partisans who fought the Germans behind the lines during World War II. Based on a true story, the novel became extremely popular and won the Stalin Prize. But in late 1947, literary critics (following Party leaders' directives) suddenly attacked the work for failing to highlight the role of the Communist Party in leading partisans' resistance. Fadeev had to rewrite the novel to add characters who were Party members – these characters were now portrayed as the true heroes of the war effort.[39]

Zhdanov launched attacks in other realms as well. He criticized leading composers, including Dmitry Shostakovich, for writing dissonant music that reminded one of "a musical gas-chamber." He claimed that such "formalist" music did not reflect "our glorious victories" or convey the ascendancy of Soviet society.[40] Leading filmmakers such as Sergey Eisenstein and Vsevolod Pudovkin similarly came under fire, and theater directors were censured for putting on too many Western plays. Zhdanovism also spread to academic fields. Social scientists were obliged to adhere to a dogmatic version of Marxism-Leninism in their work. All biological research had to conform to Trofim Lysenko's theories on the inheritability of acquired characteristics, as the field of genetics was outlawed as bourgeois science.[41]

Zhdanovism had a strong anti-Western bias. As the Cold War set in, any intellectual or artistic work that seemed to praise or imitate Western culture was viewed as disloyal. Literary critics who had noted positive influences of Western writers were denounced for "kowtowing before the West." The State Museum of Modern Western Art was closed. Soviet artists and intellectuals with connections abroad were condemned for "cosmopolitanism," and their patriotism was questioned. Russian science and the arts were proclaimed to be far superior to anything produced in western Europe or the United States. According to the logic of Zhdanovism, the preeminence of Russian and Soviet culture confirmed the supremacy of Soviet socialism. Anyone enamored with Western bourgeois culture was a traitor.

In some ways, Zhdanovism paralleled McCarthyism in the United States. In both countries, Cold War tensions led to domestic ideological crackdowns. The witch hunts conducted by Senator Joseph McCarthy and others sought to root out communists within the US government and amongst the intellectual and cultural clite. In the American case, accusations of treason were directed specifically at alleged Communist Party members and sympathizers. Zhdanovism, by contrast, cast a wider net, attacking any Western influences in the work of writers, artists, and other members of the intelligentsia. In both countries, these campaigns impinged on intellectual and cultural freedoms, though much more so in the Soviet case where both the restrictions and penalties were far greater.

Another effect of Zhdanovism was to further isolate the Soviet Union from the outside world. Soviet censors already severely limited the flow of information from other countries. Now Western contacts or travel exposed intellectuals to charges of cosmopolitanism and political treason. The Soviet press warned, "In developing subversive activity against the Soviet Union now, the predatory imperialists are trying to make use of routed anti-Soviet groups, morally corrupt people, the bearers of survivals of capitalist ideology and morality."[42] Soviet citizens interested in foreign culture could be branded corrupt agents of American imperialism. In western Europe during the postwar years, American popular culture and commercial practices exerted enormous influence, but not in the Soviet Union. While some young people in Soviet cities became infatuated with American fashions and jazz music, their interests remained part of an underground subculture, one that was repressed throughout the Stalinist era.[43]

In cultural matters the postwar years saw an ideological crackdown that reversed the relative tolerance of the war years. The Soviet government ended its wartime accommodation with the Orthodox Church, and it closed a number of churches and monasteries.[44] Zhdanov and other officials reimposed a strict Party line and harshly condemned artists and intellectuals with connections to Western culture. Russian and Soviet science and literature were deemed superior, and any praise or emulation of the West was seen as unpatriotic. While Zhdanovism mainly affected the country's intellectual and cultural elite, it further contributed to the repressive atmosphere of the postwar Stalinist period. The reading public no longer had access to the classics of Western literature, nor were foreign films or plays presented in the Soviet Union. To some degree, the xenophobia of Zhdanovism was a response to the Cold War menace posed by the United States, as any foreign threat seemed especially grave in the aftermath of the Nazi invasion. But more broadly it represented a hardening of the Stalinist system – a system of control that demanded the all-embracing loyalty of its citizens.

The Doctor's Plot and Stalin's Death

Popular anti-Semitism had long existed in the Russian empire and Soviet Union, and during the war it actually intensified in occupied regions subjected to Nazi propaganda. Officially, however, the Soviet government had always opposed anti-Semitism. And because it had defeated Germany and liberated Nazi death camps in Poland, the Soviet Union appeared to be the protector of Jews. After the war, however, Soviet leaders refused to recognize Jewish losses during the Holocaust as distinct from the losses suffered by the country as a whole. Moreover, the Soviet government disbanded the Jewish Anti-Fascist Committee, and the secret police killed the committee's leader Solomon Mikhoels in 1948. Simultaneously the anti-cosmopolitan campaign of Zhdanovism targeted many Jewish intellectuals for their ties with the West.

A key event behind the rise of Stalinist anti-Semitism was the founding of the state of Israel in 1948. The Soviet government did not initially oppose Israel's formation, viewing it as a way to lessen British control in the Middle East. But as it became clear that Israel was aligned more with the United States than the Soviet Union, the Stalinist leadership began to see it as a Cold War enemy. Now that there was a Jewish homeland outside the Soviet Union, Party leaders called into question the loyalty

Figure 5.4 Thousands of Soviet Jews greet Israeli ambassador Golda
Meir (circled) outside a Moscow synagogue on Rosh Hashanah, 1948.

of Soviet Jews. Much as had been true for ethnic Germans, Poles,
Latvians, and so forth prior to World War II, Jews as a diaspora nationality were viewed as potential traitors – their loyalty might be to Israel
instead of to the Soviet government.[45]

Party leaders' suspicions were exacerbated by the arrival of Golda Meir
in the autumn of 1948 as the first Israeli ambassador to Moscow. Meir
received an enthusiastic reception from Soviet Jews, including thousands
who greeted her at a Moscow synagogue on Rosh Hashanah (see
Figure 5.4). Stalin apparently took this occurrence as evidence of Jews'
disloyalty, and he ordered repressive measures. That year the Soviet
government closed the Moscow State Jewish Theater. It closed Yiddish
newspapers, schools, and libraries as well. A number of Jewish writers and
critics were labelled unpatriotic – most lost their jobs, and several were
even arrested. In 1949, state institutions including the secret police began
to purge Jews from their ranks. Jews were likewise expelled from many
scientific institutions and editorial boards.[46]

The climax of Stalinist anti-Semitism was the so-called Doctor's Plot.
In January 1953, the leading Soviet newspaper (*Pravda*) announced the

arrest of nine "saboteur doctors," six of whom were Jewish. The arrested doctors were among the country's leading physicians and worked at the Kremlin hospital. The article accused them of conspiring to poison Party and military leaders, blaming them for the deaths of Zhdanov, Shcherbakov, and several others. It also claimed they worked for a "Jewish bourgeois-nationalist organization" (also referred to as a "Zionist spy organization") formed by American intelligence agencies. Echoing Cold War fears, the article concluded that the United States and the United Kingdom were preparing for a new world war by sending spies into the country and attempting to create a subversive fifth column. It called on Soviet citizens to heighten their vigilance.

The announcement of this alleged plot sparked a wave of popular anti-Semitism across the country. One resident of Novocherkassk, for example, wrote to *Pravda*: "Hearing the news on the radio, I curse the vile murderers of Comrades Zhdanov and Shcherbakov. The vermin must be hanged." A worker in Moscow wrote, "It has long been necessary to chase the Jews out of the medical institutes, pharmacies, hospitals … These places are controlled by Jews."[47] Rumors began to spread that Jewish doctors were killing babies and poisoning patients. Visits to clinics and pharmacies suddenly declined. Soon more doctors were accused of crimes and arrested. One of those arrested, the prominent pathologist Yakov Rapoport, later recounted that the entire episode was a harrowing time.[48] The Doctor's Plot, however, came to an abrupt end when Stalin died in early March 1953. A decree exonerated the doctors who had been arrested, and they were released.

Perhaps fittingly, Stalin's persecution of doctors may have hastened his demise. On March 1, he suffered a stroke. His bodyguards found him on the floor of his dacha that evening, conscious but unable to speak. They called Malenkov and Beria, who arrived to check on him. But Beria pronounced that nothing was wrong and that Stalin should be left alone to rest. He and Malenkov may have been afraid to summon medical care, fearful that Stalin might hold them accountable for any treatment provided by untrustworthy doctors. Alternatively, Beria may have wished for Stalin to die, as he and other leaders feared that Stalin might launch a new purge and turn on them. Only the following evening, after a long delay, were physicians called to examine Stalin. They diagnosed a cerebral hemorrhage, but by then there was nothing they could do to save him. He died three days later on March 5, 1953. The Stalinist era came to an end.

In sum, the postwar years saw the reinforcement of the Stalinist system. Despite wartime losses and the population's hopes for liberalization, the Stalinist leadership tightened its control and prioritized heavy industry in reconstruction efforts. Victory in the war seemed to vindicate the Stalinist system and militated against any reforms. It also heightened the Soviet Union's international prestige and left it in control of eastern Europe, where it installed Communist governments. Following the Communist Revolution in China, the Soviet Union became the leader of an entire coalition of Communist countries that challenged the liberal democratic order. But this challenge also triggered the Cold War – the rivalry between the Soviet Union and United States for world domination. The prospect of war with the United States prompted the Stalinist regime to demand continued vigilance and sacrifice on the part of the population. For the Soviet people, the Stalinist era ended in the same repressive atmosphere with which it had begun.

Conclusion

The Soviet media did not immediately report Stalin's death. To prepare the populace, Radio Moscow played solemn classical music for several hours. Finally, in the early morning of March 6, broadcaster Yuri Levitan announced that the country's leader had died. When the Soviet people heard of Stalin's death, thousands of them wept. Many were utterly distraught, even some who had lost family members during dekulakization and the purges. The entire country seemed to be in mourning. How was it possible that people grieved the death of Stalin? Why did they shed tears over one of the bloodiest dictators in all human history?

First, we should note that not all people grieved. In fact, some people secretly rejoiced at Stalin's death. They understood that Stalin had been responsible for countless arrests and executions, and, while they dared not say so publicly, they were grateful that he was gone. Second, many people cried not so much from grief as from shock. For decades, Soviet propaganda had deified Stalin, and when he died, it was difficult to comprehend that he had been mortal after all. As poet Evgeny Evtushenko later remembered, "I found it almost impossible to imagine him dead, so much had he been an indispensable part of life." Third, along with shock many people felt fear. After such a momentous event, they did not know who might lead the country and what might happen next. Evtushenko went on, "Trained to believe that they were all in Stalin's care, people were lost and bewildered without him. All Russia wept. And so did I. We wept sincerely, tears of grief – and perhaps tears of fear for the future."[1]

There were those who felt genuine sorrow at Stalin's death. Soviet propaganda had portrayed him as a father figure, the protector of his people. This image was reinforced by the fact that Stalin had led the country through the war. During the darkest days of the Nazi invasion and occupation, Stalin had served as the people's leader, and he had guided them to victory. The general public did not know that Stalin's purges had greatly weakened the Red Army, or that his failures at the beginning of the war had left the country extremely vulnerable to surprise attack. Nor were they necessarily fully aware of the death and suffering caused by collectivization, famines, the mass operations, the deportation of nationalities, and so forth. It was only later that they learned the full extent of Stalin's brutality.

At the Twentieth Party Congress in 1956, the country's new leader Nikita Khrushchev confronted Stalin's crimes. In a dramatic move on the last day of the congress, Khrushchev called the delegates back to the meeting hall at midnight and delivered the so-called secret speech. He began by criticizing the Stalin cult, pointing out that glorifying one individual violated Marxist-Leninist principles. He then accused Stalin of imprisoning and executing thousands of innocent Communists during the Great Purges. He went on to cite numerous other violations of Soviet legality as well. Khrushchev also disparaged Stalin's leadership during World War II. He pointed out that Stalin did not put troops on alert despite warnings that invasion was imminent, and that his purge of the Soviet officer corps had deprived the military of leading commanders. When Khrushchev finished his speech four hours later, delegates were dumbfounded. After years of hearing nothing but adulation for Stalin, Khrushchev's sweeping condemnation of "the great leader" left them stunned.

Khrushchev's speech was secret only in that it was not published in the Soviet Union. But Party members around the country were required to read and discuss the speech. Once they knew about Stalin's misdeeds, word spread quickly to informed people throughout the population. In addition, Khrushchev took other measures to downgrade Stalin's legacy. He subsequently ordered that Stalin statues be taken down and that Stalingrad be renamed Volgograd. He had Stalin's body removed from Lenin's mausoleum and buried beside the Kremlin wall. He also authorized the publication of Alexander Solzhenitsyn's novella, *One Day in the Life of Ivan Denisovich*, which describes the suffering of Gulag inmates. His de-Stalinization campaign, however, provoked resistance from some Party leaders. He initially overrode this opposition, but after several other controversial missteps in foreign and domestic policy, Khrushchev was ousted from power in 1964. His successor, Leonid Brezhnev, was silent about Stalin's crimes, and the de-Stalinization campaign came to an end. Despite his fall, Khrushchev had put a stop to the Stalin cult and the practice of using the secret police to arrest Party members. Brezhnev and subsequent Soviet leaders never returned to Stalinist methods of state violence. To this extent, Khrushchev's de-Stalinization campaign was a success.

Equally significant, however, were aspects of Stalinism that Khrushchev did not criticize. He did not condemn the violence of dekulakization, which he had supported. He made no mention of the horrendous famine of 1932–33 that resulted from collectivization, and he reinforced collective farms rather than disbanding them. Nor did he criticize the Soviet planned economy and Stalinist industrialization, things in which he and other leaders took pride. The Soviet economy continued to be entirely controlled by the government, with no free market or private property. And while Khrushchev freed more than half of all Gulag inmates, he did not close Gulag labor camps. The secret police likewise continued to function and suppress dissent, even if it no longer arrested Party members. All these elements of Stalinism, then, outlived Stalin and continued as essential components of the Soviet system. These continuities highlight the ways in which Stalinism went beyond Stalin himself. Stalinism was more than Stalin's personal dictatorship – it was an entire system of centralized control and coercive modernization.

In explaining Stalinism, I have emphasized three factors: the need to modernize; practices of social intervention and state violence; and the ideological worldview of the Stalinist leadership. In the early twentieth century, Russia was an underdeveloped country that could not compete with industrialized nations. Lacking the factories necessary to mass-produce guns, artillery, and warships, Russia was unable to match the military power of western European countries or Japan, which defeated it in the Russo-Japanese War. Russia's catastrophic losses to the German army during World War I further discredited the tsarist government and led to its overthrow in 1917. Not coincidentally, the group that ultimately took power – the Bolsheviks/Communists – were dedicated to modernizing the country. The fact that they promised to carry out industrialization in the name of the working class (rather than through its exploitation) bolstered their support.

For the Russian intelligentsia, modernization meant not only industrialization, but also raising the population's cultural level. At the time of the October Revolution, the Russian empire was still an overwhelmingly peasant society with high rates of illiteracy, infectious disease, and infant mortality. Educated Russians were ashamed of their country's backwardness and hoped to improve the lives of peasants and workers. Many were drawn to Marxism as an ideology that promised revolutionary transformation and an alternative to the class antagonism of capitalist industrialization. But even non-Marxist professionals saw it as their duty to modernize the country and uplift the masses. In fact, many teachers, doctors, agronomists, and engineers helped develop Soviet programs for education, hygiene, and economic advancement. As in other late-developing countries, these professionals were willing to work with the state, given the absence of strong civic organizations.

Practices of social intervention provided the means to pursue social transformation. These practices did not originate in the Soviet Union, but rather in nineteenth-century western Europe, where reformers first introduced social work, housing inspections, maternal care, and other welfare programs to remake and improve society. During World War I, state officials increasingly took charge of these programs to safeguard their countries' "military manpower." The war also prompted more coercive state intervention. Combatant countries across Europe established government economic controls, surveillance systems, and internment camps. In Russia, the tsarist government used similar means, including internments and deportations to counter perceived security risks.

The Soviet state was born at this moment of war, and these interventionist practices served as the building blocks of the Soviet system. Following the Provisional Government's model, the new Soviet government established commissariats of health, labor, and welfare. State agencies ran the economy, nationalizing factories and controlling grain supplies. Surveillance systems, first established during World War I, were made permanent by Soviet leaders and placed under the newly-founded secret police. Concentration camps, used by both sides during the Civil War, also became a permanent part of the Soviet system under the Gulag administration. What we call "Stalinist" forms of intervention and state violence, then, did not derive from Stalin or from socialist ideology but rather from wartime practices. Whereas other countries stepped back from these practices in peacetime, the Soviet government institutionalized them as permanent features of governance.

Soviet leaders subsequently used these means to pursue their ideological goals. Here Marxist ideology played a role, for it shaped Communist leaders' objectives and worldview. The Communists sought to push their country along a historical timeline toward socialism and communism. Marxism provided them with no precise roadmap of how to create a socialist society. After Stalin emerged as the Party's leader in 1928, he launched a military-style campaign of collectivization and industrialization. Using a system of social cataloguing, he and his fellow leaders ordered the deportation of "kulaks" and the establishment of collective farms. They simultaneously created the equivalent of a wartime economy, with government control of resources and emphasis on heavy industry. The Stalinist leadership thus employed wartime practices to pursue ideological ends.

By 1934, Party leaders claimed they had built the foundations of socialism. Their version of socialism was based on control and coercion –

the very antitheses of socialist ideals such as liberation and equality. But for them, socialism meant the elimination of class enemies and the creation of a non-capitalist economy. Collectivization and the planned economy had, in their view, ushered in a new phase of human history. Their sense of progress was reinforced by a rapid increase in industrial production, allowing the Soviet Union to catch up to more advanced countries. The new economic base dictated changes to the superstructure as well – a new constitution, socialist realism in culture, and a shift in family policy. Paradoxically, the purported attainment of socialism also triggered additional state violence. With class enemies vanquished, Stalin sought to eliminate hidden enemies and potential fifth-columnists in preparation for war, which grew closer with the German and Japanese aggression of the late 1930s. Stalinist purges, the mass operations, and the national operations led to the arrests of more than 1.5 million people, almost half of whom were executed.

Instead of preparing the country for World War II, Stalinist state violence greatly weakened it. Among those incarcerated or executed were thousands of Party administrators and military officers. Without experienced commanders, the Red Army suffered disastrous defeats at the outset of the war. Only due to great sacrifices on the part of Soviet soldiers and citizens was the country able to rally and win the war over Nazi Germany. Though it had barely survived, the Stalinist regime became even more entrenched after the war. However unjustly, the wartime victory seemed to vindicate the Stalinist system. And despite the hopes of the population, Stalin and the Soviet government undertook no liberalization. In fact, given Cold War tensions with the United States, Party leaders demanded further vigilance and sacrifice.

As mentioned earlier, most fundamental features of Stalinism outlived Stalin. While bloody purges and the Stalin cult ended under Khrushchev, the planned economy, collective farms, the secret police, the Gulag, and the Party's monopoly on power all continued. Throughout the Cold War era, this system of centralized state control mobilized resources for national defense. But it proved ill-suited to the production of consumer goods and technological innovation. The first half of the twentieth century – the historical moment in which the Stalinist system took shape – had been an era of mass warfare and heavy industry. But the world fundamentally changed in the second half of the century. Military power now depended on nuclear missiles rather than vast armies. Economic growth shifted from iron and steel to technology and the service sector. The rigidity of the planned economy and the secrecy of the Stalinist system did not allow the Soviet economy to adapt to the postindustrial age.

Beginning in 1985, Mikhail Gorbachev tried to reform the Soviet system through economic decentralization, democratization, and the lifting of censorship. This liberalization allowed more open discussion of the Stalinist era within the Soviet Union. Initially, people limited criticism to the Stalin cult, as had been the case in the Khrushchev period. Soon, however, historians and political commentators revealed the full extent of Stalinist state violence, from dekulakization to the mass operations and national deportations. Very quickly these revelations undercut the legitimacy of the Communist Party and the Soviet system as a whole. Along with rising economic discontent and nationality unrest, this discrediting of the system led the population to reject it, and in 1991 it collapsed entirely.

The Soviet Union never escaped the stain of Stalinism. Even today Russians still debate its meaning. In recent years, Stalin's popularity among Russians has increased, as some voice nostalgia for a time when their country was more powerful.[2] Other Russian citizens, however, vehemently condemn Stalinism and strive to raise awareness of the suffering it caused. Decades after Khrushchev first proposed a monument to the victims of Stalinism, the "Wall of Grief" memorial was unveiled in Moscow in 2017. At the ceremony, President Vladimir Putin, failing to mention Stalin by name, called political repression "a tragedy for all our people," and stated, "Our duty is to not let it slip into oblivion."[3] The Stalinist era was a momentous period for the Soviet Union. In the space of twenty-five years, this underdeveloped, agrarian country was transformed into an industrial superpower that defeated Nazi Germany and rivaled the United States for world domination. But the Stalinist leadership accomplished this transformation at the cost of millions of lives shattered and lost. Only by remembering this human cost can we fully grasp the painful legacy of Stalinism.

Notes

Introduction

1. For readers who wish to know more about Stalin's personal role, there are many biographies of him, including Isaac Deutscher, *Stalin: A Political Biography*, 2nd edn (New York, NY, 1967); Adam Ulam, *Stalin: The Man and His Era* (New York, NY, 1973); Dmitrii Volkogonov, *Stalin: Triumph and Tragedy* (New York, NY, 1988); Robert H. McNeal, *Stalin: Man and Ruler* (New York, NY, 1988); Robert Service, *Stalin, A Biography* (Cambridge, MA, 2004); Hiroaki Kuromiya, *Stalin* (New York, NY, 2005); Kevin McDermott, *Stalin* (New York, NY, 2006); Sarah Davies and James Harris, *Stalin, A New History* (Cambridge, UK, 2005); Oleg V. Khlevniuk, *Stalin: New Biography of a Dictator* (New Haven, CT, 2015); Stephen Kotkin, *Stalin: Waiting for Hitler, 1929–1941* (New York, NY, 2017).
2. Richard Pipes stresses the "unmistakable affinities" between tsarist and Soviet rule; Pipes, *A Concise History of the Russian Revolution* (New York, NY, 1996), pp. 397–99.
3. Theodore von Laue, *Why Lenin? Why Stalin? Why Gorbachev? The Rise and Fall of the Soviet System* (New York, NY, 1993).
4. Laura Engelstein, "Combined Underdevelopment: Discipline and the Law in Imperial and Soviet Russia," *American Historical Review* 98: 2 (April 1993), p. 344.
5. For an explanation of Stalinism focused on ideology, see Martin Malia, *The Soviet Tragedy: A History of Socialism in Russia, 1917–1991* (New York, NY, 1994). On different historical interpretations of Stalinism, see Chris Ward, *Stalin's Russia* (London, UK, 1993).
6. See Erik van Ree, *The Political Thought of Joseph Stalin* (New York, NY, 2002).
7. On "state-sponsored evolutionism" and Soviet nationality policies, see Francine Hirsch, *Empire of Nations: Ethnographic Knowledge and the Making of the Soviet Union* (Ithaca, NY, 2005), pp. 7–8.
8. For further discussion, see David L. Hoffmann, *Cultivating the Masses: Modern State Practices and Soviet Socialism, 1914–1939* (Ithaca, NY, 2011), pp. 19–29.
9. Peter Holquist, "'Information is the Alpha and Omega of Our Work': Bolshevik Surveillance in its Pan-European Context," *The Journal of Modern History* 69: 3 (1997).

10. Eric Lohr, *Nationalizing the Russian Empire: The Campaign against Enemy Aliens during World War I* (Cambridge, MA, 2003), p. 178.

1 Prelude to Stalinism

1. Alexis de Tocqueville, *Democracy in America*, vol. 1 (New York, NY, 1954), p. 452.
2. Andreas Kappeler, *The Russian Empire: A Multi-Ethnic History* (Oklahoma City, OK, 2001).
3. Geoffrey Hosking, *Russia: People and Empire, 1552–1917* (Cambridge, MA, 1998); Jane Burbank, Mark von Hagen, and Anatoly Remnev, eds., *Russian Empire: Space, People, Power, 1700–1917* (Bloomington, IN, 2007).
4. Christine Worobec, *Peasant Russia: Family and Community in the Post-Emancipation Period* (Princeton, NJ, 1991); Esther Kingston-Mann and Timothy Mixter, eds., *Peasant Economy, Culture, and Politics of European Russia* (Princeton, NJ, 1991).
5. Alfred Rieber, *Merchants and Entrepreneurs in Imperial Russia* (Oxford, UK, 1982).
6. Daniel Kaiser, ed., *The Workers' Revolution in Russia, 1917* (Cambridge, UK, 1987); Diane Koenker, *Moscow Workers and the 1917 Revolution* (Princeton, NJ, 1981); Reginald Zelnik, *A Radical Worker in Tsarist Russia* (Stanford, CA, 1986); Charters Wynn, *Workers, Strikes, and Pogroms: The Donbass-Dnepr Bend in Late Imperial Russia* (Princeton, NJ, 1992); Heather Hogan, *Forging Revolution: Metalworkers, Managers, and the State in St. Petersburg, 1905–1914* (Bloomington, IN, 1993).
7. Robert K. Massie, *Nicholas and Alexandra* (New York, NY, 1967), p. 43.
8. Ben Eklof, *Russian Peasant Schools: Officialdom, Village Culture, and Popular Pedagogy, 1861–1914* (Berkeley, CA, 1986).
9. On professionals in late imperial Russia, see Christine Ruane, *Gender, Class, and the Professionalization of Russian City Teachers, 1860–1914* (Pittsburgh, PA, 1994); Nancy Frieden, *Russian Physicians in an Era of Reform and Revolution* (Princeton, NJ, 1981); Joseph Bradley, *Muzhik and Muscovite: Urbanization in Late Imperial Russia* (Berkeley, CA, 1985); Joan Neuberger, *Hooliganism: Crime, Culture, and Power in St. Petersburg, 1900–1914* (Berkeley, CA, 1993); Yanni Kotsonis, *Making Peasants Backwards: Managing Populations in Russian Agricultural Cooperatives* (New York, NY, 1999).
10. Michael David-Fox, "The Intelligentsia, the Masses, and the West," *Crossing Borders: Modernity, Ideology, and Culture in Russia and the Soviet Union* (Pittsburgh, PA, 2015). See also Daniel Beer, *Renovating Russia: The Human Sciences and the Fate of Liberal Modernity, 1880–1930* (Ithaca, NY, 2008); Kenneth Pinnow, *Lost to the Collective: Suicide and the Promise of Soviet Socialism, 1921–1929* (Ithaca, NY, 2010).
11. Massie, *Nicholas and Alexandra*, p. 16.
12. Vladimir Ilyich Lenin, "Imperialism, the Highest Stage of Capitalism," *The Lenin Anthology*, ed. Robert C. Tucker (New York, NY, 1975).
13. For a colorful biography focused on Stalin's early life, see Simon Sebag Montefiore, *Young Stalin* (New York, NY, 2007).

14. Abraham Ascher, *The Revolution of 1905: Russia in Disarray* (Stanford, CA, 1988).
15. As quoted in Simon Sebag Montefiore, *The Romanovs, 1613–1918* (New York, NY, 2016), p. 547.
16. Susan Gross Solomon, "The Expert and the State in Russian Public Health: Continuities and Changes Across the Revolutionary Divide," in Dorothy Porter (ed.), *The History of Public Health and the Modern State* (Amsterdam, NL, 1994); John Hutchinson, *Politics and Public Health in Revolutionary Russia, 1890–1918* (Baltimore, MD, 1990).
17. Peter Gatrell, *A Whole Empire Walking: Refugees in Russia during World War I* (Bloomington, IN, 2005).
18. Lewis H. Siegelbaum, *The Politics of Industrial Mobilization in Russia, 1914–1917: A Study of the War-Industries Committees* (London, UK, 1983).
19. Peter Holquist, *Making War, Forging Revolution: Russia's Continuum of Crisis, 1914–1921* (Cambridge, MA, 2002).
20. Hubertus Jahn, *Patriotic Culture in Russia during World War I* (Ithaca, NY, 1995). For more on the rise of mass politics in Russia, see Joshua Sanborn, *Drafting the Russian Nation: Military Conscription, Total War, and Mass Politics, 1905–1925* (DeKalb, IL, 2003).
21. Eric Lohr, *Nationalizing the Russian Empire: The Campaign against Enemy Aliens during World War I* (Cambridge, MA, 2003), p. 178.
22. Lohr, *Nationalizing the Russian Empire*, pp. 137–39; Sanborn, *Drafting the Russian Nation*, pp. 119–21.
23. Scott Seregny, "Zemstvos, Peasants, and Citizenship: The Russian Adult Education Movement and World War I," *Slavic Review* 59: 2 (Summer 2000).
24. Allan K. Wildman, *The End of the Russian Imperial Army: The Old Army and the Soldiers' Revolt (March–April 1917)* (Princeton, NJ, 1979).
25. Joshua Sanborn, *Imperial Apocalypse: The Great War and the Destruction of the Russian Empire* (Oxford, UK, 2014).
26. For a detailed description of the February Revolution, see Rex Wade, *The Russian Revolution, 1917*, 2nd edn (New York, NY, 2005), Chapter 2; Tsuyoshi Hasegawa, *The February Revolution, Petrograd, 1917* (Seattle, WA, 1981).
27. Leopold Haimson, "The Problem of Social Stability in Urban Russia, 1905–1917," *Slavic Review* 23: 4 (December 1964).
28. For further discussion, see William Rosenberg, *Liberals in the Russian Revolution* (Princeton, NJ, 1974).
29. Allan K. Wildman, *The End of the Russian Imperial Army: The Road to Soviet Power and Peace* (Princeton, NJ, 1987).
30. Orlando Figes and Boris Kolonitskii, *Interpreting the Russian Revolution: The Language and Symbols of 1917* (New Haven, CT, 1999).
31. S. A. Smith, *Russia in Revolution* (Oxford, UK, 2017).
32. For more on how people experienced these events, see Mark Steinberg, *The Russian Revolution, 1905–1917* (Oxford, UK, 2017). On the memory of the October Revolution, see Frederick Corney, *Telling October: Memory and the Making of the Bolshevik Revolution* (Ithaca, NY, 2004).

33. John Reed, *Ten Days that Shook the World* (New York, NY, 1977), p. 129.

34. Laura Engelstein, *Russia in Flames: War, Revolution, Civil War, 1914–1921* (Oxford, UK, 2017).

35. Alexander Rabinowitch, *The Bolsheviks in Power* (Bloomington, IN, 2007).

36. Zinaida Zhemchuzhnaia, "The Road to Exile," in Sheila Fitzpatrick and Yuri Slezkine (eds.), *In the Shadow of Revolution: Life Stories of Russian Women from 1917 to the Second World War* (Princeton, NJ, 2000), pp. 89–91.

37. Boris Pasternak, *Doctor Zhivago*, trans. Max Hayward and Manya Harari (London, UK, 1958), p. 448.

38. On the military history of the Civil War, see Evan Mawdsley, *The Russian Civil War* (Boston, MA, 1987).

39. Francesco Benvenuti, *The Bolsheviks and the Red Army, 1918–1922*, trans. Christopher Woodall (Cambridge, UK, 1988).

40. Holquist, *Making War*, Chapter 7.

41. George Leggett, *The Cheka: Lenin's Political Police* (New York, NY, 1981), pp. 109–10.

42. Peter Holquist, "To Count, to Extract, to Exterminate: Population Statistics in Late Imperial and Soviet Russia," in Ronald Grigor Suny and Terry Martin (eds.), *A State of Nations* (Oxford, UK, 2001), p. 131.

43. Between 1918 and 1920, Soviet officials registered 5 million typhus cases (with estimated totals running much higher), and cholera, typhoid, and malaria epidemics occurred as well; Tricia Starks, *The Body Soviet: Propaganda, Hygiene, and the Revolutionary State* (Madison, WI, 2008), pp. 48–49. See also Susan Gross Solomon and John Hutchinson, eds., *Health and Society in Revolutionary Russia* (Bloomington, IN, 1993).

44. Diane P. Koenker, *Republic of Labor: Russian Printers and Soviet Socialism, 1918–1930* (Ithaca, NY, 2005).

45. For more on grain procurements and food policy, see Lars Lih, *Bread and Authority in Russia, 1914–1921* (Berkeley, CA, 1990).

46. On requisitioning and rationing, see Donald J. Raleigh, *Experiencing Russia's Civil War: Politics, Society, and Revolutionary Culture in Saratov, 1917–1922* (Princeton, NJ, 2002), Chapter 9.

47. As quoted in Ronald Grigor Suny, *The Soviet Experiment: Russia, the USSR, and the Successor States* (Oxford, UK, 1998), p. 70.

48. Mark von Hagen, *Soldiers in the Proletarian Dictatorship: The Red Army and the Soviet Socialist State, 1917–1930* (Ithaca, NY, 1990).

49. For more on the peasantry during the Civil War, see Aaron Retish, *Russia's Peasants in Revolution and Civil War* (Cambridge, UK, 2008); Orlando Figes, *Peasant Russia, Civil War* (Oxford, UK, 1989); Sarah Babcock, *Politics and the People in Revolutionary Russia: A Provincial History* (New York, NY, 2007).

50. Evan Mawdsley, *The Russian Civil War* (Boston, MA, 1987); Diane Koenker, William Rosenberg, and Ronald Grigor Suny, eds., *Party, State, and Society in the Russian Civil War* (Bloomington, IN, 1989).

51. Alan Ball, *And Now My Soul Has Hardened: Abandoned Children in Soviet Russia, 1918–1930* (Berkeley, CA, 1994).

52. Paul Avrich, *Kronstadt, 1921* (New York, NY, 1970).

53. V. I. Lenin, "Political Report of the Central Committee to the Eleventh Party Congress," (1922) *Collected Works* (Moscow, 1966), xxxiii, p. 282, as cited in Sheila Fitzpatrick, *The Russian Revolution*, 3rd edn (Oxford, UK, 1994), p. 97.
54. On the institutions of censorship, see Arlen V. Blium, *Za kulisami "ministerstva pravdy": Tainaia istoriia sovetskoi tzenzury 1917–1929* (St. Petersburg, 1994).
55. G. M. Ivanova, *Labor Camp Socialism: The Gulag in the Soviet Totalitarian System* (Armonk, NY, 2000).
56. Alexander Marshall, "Turkfront: Frunze and the Development of Soviet Counter-Insurgency in Central Asia," in Tom Everett-Heath (ed.), *Central Asia: Aspects of Transition* (London, UK, 2003).
57. Stephen G. Wheatcroft, "Agency and Terror: Evdokimov and Mass Killing in Stalin's Great Terror," *Australian Journal of Politics and History* 53: 1 (2007), pp. 23–32.
58. Terry Martin, *The Affirmative Action Empire* (Ithaca, NY, 2001).
59. As quoted in Alexei Yurchak, "Bodies of Lenin: The Hidden Science of Communist Sovereignty," *Representations* 129: 1 (Winter 2015), p. 127.
60. Nina Tumarkin, *Lenin Lives! The Lenin Cult in Soviet Russia* (Cambridge, MA, 1997).
61. Stephen F. Cohen, *Bukharin and the Bolshevik Revolution* (Oxford, UK, 1980).
62. William Chase, *Workers, Society, and the Soviet State: Labor and Life in Moscow, 1918–1929* (Urbana, IL, 1987).
63. Anne Gorsuch, *Youth in Revolutionary Russia: Enthusiasts, Bohemians, Delinquents* (Bloomington, IN, 2000). See also Catriona Kelly, *Children's World: Growing Up in Russia, 1890–1991* (New Haven, CT, 2007).
64. As quoted in Jonathan Haslam, *Russia's Cold War: From the October Revolution to the Fall of the Wall* (New Haven, CT, 2011), p. 3.
65. John B. Hatch, "The 'Lenin Levy' and the Social Origins of Stalinism," *Slavic Review* 48: 4 (December 1989).
66. Olga Velikanova, *Popular Perceptions of Soviet Politics in the 1920s* (New York, NY, 2013), pp. 45–81.
67. S. A. Smith, *A Road is Made: Communism in Shanghai, 1920–1927* (Honolulu, HI, 2000); Martin Wilbur and Julie Lien-Ying How, *Missionaries of Revolution: Soviet Advisers and Nationalist China, 1920–1927* (Cambridge, MA, 1989).
68. Alec Nove, *An Economic History of the USSR* (New York, NY, 1969).
69. For further discussion, see Alexander Ehrlich, *The Soviet Industrialization Debate, 1924–1928* (Cambridge, MA, 1960).

2 Building Socialism (1928–1933)

1. Maurice Hindus, *Red Bread: Collectivization in a Russian Village* (Bloomington, IN, 1988).
2. David L. Hoffmann, "Land, Freedom, and Discontent: Russian Peasants of the Central Industrial Region Prior to Collectivization," *Europe-Asia Studies* 46: 4 (1994).

3. R.W. Davies, *The Socialist Offensive: The Collectivization of Soviet Agriculture, 1929–1930* (Cambridge, MA, 1980), pp. 399–408.
4. Lynne Viola, *The Unknown Gulag* (Oxford, UK, 2009), pp. 36–37. See also James Hughes, *Stalinism in a Russian Province: A Study of Collectivization and Dekulakization in Siberia* (London, UK, 1996).
5. *Sotsialisticheskoe sel'skoe khoziaistvo SSSR* (Moscow, 1939), p. 42.
6. Iosif V. Stalin, *Sochineniia*, vol. 12 (Moscow, 1952), p. 170.
7. As quoted in Viola, p. 34.
8. As quoted in Viola, p. 34. See also Tracy McDonald, *Face to the Village: The Riazan Countryside Under Soviet Rule, 1921–1930* (Toronto, 2011), Chapter 10.
9. R. W. Davies and S. G. Wheatcroft, *The Years of Hunger* (New York, NY, 2004), p. 492; Viola, pp. 30–32.
10. For more on the Gulag, see Oleg Khlevniuk, *The History of the Gulag: From Collectivization to the Great Terror*, trans. Vadim A. Staklo (New Haven, CT, 2004); Michael Jakobson, *Origins of the Gulag: The Soviet Prison Camp System, 1917–1934* (Lexington, KY, 1993).
11. For further discussion of the (often lethal) exploitation of prisoners' labor in the Gulag, see Golfo Alexopoulos, *Illness and Inhumanity in Stalin's Gulag* (New Haven, CT, 2017).
12. Viola, p. 2.
13. As quoted in Viola, p. 67.
14. J. V. Stalin, *Works* (Moscow, 1952), vol. 13, pp. 40–41.
15. E. H. Carr, *The Bolshevik Revolution*, pp. 361–74.
16. David Engerman, *Modernization from the Other Shore: American Intellectuals and the Romance of Russian Development* (Cambridge, MA, 2003), pp. 155–62; Peter G. Filene, *Americans and the Soviet Experiment, 1917–1933* (Cambridge, MA, 1967), pp. 198–99.
17. Paul Gregory, ed., *Behind the Façade of Stalin's Command Economy: Evidence from the Soviet State and Party Archives* (Stanford, CA, 2001).
18. Kevin McDermott, *Stalin: Revolutionary in an Era of War* (Basingstoke, UK, 2006), p. 74. See also R. W. Davies, *Soviet Economic Development from Lenin to Khrushchev* (Cambridge, UK, 1998).
19. Alexander Gerschenkron, *Economic Backwardness in Historical Perspective: A Book of Essays* (Cambridge, MA, 1962). See also Kurt S. Schultz, "The American Factor in Soviet Industrialization: Fordism and the First Five-Year Plan, 1928–1932," (Ph.D. dissertation, The Ohio State University, 1992).
20. S. V. Zhuravlev, *Malen'kie liudi i bol'shaia istoriia: Inostrantsy Moskovskogo Elektrozavoda v sovetskom obshchestve 1920–1930-kh godov* (Moscow, 2000). See also Zara Witkin, *An American Engineer in Stalin's Russia: The Memoirs of Zara Witkin, 1932–1934*, ed. Michael Gelb (Berkeley, CA, 1991).
21. Chauncy D. Harris, *Cities of the Soviet Union* (Chicago, IL, 1970).
22. Ivan Gudov, *Sud'ba rabochego* (Moscow, 1974), p. 7.
23. For a first-hand account of hazardous work conditions at a Magnitogorsk construction site, see John Scott, *Behind the Urals: An American Worker in Russia's City of Steel* (Bloomington, IN, 1989).

24. The classic fictional account of socialist competition is Valentin Kataev, *Time, Forward!* trans. Charles Malamuth (Evanston, IL, 1995). On the political dimensions of labor mobilization, see David Priestland, *Stalinism and the Politics of Mobilization: Ideas, Power, and Terror in Inter-War Russia* (Oxford, UK, 2007).

25. David L. Hoffmann, *Peasant Metropolis: Social Identities in Moscow, 1929–1941* (Ithaca, NY, 1994), pp. 92–93. For further discussion of socialist competition, see Donald A. Filtzer, *Soviet Workers and Stalinist Industrialization: The Formation of Modern Soviet Production Relations, 1928–1941* (New York, NY, 1986).

26. L. M. Kaganovich, *Kontrol'nye tsifry tret'ego goda piatiletki i zadachi Moskovskoi organizatsii: Rech' na V plenume MOK VKP(b), 19 fevralia 1931 g.* (Moscow, 1931), p. 34. See also E. A. Rees, *"Iron Lazar": A Political Biography of Lazar Kaganovich* (London, UK, 2012).

27. Hoffmann, *Peasant Metropolis*, pp. 94–96. For further discussion, see Hiroaki Kuromiya, *Stalin's Industrial Revolution: Politics and Workers, 1928–1932* (New York, NY, 1988), pp. 246–47.

28. Hoffmann, Peasant Metropolis, p. 1. See also Kenneth Straus, *Factory and Community in Stalin's Russia: The Making of an Industrial Working Class* (Pittsburgh, PA, 1997).

29. Andrew Smith, *I Was a Soviet Worker* (New York, NY, 1936), pp. 47–48.

30. G. K. Ordzhonikidze, *Stat'i i rechi* (Moscow, 1957), pp. 411–12.

31. Amy Randall, *The Soviet Dream World of Retail Trade and Consumption in the 1930s* (New York, NY, 2008), Chapter 1; Julie Hessler, *A Social History of Soviet Trade: Trade Policy, Retail Practices, and Consumption, 1917–1953* (Princeton, NJ, 2004), pp. 178–79.

32. Hoffmann, *Peasant Metropolis*, p. 150. For further discussion of the food supply system, see E. A. Osokina, *Our Daily Bread: Socialist Distribution and the Art of Survival in Stalin's Russia, 1927–1941*, trans. Kate Transchel and Greta Bucher (Armonk, NY, 2001).

33. Lynn Mally, *Culture of the Future: The Proletkult Movement in Revolutionary Russia* (Berkeley, CA, 1990).

34. Matthew Lenoe, *Closer to the Masses: Stalinist Culture, Social Revolution, and Soviet Newspapers* (Cambridge, MA, 2004).

35. Michael David-Fox, "What is Cultural Revolution?" *The Russian Review* 1999, no. 2.

36. *Izmeneniia sot'sialnoi struktury sovetskogo obshchestva, 1921-seredina '30-kh godov* (Moscow, 1979), p. 206. See also E. Thomas Ewing, *The Teachers of Stalinism: Policy, Practice and Power in Soviet Schools of the 1930s* (New York, NY, 2002).

37. As quoted in David L. Hoffmann, *Stalinist Values: The Cultural Norms of Soviet Modernity* (Ithaca, NY, 2003), p. 15.

38. On anti-alcohol campaigns, see Kate Transchel, *Under the Influence: Working-Class Drinking, Temperance, and Cultural Revolution in Russia, 1895–1932* (Pittsburgh, PA, 2006).

39. William Husband, *"Godless Communists": Atheism and Society in Soviet Russia, 1917–1932* (DeKalb, IL, 2000); Daniel Peris, *Storming the Heavens: The Soviet League of the Militant Godless* (Ithaca, NY, 1998).

40. As quoted in Oleg Kharkhordin, *The Collective and the Individual in Russia: A Study of Practices* (Berkeley, CA, 1999), p. 94.

41. As quoted in Lewis Siegelbaum and Andrei Sokolov, *Stalinism as a Way of Life: A Narrative in Documents* (New Haven, CT, 2000), p. 384.

42. S. Frederick Starr, "Visionary Town Planning during the Cultural Revolution," in Sheila Fitzpatrick (ed.), *Cultural Revolution in Russia, 1928–1931* (Bloomington, IN, 1978); Anatole Kopp, *Town and Revolution: Soviet Architecture and City Planning*, trans. Thomas E. Burton (New York, NY, 1970); Heather D. DeHaan, *Stalinist City Planning: Professionals, Performance, and Power* (Toronto, 2013).

43. For further discussion, see Kendall E. Bailes, *Technology and Society Under Lenin and Stalin: Origins of the Soviet Technical Intelligentsia, 1917–1941* (Princeton, NJ, 1978).

44. As quoted in Ronald Grigor Suny, *The Soviet Experiment* (Oxford, UK, 2011), p. 235.

45. As quoted in Davies, *Soviet Economy in Turmoil*, p. 114.

46. Stalin, *Works*, vol. 13, p. 69.

47. Sheila Fitzpatrick, *The Russian Revolution* (Oxford, UK, 2008), p. 145. See also Fitzpatrick, "Stalin and the Making of a New Elite," *The Cultural Front* (Ithaca, NY, 1992).

48. Sheila Fitzpatrick, *Education and Social Mobility in the Soviet Union, 1921–1934* (Cambridge, UK, 1979).

49. For a study that places both the tsarist and Soviet empires in the broader context of colonial empires, see Jeff Sahadeo, *Russian Colonial Society in Tashkent, 1865–1923* (Bloomington, IN, 2007).

50. Francine Hirsch, *Empire of Nations: Ethnographic Knowledge and the Making of the Soviet System* (Ithaca, NY, 2005).

51. For further discussion, see Hirsch.

52. Ronald Grigor Suny, *The Making of the Georgian Nation*, 2nd edn (Bloomington, IN, 1994); Ronald Grigor Suny, *Looking Toward Ararat: Armenia in Modern History* (Bloomington, IN, 1993).

53. Ian Lanzillotti, "Land, Community, and the State in the North Caucasus: Karbardino-Balkaria, 1763–1991," (Ph.D. dissertation, The Ohio State University, 2014).

54. Adeeb Khalid, *Making Uzbekistan: Nation, Empire, and Revolution in the Early USSR* (Ithaca, NY, 2015).

55. Adrienne Lynn Edgar, *Tribal Nation: The Making of Soviet Turkmenistan* (Princeton, NJ, 2006).

56. Hirsch, pp. 183–84.

57. Hirsch, pp. 166–70.

58. Robert Weinberg, *Stalin's Forgotten Zion: Birobidzhan and the Making of a Soviet Jewish Homeland: An Illustrated History, 1926–1996* (Berkeley, CA, 1998).

59. As quoted in Terry Martin, *The Affirmative Action Empire* (Ithaca, NY, 2001), p. 155.
60. Suny, *Soviet Experiment*, pp. 285–86.
61. As quoted in Martin, pp. 155–56.
62. Yuri Slezkine, "The USSR as a Communal Apartment, or How a Socialist State Promoted Ethnic Particularism," *Slavic Review* 53: 2 (Summer 1994).
63. Terry Martin, "Modernization or Neo-traditionalism? Ascribed Nationality and Soviet Primordialism," in David L. Hoffmann and Yanni Kotsonis (eds.), *Russian Modernity: Politics, Knowledge, Practices* (London, UK, 2000), p. 171.
64. Douglas Northrop, *Veiled Empire: Gender and Power in Stalinist Central Asia* (Ithaca, NY, 2004). See also Marianne Kamp, *The New Woman in Uzbekistan: Islam, Modernity, and Unveiling under Communism* (Seattle, WA, 2006).
65. Geoffrey Hosking, *The First Socialist Society: A History of the Soviet Union from Within*, 2nd enlarged edn (Cambridge, MA, 1993), p. 240.
66. Martin, *Affirmative Action Empire*, pp. 297–98.
67. Martin, *Affirmative Action Empire*, pp. 356–62.
68. Hoffmann, *Peasant Metropolis*, p. 124.
69. George O. Lieber, *Soviet Nationality Policy, Urban Growth, and Identity Change in the Ukrainian SSR, 1923–1934* (New York, NY, 1992).
70. Matthew J. Payne, *Stalin's Railroad: Turksib and the Building of Socialism* (Pittsburgh, PA, 2001), pp. 146–52, 232–41 (quotation on p. 235).
71. Paula Michaels, *Curative Powers: Medicine and Empire in Stalin's Central Asia* (Pittsburgh, PA, 2003).
72. Hoffmann, *Peasant Metropolis*, p. 39.
73. Davies and Wheatcroft, p. 448.
74. Davies and Wheatcroft, p. 449.
75. Hiroaki Kuromiya, *Stalin* (New York, NY, 2005), p. 102.
76. As quoted in Suny, *Soviet Experiment*, p. 227. See also Lev Kopelev, *The Education of a True Believer*, trans. Gary Kern (New York, NY, 1980).
77. Davies and Wheatcroft, pp. 415–21 (quotations on pp. 420–21).
78. Robert Conquest, *Harvest of Sorrow: Soviet Collectivization and the Terror-Famine* (New York, NY, 1986). For a contrary view, see Mark Tauger, "The 1932 Harvest and the Famine of 1933," *Slavic Review* 50: 1 (1991).
79. Kuromiya, *Stalin*, p. 103.
80. Martha Brill Olcott, *The Kazakhs*, 2nd edn (Stanford, CA, 1995), pp. 184–85.
81. Olcott, pp. 180–85.
82. Yuri Slezkine, *Arctic Mirrors: Russia and the Small Peoples of the North* (Ithaca, NY, 1994), pp. 187–217 (quotation on p. 203).
83. As quoted in Gijs Kessler, "The Passport System and State Control over Populations Flows in the Soviet Union, 1932–1940," *Cahiers du monde russe* 42: 2–4 (April–December 2001), p. 482.
84. Paul Hagenloh, "'Chekist in Essence, Chekist in Spirit': Regular and Political Police in the 1930s," *Cahiers du monde russe* 42: 2–4 (April–December 2001),

p. 470; David R. Shearer, *Policing Stalin's Socialism: Repressions and Social Order in the Soviet Union, 1924–1953* (New Haven, CT, 2009), p. 256.

85. Jeffrey Rossman, *Worker Resistance under Stalin: Class and Revolution on the Shop Floor* (Cambridge, MA, 2005).

86. For further discussion, see Viola, pp. 188–90.

3 Socialism Attained (1934–1938)

1. *XVII s"ezd VKP(b), 26 ianv.-10 fevr. 1934 g. Sten. Otchet* (Moscow, 1934), p. 15.

2. Golfo Alexopoulos, *Stalin's Outcasts: Aliens, Citizens, and the Soviet State, 1926–1936* (Ithaca, NY, 2002).

3. Boris Groys, *The Total Art of Stalinism* (Princeton, NJ, 1992).

4. As quoted in Jeffrey Brooks, *Thank You, Comrade Stalin* (Princeton, NJ, 2000), p. 108.

5. Both speeches are reprinted in H. G. Scott, ed., *Problems of Soviet Literature: Reports and Speeches at the First Soviet Writers' Congress* (Moscow, 1935).

6. For more on socialist realism in literature, see Thomas Lahusen, *How Life Writes the Book: Real Socialism and Socialist Realism in Stalin's Russia* (Ithaca, NY, 1997); Evgeny Dobrenko, *Political Economy of Socialist Realism* (New Haven, CT, 2007).

7. Jonathan Brooks Platt, *Greetings, Pushkin! Stalinist Cultural Politics and the Russian National Bard* (Pittsburgh, PA, 2016).

8. As quoted in Katerina Clark, *Petersburg, Crucible of Cultural Revolution* (Cambridge, MA, 1995), p. 157; Maurice Friedberg, *Russian Classics in Soviet Jackets* (New York, NY, 1962), p. 12.

9. Karen Petrone, *Life Has Become More Joyous, Comrades: Celebrations in the Time of Stalin* (Bloomington, IN, 2000).

10. Angela Brintlinger, *Writing a Usable Past: Russian Literary Culture, 1917–1937* (Evanston, IL, 2008).

11. *Sovetskoe iskusstvo*, November 17, 1935, p. 2.

12. For further discussion, see Katerina Clark and Evgeny Dobrenko, eds., *Soviet Culture and Power: A History in Documents, 1917–1953* (New Haven, CT, 2007).

13. *Pravda*, December 6, 1935, p. 3.

14. Evgeny Dobrenko, *Stalinist Cinema and the Production of History* (New Haven, CT, 2008).

15. As quoted in D. L. Brandenberger and A. M. Dubrovsky, "The People Need a Tsar," *Europe-Asia Studies* 50: 5, p. 880. See also Kevin Platt and David Brandenberger, eds., *Epic Revisionism: Russian History and Literature as Stalinist Propaganda* (Madison, WI, 2006).

16. Peter Blitstein, "Nation-Building or Russification? Obligatory Russian Instruction in the Soviet Non-Russian School, 1938–1953," in Ronald Grigor Suny and Terry Martin (eds.), *A State of Nations: Empire and Nation-State in the Age of Lenin and Stalin* (Oxford, UK, 2001).

17. Serhy Yekelchyk, *Stalin's Empire of Memory: Russian-Ukrainian Relations in the Soviet Historical Imagination* (Toronto, 2004).

18. Terry Martin, *The Affirmative Action Empire* (Ithaca, NY, 2001), pp. 444–45.
19. Nicholas Timasheff, *The Great Retreat: The Growth and Decline of Communism in Russia* (New York, NY, 1946).
20. As quoted in Sarah Davies, "The Leaders Cult: Propaganda and its Reception in Stalin's Russia," in John Channon (ed.), *Politics, Society and Stalinism in the USSR* (New York, NY, 1998), p. 117.
21. As quoted in Regine Robin, "Stalinism and Popular Culture," in Hans Gunther (ed.), *The Culture of the Stalin Period* (New York, NY, 1990), p. 29.
22. RGASPI f. 17, op. 120, d. 146, l. 34.
23. *Letchiki: Sbornik rasskazov* (Moscow, 1938), p. 567.
24. *Pravda*, August 15, 1936, p. 1.
25. Jan Plamper, *The Stalin Cult* (New Haven, CT, 2012).
26. See Sarah Davies, "Stalin and the Making of the Leader Cult in the 1930s," in B. Apor et al. (eds.), *The Leader Cult in Communist Dictatorships* (New York, NY, 2004), p. 122.
27. GARF f. 5446, op. 18a, d. 2753, l. 15.
28. Sarah Davies, *Popular Opinion in Stalin's Russia: Terror, Propaganda and Dissent, 1934–1941* (New York, NY, 1997), pp. 171, 173.
29. As quoted in Simon Sebag Montefiore, *Stalin: The Court of the Red Tsar* (London, UK, 2003), p. 4.
30. RGASPI f. 85, op. 29, d. 640, ll. 3–7. For a full discussion of Stakhanov's record, see Lewis Siegelbaum, *Stakhanovism and the Politics of Productivity in the USSR, 1935–1941* (New York, NY, 1988), pp. 67–74.
31. Janucy K. Zawodny, "Twenty-six Interviews with Former Soviet Factory Workers," Hoover Institution Archives, 11/22.
32. For more on the New Person, see Peter Fritzsche and Jochen Hellbeck, "The New Man in Stalinist Russia and Nazi Germany," in Sheila Fitzpatrick and Michael Geyer (eds.), *Beyond Totalitarianism: Stalinism and Nazism Compared* (Cambridge, UK, 2009).
33. *Labour in the Land of Socialism: Stakhanovites in Conference* (Moscow, 1936), p. 15.
34. *Labour in the Land of Socialism*, pp. 126–27, 220 and 216–17, respectively.
35. As quoted in Siegelbaum, p. 231.
36. As quoted in Jochen Hellbeck, *Revolution on My Mind: Writing a Diary under Stalin* (Cambridge, MA, 2006), pp. 74–75.
37. GARF f. 5446, op. 18a, d. 2753, l. 26.
38. I. V. Stalin, *Sochineniia*, vol. 1 [XIV], ed. Robert H. McNeal (Stanford, CA, 1967), pp. 89–90.
39. Amy Randall, *The Soviet Dreamworld of Retail Trade and Consumption in the 1930s* (New York, NY, 2008).
40. Davies, *Popular*, pp. 26–27.
41. Julie Hessler, *A Social History of Soviet Trade* (Princeton, NJ, 2004), p. 198.
42. Davies, *Popular*, pp. 35–39.
43. Wendy Goldman, *Women at the Gates: Gender and Industry in Stalin's Russia* (New York, NY, 2002), pp. 1, 269; TsMAM f. 2872, op. 2, d. 220, ll. 61–63; A. A. Tverdokhleb, "Chislennost' i sostav rabochego klassa Moskvy v 1917–1937 gg.," *Vestnik Moskovskogo universiteta* ser. 9, 1970, no. 1.

44. David L. Hoffmann, *Peasant Metropolis: Social Identities in Moscow, 1929–1941* (Ithaca, NY, 1994), pp. 42, 119.
45. L. I. Kovalev, *Metro: Sbornik posviashchennyi pusku moskovskogo metropolitena* (Moscow, 1935), p. 209.
46. Goldman, pp. 227–28.
47. See Mary Buckley, *Mobilizing Soviet Peasants: Heroines and Heroes of Stalin's Fields* (Latham, MD, 2006).
48. Melanie Ilic, *Women Workers in the Soviet Interwar Economy: From "Protection" to "Equality"* (London, UK, 1999), p. 109.
49. *Komsomol'skaia pravda*, Febuary 5, 1937, p. 2, as quoted in Elena Shulman, *Stalinism on the Frontier of Empire: Women and State Formation in the Soviet Far East* (New York, NY, 2008), p. 1.
50. For further discussion, see Choi Chatterjee, *Celebrating Women: Gender, Festival Culture and Bolshevik Ideology, 1910–1939* (Pittsburgh, PA, 2002); Barbara Evans Clements, Barbara Alpern Engel, and Christine Worobec, eds., *Russia's Women* (Berkeley, CA, 1991); Elizabeth Wood, *The Baba and the Comrade: Gender and Politics in Revolutionary Russia* (Bloomington, IN, 1997).
51. Timasheff, pp. 192–98.
52. *Sobranie zakonov i rasporiazhenii*, no. 34 (July 21, 1936), 510–11; RGASPI f. 17, op. 3, d. 976, l. 4; RGASPI f. 17, op. 3, d. 980, l. 1; d. 982, ll. 126–30.
53. *Martenovka* May 1, 1936, 5; *Rabotnitsa i krest'ianka* 1936, no. 15, 5; no. 2, 20.
54. *Sobranie zakonov i rasporiazhenii raboche-krest'ianskogo pravitel'stva Soiuza Sovetskikh Sotsialisticheskikh Respublik*, no. 34 (July 21, 1936), pp. 515–16.
55. N. V. Krylenko, "Ob izmeneniiakh i dopolneniiakh kodeksov RSFSR," *Sovetskaia iustitsiia* 1936, no. 7, as cited in Dan Healey, *Homosexual Desire in Revolutionary Russia* (Chicago, IL, 2001), p. 196.
56. For further discussion, see Frances Bernstein, *The Dictatorship of Sex: Lifestyle Advice for the Soviet Masses* (DeKalb, IL, 2007).
57. *Rabotnitsa* 1936, no. 17, p. 5, as quoted in Lynne Attwood, *Creating the New Soviet Woman: Women's Magazines as Engineers of Female Identity, 1922–1953* (New York, NY, 1999), p. 116; *Pravda*, May 28, 1936, p. 1.
58. GARF f. 5446, op. 18a, d. 2753, ll. 15, 22, 26, 35; *Izvestiia* May 29, 1936, pp. 3–4; May 30, 1936, p. 3; June 2, 1936, p. 3.
59. GARF f. 5446, op. 18a, d. 2753, l. 85; RGAE f. 1562 s.ch., op. 329, d. 407, ll. 22–25.
60. *Sovetskaia iustitsiia* 1936, no. 34, p. 16; RGAE f. 1562 s.ch., op. 329, d. 407, l. 25; TsMAM f. 819, op. 2, d. 27, ll. 12–15.
61. Frank Lorimer, *The Population of the Soviet Union* (Geneva, 1946), p. 134; Ansley Coale et al., *Human Fertility in Russia Since the Nineteenth Century* (Princeton, NJ, 1979), p. 16.
62. Matthew Lenoe, *The Kirov Murder and Soviet History* (New Haven, CT, 2010).
63. Karl Radek confessed to all charges and was sentenced to ten years' imprisonment, but he was subsequently killed in the Gulag; Yuri Slezkine, *The House of Government* (Princeton, NJ, 2017), pp. 723–33.

64. See Peter Whitewood, *The Red Army and the Great Terror* (Lawrence, KS, 2015).
65. Wendy Goldman, *Inventing the Enemy: Denunciation and Terror in Stalin's Russia* (Cambridge, UK, 2011).
66. As quoted in Orlando Figes, *The Whisperers: Private Life in Stalin's Russia* (New York, NY, 2007), p. 246.
67. Eugenia Ginzburg, *Journey into the Whirlwind* (New York, NY, 1967), p. 83.
68. V. Rogovin, *Partiia rasstreliannykh* (Moscow, 1997), pp. 487–89; O. F. Suvenirov, *Tragediia R.K.K.A., 1937–1938* (Moscow, 1998), p. 315, as cited in Figes, pp. 238–39.
69. For further discussion of the Old Bolsheviks and their fate, see Slezkine. See also Karl Schlögel, *Terror und Traum: Moskau 1937* (Munich, 2008).
70. Oleg Khlevniuk, *In Stalin's Shadow: The Career of Sergo Ordzhonikidze* (Armonk, NY, 1995).
71. Nicolas Werth, "The Mechanism of a Mass Crime," in Robert Gellately et al. (eds.), *The Specter of Genocide* (Cambridge, UK, 2003), p. 217; Werth, "A State against its People," in Stephane Courtois (ed.), *The Black Book of Communism* (Cambridge, MA, 1999), p. 204. Werth notes that these figures do not include "non-ratified execution supplements" – people who died during preliminary investigations or under torture – and that if these were added then the estimated number of executions in 1937–38 would rise to 800,000.
72. Mark Junge, Gennadii Bordiugov, and Rolf Binner, *Vertikal' bol'shogo terrora: Istoriia operatsii po prikazu NKVD no. 00447* (Moscow, 2008).
73. Robert Conquest, *The Great Terror* (New York, NY, 1968).
74. Sarah Davies and James Harris, *Stalin's World: Dictating the Soviet Order* (New Haven, CT, 2014). See also Gabor Rittersporn, "The Omnipresent Conspiracy: On Soviet Imagery of Politics and Social Relations in the 1930s," in Nick Lampert and Gabor Rittersporn (eds.), *Stalinism: Its Nature and Aftermath* (Armonk, NY, 1992).
75. Vladimir Khaustov, "Razvitie sovetskikh organov gosudarstvennoi bezopasnosti: 1917–1953 gg." *Cahiers du monde russe* 42: 2–4 (April–December 2001), pp. 369–70.
76. I. V. Stalin, *Sochineniia* (Moscow, 1946–52), vol. 13, p. 209.
77. Stephen Wheatcroft, "Agency and Terror," *Australian Journal of Politics and History* 53: 1 (2007), p. 30.
78. For further discussion of the role of the secret police, see David Shearer, *Policing Stalin's Socialism* (New Haven, CT, 2009); Paul Hagenloh, *Stalin's Police* (Washington, DC, 2009). On the judicial system, see Peter H. Solomon, *Soviet Criminal Justice under Stalin* (Cambridge, UK, 1996).
79. J. Arch Getty and Oleg Naumov, *The Road to Terror* (New Haven, CT, 1999), pp. 473–74.
80. A. G. Latyshev, "Riadom so Stalinym," *Sovershenno sekretno*, no. 12 (1990), p.19, as quoted in Kevin McDermott, *Stalin* (New York, NY, 2006), p. 88.
81. On the Manichean worldview of Soviet Communist Party members, see Igal Halfin, *Terror in My Soul: Communist Autobiographies on Trial* (Cambridge, MA, 2003).

82. Oleg V. Khlevniuk, *A History of the Gulag* (New Haven, CT, 2004), p. 165; Martin, p. 338.
83. Stalin, *Sochineniia*, vol. 1 [XIV], p. 197.
84. Khlevniuk, *History of the Gulag*, pp. 144–45.
85. Martin, p. 337.
86. *Stalinskie deportatsii, 1928–1953*, comp. N. I. Povol' and M. Polian (Moscow, 2005), p. 83. See also Michael Gelb, "An Early Soviet Ethnic Deportation: The Far Eastern Koreans," *The Russian Review*, 54: 3 (1995).
87. As quoted in Barry McLoughlin, "Mass Operations of the NKVD, 1937–1939," in Barry McLoughlin and Kevin McDermott (eds.), *Stalin's Terror* (Basingstoke, UK, 2003), p. 122.
88. Martin, pp. 337–38.
89. For a discussion that applies the word "genocide" to the Soviet case but nonetheless points out differences between Nazi and Soviet state violence, see Norman M. Naimark, *Stalin's Genocides* (Princeton, NJ, 2010), pp. 122–28.
90. For further discussion, see Hiroaki Kuromiya, *The Voices of the Dead* (New Haven, CT, 2007), pp. 131–32, 256.
91. Stephen Kotkin, *Stalin: Waiting for Hitler, 1929–1941* (New York, NY, 2017), pp. 485–87.
92. Marc Jansen and Nikita Petrov, *Stalin's Loyal Executioner: People's Commissar Nikolai Ezhov, 1895–1940* (Stanford, CA, 2002).
93. *XVIII s''ezd Vsesoiuznoi kommunisticheskoi partii (b): 10–21 marta 1939 g.: Stenograficheskii otchet* (Moscow, 1939), pp. 26–27.
94. As quoted in Oleg V. Khlevniuk, *Master of the House: Stalin and His Inner Circle*, trans. Nora Seligman Favorov (New Haven, CT, 2009), p. 174.

4 World War II (1939–1945)

1. Silvio Pons, *Stalin and the Inevitable War: 1936–1941* (London, UK, 2002).
2. R. W. Davies and Mark Harrison, "Defence Spending and Defence Industry in the 1930s," in John Barber and Mark Harrison (eds.), *The Soviet Defence-Industry Complex from Stalin to Khrushchev* (London, UK, 2000); Lennart Samuelson, "Wartime Perspectives and Economic Planning: Tukhachevsky and the Military-Industrial Complex, 1925–1937," in Silvio Pons and Andrea Romano (eds.), *Russia in the Age of Wars, 1914–1945* (Milan, 2000); David Stone, *Hammer and Rifle: The Militarization of the Soviet Union, 1926–1933* (Lawrence, KS, 2000).
3. *Molotov Remembers: Inside Kremlin Politics, Conversations with Felix Chuev*, ed. Albert Resis (Chicago, IL, 1993), p. 22.
4. Alfred Rieber, *Stalin and the Struggle for Supremacy in Eurasia* (Cambridge, UK, 2015).
5. For an in-depth discussion of Soviet prewar diplomacy, see Gabriel Gorodetsky, *Grand Delusion: Stalin and the German Invasion of Russia* (New Haven, CT, 1999).
6. Jan Gross, *Revolution from Abroad: The Soviet Conquest of Poland's Western Ukraine and Western Belorussia* (Princeton, NJ, 1988).

7. Ivo Banac, ed., *The Diary of Georgi Dimitrov, 1933–1949* (New Haven, CT, 2003), pp. 115–16.
8. In the early hours of June 22, 1941, Timoshenko and Zhukov finally convinced Stalin to put troops on high alert, though he still ordered the military to avoid war and not to respond to provocations. With the German invasion only a couple hours away, the high alert directive did not have time to reach officers at the front until it was too late. See Stephen Kotkin, *Stalin: Waiting for Hitler* (New York, NY, 2017), pp. 899–901.
9. As quoted in Alexander Werth, *Russia at War* (London, UK, 1964), p. 151.
10. O. V. Druzhba, *Velikaia otechestvennaia voina v soznanii sovetskogo i postsovetskogo obshchestva* (Rostov, 2000), p. 20, as quoted in Catherine Merridale, *Ivan's War: Life and Death in the Red Army, 1939–1945* (New York, NY, 2006), p. 111.
11. Werth, *Russia at War*, p. 235.
12. As quoted in Werth, *Russia at War*, p. 240.
13. Joseph Stalin, *The Great Patriotic War of the Soviet Union* (New York, NY, 1945), pp. 37–38.
14. For Zhukov's own account of the battle, see Georgii Zhukov, *The Memoirs of Marshal Zhukov* (London, UK, 1971).
15. For further discussion, see Yitzhak Arad, *The Holocaust in the Soviet Union* (Lincoln, NE, 2009).
16. Cynthia Simmons and Nina Perlina, eds., *Writing the Siege of Leningrad: Women's Diaries, Memoirs, and Documentary Prose* (Pittsburgh, PA, 2002), pp. 59–60.
17. Richard Bidlack and Nikita Lomagin calculate that between 1.6 and 2 million Soviet citizens died within the city and in battles surrounding it during the siege, including some 900,000 civilians who died of starvation, cold, and bombardment; Bidlack and Lomagin, eds., *The Leningrad Blockade, 1941–1944*, trans. Marion Schwatz (New Haven, CT, 2012), pp. 1, 270–75.
18. See John Barber, "Popular Reactions in Moscow to the German Invasion of June 22, 1941," *Soviet Union*, 18: 1–3 (1991).
19. Stalin, p. 38.
20. As quoted in Walter Kolarz, "Soviet Patriotism and the War," *Fortnightly Review* 44 (1943), p. 379. For further discussion, see Richard Stites, ed., *Culture and Entertainment in Wartime Russia* (Bloomington, IN, 1995).
21. Steven Miner, *Stalin's Holy War: Religion, Nationalism, and Alliance Politics, 1941–1945* (Chapel Hill, NC, 2003).
22. As quoted in Alexander Werth, *The Year of Stalingrad* (New York, NY, 1947), p. 172.
23. Werth, *Russia at War*, p. 194.
24. Rebecca Manley, *To the Tashkent Station: Evacuation and Survival in the Soviet Union at War* (Ithaca, NY, 2009).
25. See John Barber and Mark Harrison, *The Soviet Home Front, 1941–1945* (London, UK, 1991).
26. As quoted in Steven George Jug, "All Stalin's Men? Soldierly Masculinities in the Soviet War Effort, 1938–1945" (Ph.D. dissertation, University of Illinois, 2013), pp. 35–36.

27. *Krasnaia zvezda*, April 7, 1942, p. 3; April 10, 1942, p. 1, as quoted in Jug, pp. 102, 104.

28. David M. Glantz, *Stumbling Colossus: The Red Army on the Eve of World War II* (Lawrence, KS, 1998), p. 15.

29. Orlando Figes, *The Whisperers: Private Life in Stalin's Russia* (New York, NY, 2007), p. 419.

30. See Reina Pennington, *Wings, Women, and War: Soviet Airwomen in World War II Combat* (Lawrence, KS, 2002).

31. Anna Krylova, *Soviet Women in Combat: A History of Violence on the Eastern Front* (New York, NY, 2010), pp. 121–23, 145–59.

32. Roger Reese, "Soviet Women at War," *Military History* 28: 1 (May 2011).

33. For this quotation and further discussion of female partisans, see Roger D. Markwick and Euridice Charon Cardona, *Soviet Women on the Frontline in the Second World War* (New York, NY, 2012), Chapter 5.

34. *Krasnaia zvezda*, March 10, 1942, p. 3, as quoted in Jug, p. 111.

35. Rudolf Schlesinger, ed., *The Family in the USSR* (London, UK, 1949), pp. 367–72.

36. *Krasnaia zvezda*, October 28, 1944, p. 1, as quoted in Jug, p. 210.

37. Reese, p. 51.

38. Reese, p. 52.

39. For a discussion of relations between male and female soldiers, see Oleg Budnitskii, "Muzhchini i zhenshchiny v Krasnoi armii (1941–1945)," *Cahiers du monde russe* 52: 2/3 (2011).

40. As quoted in Werth, *Russia at War*, p. 453. For other eyewitness accounts, see Jochen Hellbeck, *Stalingrad: The City that Defeated the Third Reich* (New York, NY, 2015).

41. As quoted in Werth, *Russia at War*, p. 464.

42. For further discussion, see Roger Reese, *Why Stalin's Soldiers Fought: The Red Army's Military Effectiveness in World War II* (Lawrence, KS, 2011).

43. Svetlana Alexievich, *The Unwomanly Face of War: An Oral History of Women in World War II* (New York, NY, 2017), p. 134.

44. For more on the partisan movement, see Kenneth Slepyan, *Stalin's Guerrillas: Soviet Partisans in World War II* (Lawrence, KS, 2006).

45. John Erickson, *The Road to Berlin* (Boulder, CO, 1983).

46. Norman Davies, *Rising '44: The Battle for Warsaw* (New York, NY, 2004), p. 444; Werth, *Russia at War*, pp. 876–77.

47. Alexievich, p. 307.

48. Werth, *Russia at War*, p. 965.

49. As quoted in Werth, *Russia at War*, p. 966.

50. Norman Naimark, *The Russians in Germany* (Cambridge, MA, 1995), pp. 108–15.

51. Antony Beevor, *Berlin: The Downfall 1945* (New York, NY, 2002).

52. Werth, *Russia at War*, p. 969.

53. See Amir Weiner, *Making Sense of the War* (Princeton, NJ, 2002).

54. For further discussion of wartime propaganda concerning Soviet national-ities, see David Brandenberger, *National Bolshevism: Stalinist Mass Culture*

and the Formation of Modern Russian National Identity, 1931–1956 (Cambridge, MA, 2002), pp. 168–80.

55. For a discussion of all wartime deportations, see Pavel Polian, *Against Their Will: The History and Geography of Forced Migrations in the USSR* (Budapest, 2004).
56. John Hiden and Patrick Salmon, *The Baltic Nations and Europe: Estonia, Latvia, and Lithuania in the Twentieth Century* (New York, NY, 1994).
57. William Taubman, *Khrushchev: The Man and His Era* (New York, NY, 2004), p. 195.
58. RGASPI f. 77, op. 1, d. 938, l. 5, as quoted in Jug, p. 111.

5 The Postwar Years (1946–1953)

1. As quoted in Ronald Grigor Suny, *The Soviet Experiment* (Oxford, UK, 2011), p. 367.
2. See the website of the International Churchill Society, www.winstonchurch ill.org.
3. For further discussion, see Walter LaFeber, *America, Russia, and the Cold War, 1945–2006*, 10th edn (New York, NY, 2012).
4. Alfred Rieber, *Stalin and the Struggle for Supremacy in Eurasia* (Cambridge, UK, 2015), pp. 324–25.
5. For further discussion, see Tony Judt, *Postwar: A History of Europe Since 1945* (New York, NY, 2005), Chapters 5–6.
6. The Cominform replaced the Comintern, which had been disbanded during the war; see Kevin McDermott and Jeremy Agnew, *The Comintern: A History of International Communism from Lenin to Stalin* (Basingstoke, UK, 1996).
7. As quoted in Suny, p. 371.
8. Jonathan Haslam, *Russia's Cold War* (New Haven, CT, 2011), p. 108.
9. http://digitalarchive.wilsoncenter.org/document116179. See also Alexei Kojevnikov, *Stalin's Great Science: The Times and Adventures of Soviet Physicists* (London, UK, 2004).
10. For more on the Soviet nuclear program, see David Holloway, *Stalin and the Bomb* (New Haven, CT, 1994).
11. As quoted in Gerald J. DeGroot, *The Bomb: A Life* (Cambridge, MA, 2005), p. 141.
12. Kate Brown, *Plutopia: Nuclear Families, Atomic Cities, and the Great Soviet and American Plutonium Disasters* (Oxford, UK, 2013), pp. 115–23.
13. Brown, pp. 3, 165–69.
14. See Andy Bruno, *The Nature of Soviet Power: An Arctic Environmental History* (Cambridge, UK, 2017); Stephen Brain, *Song of the Forest: Russian Forestry and Stalinist Environmentalism, 1905–1953* (Pittsburgh, PA, 2011).
15. For further discussion, see Douglas Weiner, *Models of Nature: Ecology, Conservation, and Cultural Revolution in Soviet Russia* (Pittsburgh, PA, 2000).
16. Haslam, pp. 126–28.
17. Kathryn Weathersby, "Soviet Aims in Korea and the Origins of the Korean War, 1945–1950: New Evidence from the Russian Archives," Cold War International History Project, Working Paper No. 8 (1993), pp. 31–32.

18. For further discussion, see Bruce Cumings, *The Korean War: A History* (New York, NY, 2011).
19. Orlando Figes, *The Whisperers: Private Life in Stalin's Russia* (New York, NY, 2007), pp. 455–58.
20. As quoted in Figes, p. 459.
21. See Elena Zubkova, *Russia after the War: Hopes, Illusions, and Disappointments, 1945–1957*, trans. Hugh Ragsdale (Armonk, NY, 1998), p. 37.
22. As quoted in Zubkova, p. 60.
23. For further discussion, see Greta Bucher, *Women, the Bureaucracy, and Daily Life in Postwar Moscow, 1945–1953* (Boulder, CO, 2006).
24. As quoted in Figes, pp. 433–34.
25. Figes, p. 442.
26. As quoted in Zubkova, p. 63.
27. Given the poverty of the postwar years, this aid was often lacking, and veterans subsequently worked to obtain greater recognition and benefits; see Mark Edele, *Soviet Veterans of World War II: A Popular Movement in an Authoritarian Society, 1941–1991* (Oxford, UK, 2008).
28. For further discussion, see Amir Weiner, *Making Sense of the War: The Second World War and the Fate of the Bolshevik Revolution* (Princeton, NJ, 2002).
29. As quoted in Zubkova, pp. 83–84.
30. As quoted in Figes, p. 448.
31. See Juliane Fürst, *Stalin's Last Generation: Soviet Post-War Youth and the Emergence of Mature Socialism* (Oxford, UK, 2010).
32. Yoram Gorlizki and Oleg Khlevniuk, *Cold Peace: Stalin and the Soviet Ruling Circle, 1945–1953* (Oxford, UK, 2004).
33. For further discussion, see Richard Overy, *Russia's War* (London, UK, 1997), pp. 304–07.
34. Blair A. Ruble, "The Leningrad Affair and the Provincialization of Leningrad," *The Russian Review*, 42: 3 (July 1983).
35. Galina Mikhailovna Ivanova, *Labor Camp Socialism: The Gulag in the Soviet Totalitarian System* (Armonk, NY, 2000), p. 98.
36. Figes, p. 453.
37. As quoted in Zubkova, p. 77.
38. As quoted in Figes, p. 489.
39. Katerina Clark, *The Soviet Novel: History as Ritual*, 3rd edn (Bloomington, IN, 2000), pp. 160–61.
40. As quoted in Suny, p. 396.
41. See Ethan Pollock, *Stalin and Soviet Science Wars* (Princeton, NJ, 2008).
42. L. Smirnov, "Material for Talks," *Bloknot agitatora*, 3 (January 30, 1953), pp. 10–22, as posted on http://soviethistory.msu.edu/1947–2/xenophobia/xenophobia-texts/spies-saboteurs-embezzlers-and-swindlers.
43. Mark Edele, "Strange Young Men in Stalin's Moscow: The Birth and Life of the Stiliagi, 1945–1953," *Jahrbücher für Geschichte Osteuropas*, 50: 1 (2002).
44. For further discussion, see Zubkova, pp. 72–73.
45. Jeffrey Veidlinger, "Soviet Jewry as a Diaspora Nationality" *East European Jewish Affairs* 33: 1 (2003).

46. For further discussion, see Benjamin Pinkus, *The Jews of the Soviet Union* (Cambridge, UK, 1990).
47. As quoted in Zubkova, p. 137.
48. Yakov Rapoport, *The Doctor's Plot of 1953: A Survivor's Memoir of Stalin's Last Act of Terror against Jews and Science* (Cambridge, MA, 1991).

Conclusion

1. As quoted in Ronald Grigor Suny, *The Soviet Experiment* (Oxford, UK, 2011), p. 413.
2. See Alec Luhn, "Stalin, Russia's New Hero," *The New York Times*, March 11, 2016; David L. Hoffmann, "Stalin Rises from the Ashes in Putin's Russia," *The Moscow Times*, April 14, 2015.
3. http://en.kremlin.ru/events/president/news/55948

Index